# Advertising Management in a Digital Environment

*Advertising Management in a Digital Environment: Text and Cases* blends the latest methods for digital communication and an understanding of the global landscape with the best practices of the functional areas of management.

Divided into three core sections, the book provides a truly holistic approach to Advertising Management. The first part considers the fundamentals of advertising management, including leadership, ethics and corporate social responsibility, and finance and budgeting. The second part considers human capital management and managing across cultures, whilst the third part discusses strategic planning, decision making and brand strategy. To demonstrate how theory translates to practice in advertising, each chapter is illustrated with real-life case studies from a broad range of sectors, and practical exercises allow case analysis and further learning.

This new textbook offers an integrated and global approach to Advertising Management and should be core or recommended reading for undergraduate and postgraduate students of Media Management, Advertising, Marketing Management and Strategy, Communications and Public Relations. The applied approach provided by case study analysis makes it equally suitable for those in executive education and studying for professional qualifications.

**Larry D. Kelley** is Professor of Advertising at the Jack J. Valenti School of Communication at the University of Houston, USA.

**Kim Bartel Sheehan** is Professor and Director of the Master's in Advertising and Brand Responsibility at the University of Oregon, USA.

# Advertising Management in a Digital Environment

## Text and Cases

Larry D. Kelley and
Kim Bartel Sheehan

Routledge
Taylor & Francis Group
LONDON AND NEW YORK

First published 2022
by Routledge
2 Park Square, Milton Park, Abingdon, Oxon OX14 4RN

and by Routledge
605 Third Avenue, New York, NY 10158

*Routledge is an imprint of the Taylor & Francis Group, an informa business*



*British Library Cataloguing-in-Publication Data*
A catalogue record for this book is available from the British Library

*Library of Congress Cataloging-in-Publication Data*
Names: Kelley, Larry D., 1955– author. | Bartel Sheehan, Kim, 1958– author.
Title: Advertising management in a digital environment: text and cases / Larry D. Kelley and Kim Bartel Sheehan.
Description: New York: Routledge, 2021. | Includes bibliographical references and index.
Identifiers: LCCN 2021004619 (print) | LCCN 2021004620 (ebook)
Subjects: LCSH: Advertising—Management. | Advertising media planning. | Relationship marketing. | Digital media.
Classification: LCC HF5823 .K34425 2021 (print) | LCC HF5823 (ebook) | DDC 659.14/4—dc23
LC record available at https://lccn.loc.gov/2021004619
LC ebook record available at https://lccn.loc.gov/2021004620

ISBN: 978-0-367-62071-4 (hbk)
ISBN: 978-0-367-62074-5 (pbk)
ISBN: 978-1-003-10782-8 (ebk)

Typeset in Bembo
by codeMantra

Access the Support Material: www.routledge.com/9780367620745

# Contents

**Introduction: Applied learning: the case study approach** 1

1 **The new world of advertising management: digital and global** 9
*Case 1.1 Boswell Agency 19*

2 **Culture, administration and leadership in a global market** 25
*Case 2.1 Prime Media 35*

3 **Advertising ethics and social responsibility across cultures** 37
*Case 3.1 KMF Agency 46*

4 **Understanding the role of finance and budgeting** 48
*Case 4.1 The Southern Rice Company 60*
*Case 4.2 Vineyard Agency 64*

5 **Managing means measuring: what and how to measure** 68
*Case 5.1 Randall White Dog Food 78*
*Case 5.2 Tinsdale Agency and Design 83*

6 **An overview of advertising personnel management** 85
*Case 6.1 IPortal Media Company 94*

7 **Adjusting to being a new manager in advertising** 96
*Case 7.1 Metropolitan Media Company 103*
*Case 7.2 Gotham Media 104*

8 **Managing creative people** 107
*Case 8.1 JPT Agency 113*

9 **Managing across cultures** 115
*Case 9.1 The Davis Group 122*

10 **Handling tricky situations** **126**
*Case 10.1 The Leaky Oil Company 134*

11 **Management and creative strategy** **136**
*Case 11.1 Go Organic Company 142*

12 **Making strategic decisions in advertising management within a brand perspective** **146**
*Case 12.1 Boston Life Insurance Company 154*

13 **Aligning strategy to cultural differences in advertising management** **160**
*Case 13.1 Barrands Agency 168*

14 **Managing the brand's digital assets** **171**
*Case 14.1 AdLeaders 177*

15 **Advertising management when things go wrong** **179**
*Case 15.1 Phoenix Power Company 186*

*Index* 189

# Introduction

## Applied learning: the case study approach

This text is designed to be learn a concept and then learn how to apply that concept. Management in general and advertising management are about putting principles into action. Management is decision-making. You need tools to make decisions. That is why it is so important to have a resource where you can learn fundamental advertising management concepts and then have the opportunity to put those concepts into practice through analyzing a case study.

The objective of the case study method is very simple. It is to provide a framework for putting into practice what you learn in the classroom. Case studies offer a realistic look at business situations and how you might solve them. Sometimes, the answers are strictly academic. However, sometimes, the answers may go against everything that you have learned.

That is why the case method is so important. It is the one opportunity to make mistakes, take risks and challenge conventional wisdom without the fear of failure. Since each case is unique, you must apply your knowledge and skill to solve problems that are not always interrelated. This will raise your critical thinking skill level plus improve your written and oral communication.

Both developing your analytical ability to quickly determine a course of action and the ability to articulate that action in terms of concise communication are the keys to becoming a successful manager.

Most cases in this book are drawn from real experiences. The names and locations are disguised to protect the interest of the companies involved. The overall situations are true. The final decisions are omitted, enabling you to reach your own conclusions. That is a much more powerful approach rather than simply critiquing the past thinking of others.

The case method is as close to real world as possible. However, there is one big difference between real-world advertising management and this text. In a typical business situation, advertising managers do not usually have the facts presented in an organized and clear manner such as you find in these cases. Advertising managers must do their own research and find their own information so that they can solve the problem as efficiently and effectively as possible.

That leads us to the second big difference. Time. You have the luxury of reading a case, pondering the problem and developing a cogent response in a few days or weeks depending on the assignment. In any business day, a manager may need to react to a problem immediately or within a limited timeframe. Because of this, they may only be able to gather limited information on which to make the best decision within that time.

Plus a manager may be presented with a variety of decisions at the same time rather than one case.

The third big difference between the boardroom and classroom are the stakes. The stakes for writing a paper may be a part of your overall grade. A manager may be dealing with profit issues, client relationships or employees' livelihoods. The stakes are much greater. And that makes the lack of time to make decisions even more intense.

Even with these differences, the case method is, perhaps, the best and only way to simulate these conditions. It will certainly make you a much better advertising manager. It will also make you a better and better-rounded person.

## Case analysis procedure

You can approach a case analysis in a wide variety of ways. We recommend that you follow the traditional business framework for writing a memorandum or what is sometimes termed "a white paper." A white paper is a point-of-view document. In today's fast-paced business climate, there are less and less formal white papers presented or written. However, the framework of doing so provides you with a proven method for analyzing any situation.

The following steps form the analysis framework.

1 Purpose: statement of the problem
2 Background or situation analysis (gathering data)
3 Discussion of alternatives
4 Recommendation/rationale for why it is the best course of action
5 Action plan (how to put the plan into motion)
6 Contingency plan (backup plan) (optional)

This framework will help organize your thoughts. While you may not write a formal paper with each of these headers for every business problem you encounter, it will help you quickly organize your thoughts.

Many business managers request that you keep your written recommendations to a single page. This is done to aid in time spent reading, plus it forces the communicator to become very focused in their thoughts.

If you eliminate the discussion of alternatives plus the contingency plan, you can produce a focused single-page recommendation without much difficulty.

For the purpose of writing an analysis of a case study for a class project, this complete framework will be an excellent guide for you.

## Purpose: statement of problem

Once you have read a case study and become familiar with the issues, you can then define the purpose of your analysis. It is good practice to assume that you are writing this analysis to a senior manager within your company. You can pretend that the professor is the CEO.

You should also assume that you have been given this project because it is important to the company. Since you are writing this analysis to a senior manager, they must quickly assess how important this analysis is to the company's future. Is it nice-to-know information, or is it something that he/she would need to act on the issue immediately?

By clearly defining the purpose, you help the reader determine how they should budget their time. If the purpose or statement of problem is not clear, it is likely to get put into the pile of reading that is saved for another time.

The following is an example of a purpose statement that introduces a problem that needs to be solved.

> This provides an analysis and recommendation to blunt the recent competitive advertising push of Dean's Beans into Bob's Beans heartland markets.

This clearly states that a competitor (Dean's) is intruding on your client's (Bob's) territory. Something needs to be done. You have the solution. Any manager who would receive this document would be quick to read it and respond.

The key to the purpose is to clearly articulate why you are providing this document to your manager. Be succinct in your approach. Use words that clearly paint the picture of the issue at hand.

## Background or situation analysis

The background or situation analysis provides the contest for the problem. It spells out why there is a problem. Some background or situation analysis sections of a plan are extensive. There may be a tremendous amount of research devoted to the problem.

Your task is to assess the research and make quick work of it. Think about your reader. They don't want to wade through an entire research report. They hired you to do that. You need to provide a quick summary of key points. Usually this is done in a bullet point fashion. For example, in the above problem of Dean's intrusion into Bob's territory, here is a summary of three pieces of research.

- *Dean's Baked Beans has increased their advertising spending from $5 million to $15 million within Bob's heartland territory.*
- *Bob's recent AAU study (awareness, attitude and usage) shows that Dean's Baked Beans has increased unaided awareness by 50% while Bob's Baked Beans awareness is sliding from 20% unaided to 15% unaided.*
- *Dean's message strategy is directly aimed at Bob's Beans with a comparative campaign centered on health claims.*

The latter recaps hundreds of pages of research. If your manager wants to dive further into the issue, you can offer up those studies. Your goal is to make the context clear for your manager.

Background or situation analysis for an advertising manager fall into two broad camps.

- The first is external. This is likely something that impacts a business situation such as the one we have just discussed.
- The second is internal. This is usually around people or personnel.

Let's take a look at each of these areas and discuss some of the typical background or situational areas that arise.

## External factors

For most advertising problems, there are four key areas to consider in a situation analysis. Sometimes, called the 4C's, the broad areas are as follows.

- Company: the company or brand business environment
- Consumer: trends and the environment
- Competition: competing companies
- Communication: trends and strategies

These four areas are forces that can impact the company, brand or organization from a strategic communication perspective. The key to the situation analysis or background section is to highlight factors that will impact the decision that the manager needs to make. Let's briefly look at each area.

The company or brand that you are working with should be the initial aspect of any background analysis. This is a bit of a hybrid situation where you may need to review current internal as well as external factors when considering advertising. For example, if you are developing a campaign for a brand that is expanding its distribution, you will need to understand what the plans are, whether they can deliver product in time and whether there are special circumstances you need to account for.

From an external perspective, what is the business environment that the company is facing? Is it a growing category? What is going on in the marketplace?

This ties nicely to consumer trends and the environment. You need to be aware of changing consumer attitudes. What could have been cool last year could be passé today. Last year the economy may have gone great. This year may be more of a rocky road. The economy, social trends and consumer attitudes are all a part of the changing landscape that any communicator needs to be cognizant of.

The competition is a crucial component to any background analysis. Understanding who the competition is and what they are doing greatly impacts your message and how you go to market.

The last area is the field of communication itself. Communication is a rapidly changing field with new ways to communicate popping up every day. Technology is a tremendous force in communication, moving the field from analog to digital communication. Communication strategies also change. What could have been relevant one day may be less relevant tomorrow.

The purpose of this section is to discuss the most important facts that provide context for the problem. It isn't to show the reader how much you know. If the context is focused on just one of these areas, that is fine. If the reader needs to understand all these areas to better make a decision, then just provide the key points for each. The trick to the background section is to not make it a term paper, but to make it relevant to the single focused problem that needs to be solved.

## Internal factors and personnel

As a manager, much of your responsibilities revolve around the internal workings of your company and the people that you manage. The big three areas of internal focus for a manager are the following.

- Operations
- Finance
- Personnel

The first area is how the company works. In a fast-paced industry such as advertising, having a sluggish or dysfunctional workplace is going to wreak havoc on getting the work done and getting it done in a manner that meets your standards.

Most advertising campaigns and projects require collaboration. Setting up systems and processes to facilitate work flow without stifling creativity can be a tricky balancing act.

Managing projects also means properly allocating manpower. There is nothing worse than having a small group of your employees working 60 hours a week while another group is idle. Shifting people to meet workflow demands is also a key part of the management challenge.

Every company needs to make a profit to exist. As a manager, you will be responsible for managing a budget. This will likely include personnel salaries as well as resources for people to do their jobs. You may also be a part of a larger management team where you discuss the entire financial performance of the company. Obviously the overall health and well-being of the company will impact all your future internal management decisions.

The most time-consuming part of your job as a manager is likely to be personnel. Advertising is a people business. And unlike many other businesses, advertising is a collection of unique talents and personalities. The "creative class" is different from other professions. Understanding how to not only manage your team but also get your team to give their best will be critical to your and the company's success. In this role, you will be hiring/firing people. You will be providing performance reviews, career enhancements and, ultimately, salary adjustments.

Typically, internal issues are all intertwined. Who is hired, what their talents are and how they are used within the team all impact the team's performance and the company's profitability.

The greatest challenge in providing context to any personnel issue is to pull up and look at the larger picture. That is why context is important. With any personnel issue, there is the person. That is the most important thing. As a manager, you need to be sensitive to the person but also understand that every personnel decision is also a business decision.

## Discussion of alternatives

Once you have completed the background or situation analysis, your next step is to define possible alternatives. In the process of generating alternatives, you may come up with a wide variety of solution ideas. Just remember, senior management is not interested in wading through a litany of ideas. They want to see that you have considered alternatives and that there are viable options to solving the problem at hand. If management wants to see every idea you have considered, they can ask for them. Your task is to provide approximately three alternatives for discussion. One of these alternatives should be to maintain the status quo or do nothing to solve the problem. This is an important alternative because the first decision a senior manager must make is to actually take action or not take action. Many times, the best decision a senior leader can take is to not take action or overreact to a situation.

With no action as one alternative, then you can provide two alternatives to consider if action is recommended. This gives management a plan A and plan B to consider.

The following is an example based on the situation that a competitive brand has significantly increased its advertising spending.

- *Monitor the situation until you see evidence that brand sales are eroding as a result of the competitive advertising spending.*
- *Immediately increase your brand's advertising spending to match the competitor.*
- *Test different spending levels to determine the optimum advertising spend in light of this changing competitive landscape.*

Senior management can clearly see that there are three viable paths to take. One is the status quo. Another is to become very aggressive. And the third is to test a variety of approaches.

You will note that these alternatives are markedly different. When you provide an alternative, it is important that it is clearly different from other options and not just a nuanced approach. Once a path is determined, you can then discuss nuances to that recommended approach.

From the alternatives, you can then discuss the pros and cons or advantages and disadvantages of each. Sometimes, it helps to actually make a list of pros and cons. This makes it easy for management to understand the risks or rewards of each alternative you have outlined.

## Recommendation/rationale

Once you have outlined the alternatives, it is then time to make a recommendation. This is not a time to be "wishy washy." Senior management is looking to you to provide the solution, so you need to provide a recommendation that has a strong persuasive argument. You must have a rationale that is compelling to support your point of view. Otherwise, management will wonder if you really believe that this is the best approach.

Continuing with our problem that a competitor has significantly increased advertising spending, the following is an example of a recommendation and supporting rationale to address that problem.

*Based on the above analysis, we recommend that the brand immediately match our competitor's advertising spending levels.*

- *If we don't take immediate action, we are at risk of losing distribution to our top retail outlet that controls 30% of the market.*
- *If we just test different levels, it will be at least a year before we can read the results and by then the brand may have suffered a significant sales erosion.*
- *The company and brand's financial position is stronger than the competitor, which suggests that a matching strategy will ultimately hurt the competition because they will not be able to sustain their current spending.*

That is a straightforward recommendation with a compelling rationale. Most managers look for three bullet point reasons why you recommend a course of action. You should review your rationale to make sure that it is clearly written.

Some students may feel that they do not have enough information to make a decision. So they may recommend postponing the decision to gather more information or do more research. While this may be acceptable from an academic perspective, many business leaders would find this unacceptable. Academics work on a very high confidence level. Academic research is usually at a 95% degree of confidence, which means that the research will be right 95% of the time. In business, most decisions are made within a 60%–80% level of confidence. In other words, business leaders accept some level of ambiguity since the world moves fast. So you make the best decision with the information available.

That is how you should approach the case studies. Look at it as a simulation of the real world.

## Action plan or next step

Once you have made a recommendation, the next step is detailing a plan to implement it. This is the action plan or next step. Here you detail the necessary steps needed to put your plan into motion.

The key items to include for management are a time frame and any resources required. The latter could be dollars and/or people. Managers are prone to action, so be sure to spell out the specifics of the next step.

Continuing our example for the competitive advertising spending situation, the following are the action items.

- *Authorize an incremental $5 million of advertising for the year.*
- *Approve a media plan that details the use of the funds by 7/25.*
- *Begin the incremental spending by 8/21.*
- *Add one more wave to the research study to track effectiveness.*

Note that this action plan is very detailed. It details specific dollars, timing and actions needed to accomplish the task. This is required in any recommendation so that management can understand the details. Keep it short and to the point.

## Contingency plan (optional)

Some organizations like to see a contingency plan just in case the future unfolds differently than you are currently thinking. Contingency plans could be based on economic conditions, competitive conditions and other outside influences that may alter the current recommendation.

Regardless of the issue, it is good to have some thinking ready so that you can rapidly adjust your plan. Contingency plans need not be long. They can be as simple as if this happens, we do that.

Continuing on the current competitive intrusion problem, you may have a contingency plan based on the competitor not succeeding. Or you may have a tactical plan for adjusting your media mix.

As a manager, it is always a good idea to do "what if" scenarios. That way, you are prepared in case adjustments need to be made.

## Summary

The case study method is designed to give you the opportunity to solve real-world problems. It teaches you critical thinking. As you move into the business world, you will find that your daily activities are a series of mini case studies. The only difference is that the real-world case studies are not neatly packaged like they are in this book. The decision process remains the same. The sooner you can rapidly adopt a "case study thinking" mentality, the better prepared you will be to solve problems in the workplace.

Chapter 1

# The new world of advertising management

## Digital and global

### LEARNING OBJECTIVES

This chapter is intended to help you:

- Learn the foundation principles of advertising management.
- Understand the different managerial roles in advertising.
- Learn about the impact of digital advertising on management.
- Learn about the impact of globalization on management.
- Understand daily management challenges dealing with change.

Every organization needs managers. You would have likely witnessed organizations that are not well managed and some that are well managed. You may have seen the old sitcom The Office and wondered if that is what managers really do. Or perhaps you have watched the Mad Men television series about the advertising industry in the 1960s and wondered if that is what it is like in the real world today.

Management seems like such an ambiguous job. Is it just about sitting in an office or going to meetings or filling out mind-numbing amounts of paperwork? Is there more to it than that? And how is management different in the advertising industry? Or is it really? Are all managers the same?

Throughout this text, we will answer these questions. Management is largely a generic term. Some popular definitions include the following.

- The process of dealing with or controlling things or people
- The act of supervising something
- The collective body of those who direct an enterprise or organization

Just about any enterprise or organization needs someone or a group to direct that enterprise or organization. Not all enterprises and organizations are the same. Being an advertising manager is a very different experience than being a manager at a McDonalds. While they both may direct an enterprise, the enterprise itself is so radically different that it does require a unique skill set.

If you can manage a McDonalds, I would dare say you could likely manage any other restaurant. Those skills are quite transferable. In fact, you might make a case that a McDonald's manager could manage just about any retail store. The basics are relatively the same. All retailers sell a tangible product (or products).

Advertising is different. It is in the business of selling ideas—not just any idea; it is communication ideas that change the way people think and/or behave about a specific product, service or organization. And this difference demands different ways of looking at managing. Let's take a look at the foundation principles of advertising management.

## Advertising management foundation principles

Advertising management has four broad components. We call them the 4Ps of advertising management. They are as follows.

- People
- Process
- Planning
- Profit

Advertising management involves managing people, developing processes to ensure that work is done both effectively yet efficiently, planning for the future and helping the company make a profit.

While just about every manager is involved in some form of these four components of management, each of these areas has unique aspects specific to the advertising industry.

## People are the product

Advertising is a creative business. It is an idea-driven business. As a result, the people that are attracted to the advertising industry are different. They are not like engineers who build a building. They are content creators who build strategic communication campaigns.

The job of the manager is to find ways to make the people employed with an organization thrive. That means hiring the right people, rewarding them properly and giving them the space to do their job. Many view advertising managers more as a coach than as a traditional manager. The management challenge is to help your team stay motivated. Since advertising is about being "creative on demand," sometimes that is no easy task. It is difficult to be "on" all the time. Yet that is what the advertising industry demands. The client or project dictates when you need to be "creative," whereby you think about things in a new and unique way. As a manager, your job then becomes to help mold or take others' ideas and push them forward—make them even better. This is no simple task. It requires a deft touch whereby the manager pushes their associates to think better without alienating them.

Another key part of managing people is to make sure they work together. Developing an advertising campaign is a collaborative process. It requires creative content that may begin with writers and art directors and end up with producers or information architects. It also requires content connectors, media planners and buyers, digital specialists, social media specialists and many others to determine how best to connect the content to the audience. All of this must focus on strategy, so there are account planners, brand strategists and others who provide strategic input. Account managers, then, are the team leaders. They ensure that all of these groups work together. It is a complex dance with a variety pack of people and egos.

As we will discuss in later chapters, the other side of managing is firing people. This may be for poor performance or for not fitting in. Or they may be doing a great job and the company needs to let them go for economic reasons.

The manager needs to be in constant communication with his or her associates so that they are not "blindsided" by bad news. This also requires a deft touch so that you have provided important information yet haven't demotivated your staff.

Working with people is the cornerstone of advertising management.

## Process: making things run smoothly

You've hired the right team. Now they have to do the work. Another key advertising management function is to make sure that things run smoothly. Determining if your team has the right resources to do the job is a part of management. Do they have the right information? Do you have a system where there is seamless collaboration?

Setting up advertising processes is not like building a car or like setting up an assembly line. Persuasive communication comes from the understanding of consumer insights. Compelling communication taps into emotional nerve ends that may not have been previously explored. Campaigns can't go viral just like that. Going viral is something that isn't ordered like a hamburger. Sometimes advertising campaigns come into existence as the result of "happy circumstances" where two or three associates are discussing ideas or alternatives and that triggers an even better idea.

On the flip side, there are demanding timetables. A client can't wait forever for the "happy circumstance" to happen. They may need to be in the market with a message in a day or a week.

That is the management challenge—setting up a process that gets the best and most innovative thinking in the shortest amount of time, and then executing the ideas quickly in consideration of the budget parameters.

Well, are you beginning to see why managers get paid well? Their job simply isn't easy.

## Planning: making the future bright

One of the bigger management challenges is to be in the moment with people and processes yet have an eye to the future endeavors. As a manager, one of your roles is to always be thinking ahead. You need to have a plan. That plan might include what kind of people you may need in the future, what resources will you need and, more importantly, where the business will be in the next three to five years.

As a manager, you need to be constantly looking at the horizon; in the advertising industry, that means understanding where consumer trends are going. It means understanding where communication is going. What will be the new media channels or platforms of tomorrow?

Your employees or associates are counting on you to lead them to a brighter future. You can't do that without trying to figure out where the future is going.

As you wrestle with the daily work routine and the flow of work, you must continue to be curious about all aspects of business and society. Those factors will ultimately impact your management plan.

## Make a profit

All managers must deal with a budget; there is likely a budget for personnel and there could be a budget for resources. Budget management is certainly a part of every manager's life.

The broader picture of financial management is helping the organization make a profit, for without a profit, the company will not exist. Advertising managers must understand the basics of finance. They must also understand the role they play in making the company profitable. Those are core management functions.

The other big picture regarding profit is how to measure the impact of an advertising program. Is the program generating the impact it was designed to create? And how does that impact translate to some form of return on investment.

All advertising programs are an investment for the company and/or brand. Many times, the investment in advertising is one of the larger dollar commitments made by a company. This is especially true if a company is investing a large amount of dollars into paid media. This can be millions of dollars. Thus, there is pressure to understand what the brand got in return for that investment.

Advertising managers must know their way around the fundamentals of budgeting, accounting, finance and financial analysis. It is a necessary part of being a manager.

## Advertising management roles and organization structure

There are many different companies that are part of the advertising ecosystem.

The type of organization, its ownership structure and its organizational structure will dictate the type of advertising management needed.

We will deal with four overall categories of organizations that are involved with the advertising industry. They are as follows.

- Advertiser
- Advertising agencies
- Media
- Specialty vendors

The advertiser is a company or organization that is being promoted by the advertising. This could be a large corporation such as General Motors, Procter & Gamble, Nike or Apple. Or it can be a small retailer such as a local pet store, a florist or even a barbershop.

Some large advertisers such as a General Motors may have their own in-house advertising department. Or they may use an outside advertising agency. Or they may do a bit of both. A small advertiser such as a florist may handle their own advertising or they may hire a consultant to help them.

How a client structures their advertising program will dictate the need for management roles. Some may have a large team that requires many managers; others may have a single person or a small team, and still others may be doing advertising as a part of all the necessary business activities needed to make their business run.

Advertising agencies work for advertisers to help conceptualize, develop and place advertising on their behalf. Some advertising agencies do all of these activities, and some agencies just focus on a specific function such as media planning and buying, while others may focus on a part of the process such as digital marketing. The size and scope of the agency will dictate the type of managers required.

The media is another large part of the advertising ecosystem. Media properties, whether it be large digital media companies like Google or Facebook, or broadcast companies such as Disney or out-of-home companies such as Clear Channel Communications, all depend on advertising as their revenue source. Their management structure reflects the need to build an audience and people to generate revenue based on the same.

The fourth big area of advertising is specialty companies that serve various niche aspects of the advertising industry. This includes many creative content makers such as film producers, graphic designers, photographers and digital artists. It also includes niche companies such as trade shows, events and app producers. These companies all require management to organize their activities.

## Management titles and structures

How a company is owned has a big impact on management. There are two basic types of ownership structures.

- Privately owned companies dominate the landscape of advertising agencies, smaller advertisers and smaller niche companies. A privately owned company may be owned by a single person or a group of people. A privately owned or held company is usually structured as a limited liability company (LLC).
- Publicly traded companies dominate the landscape of large advertisers and media companies. A publicly traded company is one that issues stock to the public. Its ownership is shared among a wide range of people called shareholders. A shareholder can own just a few shares of a company or a large percentage of the company.
- Because publicly traded companies have a fiduciary responsibility to their shareholders, there is an independent board of directors elected to oversee management. In the case of a public company, management ultimately reports to a board of directors. Both answer to the shareholder base.

Regardless of being a private or a public company, there are similar types of managers. They just have different reporting structures. Private managers report to company owners or partners, while public managers report to shareholders.

Managers come in a wide variety of roles and titles. There are two fundamental layers of management. The first is senior management, which is sometimes called the C-level since their titles all begin with the letter C. The second is functional or department management, which is managers with specific responsibility. For example, a media director is a functional manager whose responsibility is with the media department, and a creative director is responsible for the creative department and so on.

Top managers have titles such as CEO, COO, CFO, CIO and CMO. A CEO is the chief executive officer. He or she is ultimately in charge of everyone in the company. Within a publicly traded company, the CEO reports to the board of directors. A CEO has a unique management role. CEOs are responsible for how the company grows and how the company allocates its capital. Everyone else in the company is focused on generating income and profit for the company. The CEO's role is to best determine how to deploy that profit.

A CEO then needs to determine what that money will be used for. This is especially true of a publicly traded company where the price of the company's stock is an important factor in the overall success of the CEO.

Capital can be used to reward employees. It can also be used to potentially acquire a new capability or to acquire a company that can accelerate their growth. Financial pressure may be on the CEO in a publicly traded company to increase its dividend which goes directly to the shareholders or to buy back company stock, which in theory helps increase the share price of the company.

In this text, we will focus more on the day-to-day management of advertising than on the C-level. Beyond the CEO, there are other C-suite positions within many companies.

A COO is the chief operating officer. Their role is the day-to-day management of the company while that of the CEO is more focused on long-term projects and vision of the organization. Then there are senior level positions such as CFO or chief financial officer who is responsible for the financial results and reporting of the company. A CIO or chief information officer may be responsible for all information and technology activity, and a chief marketing officer (CMO) is a standard title, among advertisers, for the head of all marketing and advertising.

Every advertising industry business has its own unique organizational structure. It is simply not possible to discuss or demonstrate all the various organizational settings in use. However, let's take the typical advertising agency as a framework for discussion.

Advertising agencies are typically organized in a departmental structure. This means that the functions of the agency are organized in various departments. Work flows from one department to another. Most advertising agencies have the following departments.

- Creative: includes writers, art directors, digital designers
- Production: includes print, video and digital production
- Media: includes media planners and buyers with print, broadcast and digital represented
- Account Service: includes account/client interface or account executives as well as project managers, those who work internally on the account
- Research/Account Planning: includes strategists for developing consumer insights
- Human Resources: manages personnel benefits and does talent acquisition
- Accounting: manages account payables for the agency

There are managers for each of these areas. Depending on the size of the organization, there can be managers for managers. For example, a media director may have a planning director and buying director reporting to him or her. Those two managers many have supervisors who manage a variety of people. There can be layers in each area.

The senior management at an advertising firm, many times, consists of a CEO or president and a CFO or chief financial officer. Other senior management may be drawn from the functional areas of Creative, Media, Account Service and/or Planning. It just depends on the size and scope of the agency.

Advertisers have a variety of organizational structures to manage their marketing and advertising. Many companies use a brand management approach. A brand manager is responsible for all the marketing and advertising needs of a specific brand or company. The role of this structure began with consumer package goods, but, over time, it has extended to many other companies.

In this structure, brand managers hire advertising agencies and other marketing communication partners to help develop marketing and advertising strategy and support. In this structure, advertising is done outside the brand. It is the brand manager's job to ensure that it is being done correctly.

In the case of other advertisers, there are a range of in-house capabilities. Some advertisers have in-house media planning and buying, and use outside agencies for creative development. Other advertisers do their digital advertising in-house and then use outside resources for other activities. In this case, the advertising manager or CMO may be the head of the department.

An in-house operation, whether it is media, digital or a complete in-house agency, is structured similarly to an advertising agency or that specific department within the advertising agency. The difference is that unlike an advertising agency that has its senior management devoted to the agency's growth, the in-house agency is focused on specific advertising programs for that advertiser.

Media company organizations are composed of those who are create content for the media property and those who sell advertising. Management on the content side of the business is set up from an editorial perspective. There is a head of the editorial who is in charge of content. On the revenue side, there is a sales manager who is in charge of sales account executives. Those sales account executives may have assistants who help them secure and manage an account.

Media companies are largely a very flat organization. This means that there are not many layers of management. It usually has a manager as the department head. Most of the staff do their specific job duties.

## Impact of digital advertising

One of the biggest transformations in the advertising industry in the past decade has been the rapid rise of digital media and advertising.

Digital media has had a profound impact on management decisions.

The biggest change from a digital media perspective is the new way consumers communicate with brands and companies. Prior to digital communication, advertising was a one-way street; advertisers would put out a message for consumers to see or hear, and the action was either a change of attitude or a change in behavior.

Today, that is still true, but digital advertising and media has added the element of instant consumer engagement and response. Consumers can rapidly respond to a brand or a message. Consumers can give feedback and have large digital social media platforms to amplify their message.

It is no longer enough to just do advertising. Advertising has moved from being a monologue to being a dialogue. This has changed how managers view the role of advertising and what is required to be effective.

From a people perspective, digital advertising has ushered in a variety of new skills and positions. Every brand has a website. Nearly every brand has their own social media platforms. It is very common for the smallest company to have a Facebook business page or a Twitter feed. The skills to update content on the website and social media are crucial for any business.

There are specific media positions such as search or pay-per-click specialists who help drive traffic to the brand's website. There are social media specialists for both paid advertising and unpaid brand content. There are special jobs such as an information architect, coders and software engineers who are now a part of advertising instead of the IT department.

With new media comes new processes. Traditional advertising was developed and placed and results were monitored. Digital advertising, on the contrary, is ongoing and dynamic. Feedback is instant and changes must be made. This requires a much more aggressive process of "do, monitor, and change" than that before digital advertising. Integrating digital and analog media at the same company or agency is also a challenge. The processes, in general, are the same. But the speed of change is much different.

Large communication technology firms such as Google, Facebook, Amazon and Apple all provide tools so that just about any business can use their platform, bypassing the advertising agency model.

This has led managers to revisit their planning for the future. Should a company staff up with tech-savvy people or is it more advantageous to outsource this function? The first approach maintains control, while the latter maintains flexibility.

The other impact digital advertising has had on the industry is one of profitability. The large tech communication firms are highly profitable. They have size and scale. For a smaller firm, it is difficult to replicate what is needed to compete in the marketplace. While the revenue from digital advertising is great, it may not be profitable for a smaller company or agency to get deeply invested in it.

As you go through the text, you will see that digital plays a huge role in current and future management decisions.

## Impact of globalization

The other large macro trend impacting management is globalization. We live and work in a global community. Many companies are global. And many brands are global. Add to this the ability to communicate with new digital tools and you have a tremendous management opportunity.

Globalization has a huge impact on the advertising industry. If a company has a website, it now has a global footprint. Anyone from anywhere can access your products or communicate with you.

How you deal with such a change is a true management challenge. If you market on a global basis, you need to understand different country business practices, different cultures and different ways of communicating.

As an advertiser, your management challenge is how you organize your team to compete in a global market. Do you hire people in different countries to advise you on advertising strategies? Or do you hire a global communication company? Or do you have a mix of those strategies? Setting up the right people and structure is a major challenge for managers.

Globalization has led to the ability to tap into talent from across the world. You may find a graphic artist in Brazil who has the perfect style you need for communicating your brand. Or you may find that coders in Hungary can work for a fraction of what you pay someone in the United States to do the same task.

Balancing and managing who you bring onto your team is a real challenge. When you have team members from different cultures and countries, you typically run into communication style issues. Americans have a very direct communication style that can be off-putting to other cultures. On the other hand, Japan has a very subtle communication style that doesn't always connect with westerners.

A big challenge for a manager in a global world is to help smooth the path of how people can work together. As we will discuss later in the text, working remotely has its unique challenges. This is true even when it is working with people in the same culture. Throwing different countries and cultures into the mix and having a process that works for everyone can be daunting.

The more complicated the structure and market, the more challenging it is to make a profit. There are a myriad of financial issues to take into account. Different tax laws, different monetary policy and other government policies can make it more challenging to make a profit and to allocate capital.

On the other hand, globalization is a real opportunity for advertisers. Approximately 1/3 of all advertising dollars are focused on the United States. Yet the United States only represents only 4.5% of the world's population. There is a tremendous opportunity for growth of advertising in emerging markets around the globe.

For this reason alone, those working in advertising and marketing will continue to see the impact of globalization. It is a key trend that will factor heavily in the balance of this text.

## Dealing with daily changes

The biggest challenge for any manager is adapting to change. This is true of any job. It is especially true of a management position. The higher you rise in the management world, the more you have to rapidly adapt.

The following is a five-minute window into the day in the life of an advertising agency CEO. Let's call her Sarah.

"Sarah, Bob just resigned today. What do we tell the client?"

"Sarah, there is a meeting at 10am to discuss agency financial projections."

"Sarah, you may be double booked. There is also a client strategy meeting at 10am. What do you want to do?"

"Sarah, your sitter just called. Your son may be coming down with the flu. Do you want to talk to her?"

"I just learned that our largest client's marketing director has just left. Do you want to talk to the CEO about a replacement?"

And so it goes. This is an actual five minutes in the life of an advertising agency CEO's day. It is maddening. Things are coming at you from all sides—internal issues, external issues and personal issues. The worlds sometimes collide.

This is a daily balancing act that managers must deal with. As a manager, you must make solid decisions, not get ruffled, and provide constant leadership to your team. Just think, an average business leader makes around 35,000 decisions in an average day.

There is not a day that goes by that does not have issues with personnel, budgets and changes to a business. These are internal issues. Of course, the manager must change or adapt to new communication tools and communication methods.

The greatest adaption usually comes from unexpected outside forces. As we write this text, we are in the midst of a global health pandemic. The pandemic, COVID-19, originated in Wuhan, China and then rapidly spread to the rest of the world.

The impact was immense. Many countries implemented public health policies that included "stay at home" orders for a month or more. The goal was to ensure that the spread of the virus didn't overwhelm the health system of these countries.

Businesses were immediately closed. Only essential businesses were open. This included some retailers like grocers and pharmacies. Hospitals and doctors could not arrange for elective surgery. Basically, the world stopped on a country-by-country basis to deal with this novel virus.

Advertising managers had to adapt quickly. Their teams were working from home. If they were an advertising agency, their clients were changing their strategies on the fly. Budgets were being cancelled. Yet, for other businesses, messages were being changed. Lives were suddenly turned upside down.

As a manager, you must deal with the situation. You must make rapid decisions. You don't know all the information. In the case of COVID-19 health crisis, no one really knew the situation. That included the public health professionals. The situation was unprecedented. Things changed on nearly a daily basis.

As we will discuss in this text, management is all about adapting to change and making the best possible decisions. It isn't always easy; however, it can be very rewarding.

## Summary

Being a manager is not just about "being in charge." It involves taking responsibility, leading others and working long hours to achieve corporate and personal goals.

There are many ways to organize the role of advertising. Advertising agencies, advertisers, media companies and various niche advertising vendors all have unique business models and approaches to structuring the advertising function.

Regardless of the structure, advertising managers deal with personnel, process, and planning and profit issues relating to their department, company or brand.

Two key macro trends have impacted advertising management. They are digital communication and globalization. Together, these two influences shape many management decisions.

A good manager must be able to rapidly adapt to a variety of internal and external forces. The next chapter will provide deeper insights into the role of an advertising manager.

## Review questions

1. What are the key components of advertising management? How are they interrelated?
2. What are the different advertising industry organizations? How are they similar? How are they different?

3 What are different managerial roles in advertising? How is the CEO's role special?
4 What has been the impact of digital communication on advertising management?
5 What has been the impact of globalization on advertising management?

## Case 1.1 Boswell Agency

### *Issue: structuring of an advertising agency*

Jill Williams arrived at DFW airport at 9pm on Blue Sky Airlines from New York.

The flight was on time.

"Thank goodness we came in on time," she thought. "I've got enough on my plate without having to discuss a flight delay when I meet with Tom Bradley tomorrow."

Tom Bradley was the president of Blue Sky Airlines. He was a real no-nonsense figure who had many run-ins with labor unions in the past. He was a tough negotiator and an equally tough client.

In fact, he was the largest client of Boswell Agency. Jill was being asked to head up the Dallas office of Boswell after being a top executive with the agency's New York office. The president of the Dallas Boswell office had recently resigned. Since Jill had prior airline experience with Continental Airlines and had run the tourism group for Boswell's New York office, she was the choice to run Dallas office.

Naturally, this was stressful for her family. Her husband was an IBM salesman, so the move wouldn't disrupt his work. He could work from any location. However, her son and daughter were not excited about relocating. Both were in high school. Her daughter was especially distraught since she had recently performed at the New York City Ballet. She was in a special performing arts school in Manhattan. The family all liked the Manhattan lifestyle. They loved the arts and the energy of New York. Dallas seemed like a foreign country to them.

### *Company*

The Boswell Agency had grown out of Des Moines, Iowa, where it still maintained its accounting and financial activities. It began as an agricultural agency, but after its early success, Charles Bowell went on an acquisition spree. He purchased agencies across the United States, including New York, Los Angeles, Dallas, Atlanta, Chicago and Boston. Through these acquisitions, he built a network of agencies that was now the twentieth largest in the United States.

This acquisition strategy brought many challenges. Each office was largely independent and had its own financial goals. Although there were benefits to the network, it was not always easy to get the offices to work together. While Charles Boswell worked to bring a common culture to the company, power struggles and jealousies among the offices were a part of life (Exhibit 1.1).

**Exhibit 1.1 Boswell Agency: Dallas Office's client roster**

| *Account* | *Billing (millions)* | *Total office % income* |
|---|---|---|
| Blue Sky Airlines | 100.0 | 50 |
| Goodmark Foods | 30.0 | 15 |
| Oberon Printers | 22.0 | 11 |
| Bell Cellular | 18.0 | 9 |
| Roscoe's Sausages | 8.0 | 4 |
| Bluebonnet Cosmetics | 8.0 | 4 |
| Plains Bank | 6.0 | 3 |
| WPBA-TV | 4.0 | 2 |
| Singleman Auto Group | 4.0 | 2 |
| | $200.0 | 100 |

The Dallas office, which had been recently headed by Peter Finch, was the largest in the Bowell system. It was driven by its largest account, Blue Sky Airlines. Blue Sky Airlines was a relatively new account in the Dallas office which they picked up in a high-profile agency search. The Dallas office beat many larger New York and Chicago agencies for the account. This acquisition pushed them past the Boswell New York in terms of billings.

There was a rivalry between the New York and Dallas office. New York had the second largest account in the system, Unimar Foods, and a variety of nationally marketed food brands. However, Blue Sky Airlines was a higher-profile account than Unimar. The creative work for Blue Sky Airlines was winning awards. This galled New York office, which considered themselves the creative hub of the agency.

### *Dallas office*

In her hotel room, Jill studied the Dallas office client roster. It was very telling. There was Blue Sky Airlines at the top of the list. It represented half the income of the office.

"It also represents more than 10 percent of Boswell's entire agency network income." thought Jill. "It is a monster," she sighed.

The rest of the accounts consisted of a variety of categories. Jill segmented them into three overall groups. There were package goods brand such as Goodmark Foods and Roscoe's Sausages. There were high-tech accounts such as Oberon Printers and Bell Cellular. There were a number of local accounts such as Plains Bank, WPBA-TV and Singleman Auto Group. The oddball account was Bluebonnet Cosmetics, which was patterned after Mary Kay Cosmetics.

The local accounts had not grown significantly in years. But they were steady and from what Jill had heard the agency had good relationships with the senior people in those organizations. The packaged goods companies were also steady pluggers. There was not a lot of new product activity from either company, but they had to maintain support of their current brands or be forced off the grocery shelf by their competitors. They would continue to need support. The wild cards were the high-tech accounts. Oberon Printers had moved from manufacturing printers to software development. As a result, it had doubled in the past year. Bell Cellular was growing at a rapid rate as well. Bell Cellular was a national cellular service provider and also had an innovative lab that was constantly inventing new technologies.

Jill knew that as quickly as high-tech accounts go up, they can rapidly go down. The cycle of new tech products/software was so rapid that one day you had a big brand and the next day another company stole your thunder.

Then, of course, there was Blue Sky Airlines. Blue Sky was an aggressive advertiser. They were adding new routes and markets to their system. They had plans to expand internationally, which could add substantial growth to the account. Jill wondered how Boswell was going to handle this. Boswell didn't have international offices. She wasn't sure if Charles Boswell wanted to acquire or open offices in Europe or Latin America. These were the markets where Blue Sky was considering entering in the next few years.

### *Agency structure*

Jill then began to review the agency structure. Each office in the Boswell network was set up a bit differently. The only corporate functions impacting Dallas were financial controls, which were centralized in Des Moines, and network broadcast, which was centralized in the New York media department. Otherwise, each office had autonomy to set up its own structure as long as it met the corporate profit goals (Exhibit 1.2).

## Exhibit 1.2 Boswell Agency: Dallas Office's agency structure (conventional)

The Dallas office had never met the Boswell profit goals. This was largely due to Blue Sky, which took a sizeable portion of staff to manage all aspects of their business. Since Blue Sky was so large, agency management had been reluctant to cut back on staff or to ask for additional fees from the client to pay for the staff. The fact that Dallas office didn't meet profit goals had always galled the New York office, including Jill.

On the surface, the Dallas office had a conventional agency structure. There was a financial group that reported to her as well as to the corporate CFO in Des Moines. The creative group was headed by Jim Clark, a funny man who always wore a Hawaiian shirt. He had four creative directors and a number of writer/art director teams reporting to them. Jim personally wrote and directed the majority of Blue Sky's advertising. He left much of the rest of the work to the creative directors and rarely reviewed their work.

The media director was Carole Chan, a self-made woman, who began her career as a secretary and rose up through the ranks in media. She was noted as a hard-nosed negotiator who ruled her group with an iron fist. She had three group media directors who reported to her and oversaw the planning on the accounts. Then she had planner/buyers who did the planning and execution of the media, with the exception of digital. She had set up the planner/buyer model to serve Blue Sky, which relied on an extensive amount of local advertising media. Each planner/buyer had a number of markets that they were responsible for. They purchased all the media for those markets.

Jim Able was one of the group media directors. He was responsible for Blue Sky, plus he had built a small digital buying team that largely served Blue Sky. They were a small group and constantly under stress with the growing demands of digital media.

The production director was Raul Steele. Raul was a former New Yorker who had a print production background. He had a keen eye for design and worked well with the creative group. He had both print and broadcast production plus traffic reporting to him. Raul was not very tech savvy, so he relied on Millie Klein, one of the four creative directors to help him with digital production. Millie had a few junior creative people who were doing most of the digital production work. Mark's first priority was creative, so he left much of the actual management to Richard. Richard had also set up a business manager for the department, Emily Litrell, to help him keep control of costs. By most counts, she was the one who really ran the department.

The planning department was headed by Ian Howell. Ian was recruited to Boswell from London and was the first account planner in the office. He soon recruited a research person and a junior planner to help him. Ian was extremely gifted in developing insights and was a very valuable member of the team. His insights had led to recent work on Blue Sky that had won numerous industry creative awards. However, Ian often clashed with the creative department. He felt that the creative team shouldn't be involved in overall strategy. Although the creative group respected his ability to generate insights, they often felt that he went too far in leading the client into a certain type of creative execution before they got involved.

Finally, there was the account management group. There were four account directors. Hal Green ran the Blue Sky account. Hal was the former marketing director for Blue Sky and was a close personal friend of Tom Bradley. They had been college roommates. Boswell had been required to take on Hal as one of the conditions for gaining the account. It was an odd relationship since Hal worked nearly as much from the client perspective as from the agency viewpoint. He ran the account like an in-house advertising agency. Nearly all he key people on the account reported to him on a de facto basis, regardless of department. He was the only account director to have two personal assistants. One worked at the agency and the other at the client. Hal still maintained an office at Blue Sky. Many in the agency felt that while Hal certainly had a great relationship with Tom, he was reluctant to speak up for the agency when there was a conflict.

The other three account directors managed the other accounts: Crystal Heep was the only one on Bluebonnet; Bob Pugh oversaw Goodmark, Bell Cellular,

Roscoe's Sausages and Plains Bank; Jennifer Meade oversaw Oberon Printers, WPBA-TV and Singleman Auto Group.

Jill didn't know much about this group. Bob was a relatively new hire from Chicago. Having managed a number of national brands at his prior agency, he had a very strong background. Crystal and Jennifer had been with the agency for a number of years. Each of these account directors had a variety of supervisors, account executives and assistants reporting to them.

### *Decisions*

Jill sat back on her hotel room bed and pondered. She had to make a number of decisions regarding how she serviced Blue Sky Airlines and how to structure the Dallas office to make it more efficient. These goals seemed to be at odds with each other. She had heard of other agencies that had deployed an "agency within an agency" concept. This meant that they set up a dedicated account group with all disciplines housed together to serve a single account. Boswell didn't have another mega-account like Blue Sky Airlines anywhere in the system. As a result, Jill was not familiar with this approach first hand. However, she had friends at a competing agency, C+E, which handled General Motors. They had moved to adopt this approach. She really needed to find out more about how it worked.

On the other hand, an efficient agency structure should be able to handle any account, regardless of size. If she set up a separate group just for Blue Sky, she wondered whether she would be perpetuating the domination of the account within the office. She had heard that the agency had not won as much new business as they should have, because they were known as the in-house Blue Sky agency. Potential clients felt that they would always be a "second class citizen" to Blue Sky.

She also thought about what she might offer Tom Bradley of Blue Sky. He was a hard-edged guy and she must have a game plan ready for his account. She knew that he would ask her about the agency's plans to handle his international business. And she worried that the agency's ragtag approach to building out a digital media capability left them very vulnerable. She had heard through the grapevine that Tom Bradley had been asking more about digital technology and its role in his business; she needed to be in a position to lead him and not just react to new technologies coming out.

Her head throbbed as she went to bed that night. Tomorrow, she must meet with Tom Bradley and then the agency staff. She then owed a preliminary report to corporate management, including Charles Boswell, within two weeks.

She thought about not only the structure of the organization but how she should come across as a leader. She had a very collaborative style in the New York Office. But with a strong personality such as Tom Bradley, she wondered if she should modify her style to be stronger and more aggressive. And she wondered about the Hal/Tom relationship. It worried her that she may not be able to confide in either man without the other knowing.

The next few weeks were going to be long and stressful for Jill. She had to smooth the feathers of the agency's largest account, figure out a structure that would be more efficient and demonstrate to the staff that she was a capable leader. Of course, she was trying to understand how best to move her family to Dallas.

### *Questions*

1. How should Jill prioritize her agenda? What do you think should be her 90-day plan?
2. What questions should she ask of Tom Bradley, the head of Blue Sky Airlines, to assess the best course of action with this account?
3. What are the pros and cons of setting up a dedicated unit to serve a single large account?
4. Should Jill change any of the reporting structures in the agency? Should she add or delete any functions?
5. What steps should Jill take to make the agency more profitable?
6. What steps should Jill take to raise the creative product of the entire agency?
7. What information is missing that Jill needs before she can make a strong recommendation to her senior management?

Chapter 2

# Culture, administration and leadership in a global market

## LEARNING OBJECTIVES

This chapter is intended to help you:

- Learn about setting organizational culture.
- Learn about cultural and personal values.
- Understand the difference between administration, management and leadership.
- Understand the fundamentals of leadership communication.

Establishing the organization's culture is one of the most important roles for any manager. It is even more true for an advertising manager since culture can become a defining characteristic for the company.

The culture of an organization involves such factors as beliefs, practices and behaviors of the company. Culture is also the personality of the organization. It includes the values and norms.

Culture answers the following questions.

- What do you believe in?
- How do you work?
- What is it like to work here?
- What is your view of advertising?

Organizational culture varies from organization to organization. The culture of a small local advertising agency may vary greatly from some large multinational advertising holding company. Likewise, the advertising department at a national retailer may differ greatly from that of a fashion company. Media companies may differ based on their media. A communication technology company such as Google is very different from a traditional media company such as Hearst Corporation.

Why is culture important? It sets the tone and standard for all employees. Usually, senior management, including the CEO, are responsible for establishing the culture of an organization. However, it is every manager's responsibility to apply that culture to their own area.

According to Robert E. Quinn and Kim S. Cameron of the University of Michigan, there are four fundamental types of organizational cultures.

- Clan: a family-oriented culture, focused on mentoring, nurturing and "doing things together."
- Adhocracy: dynamic and entrepreneurial, focused on risk taking, innovation and "doing things first."
- Market: results-oriented culture, focused on competition, achievement and "getting the job done."
- Hierarchy: structured and controlled, focused on efficiency, stability and "doing things right."

Let's take a look at how some advertising agencies position themselves that suggests their culture.

- TBWA: TBWA is The Disruption® Company. We create disruptive ideas that locate and involve brands in culture, giving them a larger share of the future.
- Zimmerman: Hold Tight. The ride starts here. This is a non-stop, white-knuckle ride to the battle where our only weapons are ideas and passion and our only clients are fast-paced retailers.
- Omnicom: Omnicom and its agencies share in the priorities of investing in our people, protecting the environment and giving back to the communities in which we serve.
- GSD&M: We are not your typical agency, but we are your typical family.

These four advertising agencies range in size and scope. TBWA is a global agency with offices around the world. They have very high-profile clients such as Apple, Unilever and Absolut. Zimmerman is a US domestic advertising agency that specializes in retail brands. They have large retailers such as Kay Jewelers, AutoNation and Tire Kingdom. GSD&M is also a US domestic agency with a variety of clients such as Southwest Airlines, Popeyes Chicken Restaurants and Texas Department of Transportation. Omnicom is one of the largest publicly traded advertising agency holding companies. Omnicom owns hundreds of advertising and marketing services companies. Ironically, TBWA, Zimmerman and GSD&M are all owned by Omnicom.

While these three advertising agencies have common ownership, they have markedly different cultures.

TBWA is a classic *adhocracy* model. Their positioning is all about disrupting the status quo. In fact, they have an entire process built around the idea of disruption. Jean-Marie Dru, the head of TBWA in Paris, has written two books describing the agency's process, *Disruption* and *Beyond Disruption*. If you were a manager at TBWA, you mission would be to reinforce the idea of disrupting current thinking. Thus, their agency is built around a single point of view. This likely helps bring their agency together whether it is the office in Paris, Singapore or Los Angeles.

Zimmerman is a classic *market* model. Retail is a results-oriented business category. It is fast-paced. Zimmerman makes no bones about it. In fact, if you read more deeply about their culture, they almost challenge new employees to see if they can keep up with this fast pace. The mindset of a manager at Zimmerman is likely to be very different than that of TBWA.

GSD&M is a classic *clan* model. The agency was founded in the 1970s by a group of former University of Texas college students in Austin, Texas. The cofounders still live in the area and have some contact with the agency. Of the three agencies, it seems like GSD&M would be the most "warm and fuzzy."

Omnicom is the corporate entity. As such, they reflect a classic *hierarchy* model. The corporation wants its companies to "do the right thing." It is important to be a good community partner whether it is in Austin, Texas or Paris, France. Many corporations take on this type of culture.

As an advertising manager within one of these cultures, it is your job to help reinforce that culture within your department or as a part of senior management. If you were the creative director of a branch office of TBWA, you would be focused on helping your creative team develop "disruptive ideas." You would likely hold them to a very high standard which some on the team may not be able to reach. Contrast that to an agency like GSD&M, where as a manager, your culture may be to help mentor and bring along young talent; you have the same passion for compelling ideas as in TBWA but perhaps a more nurturing culture in which to foster them. For a Zimmerman manager, it is all about getting things done quickly. Responding to market conditions rapidly and beating the competition to the punch are all parts of their culture.

As you can see culture plays a big role in the makeup of any firm in the advertising industry. The next aspect to establishing a strong culture is establishing core values.

## Core values and personal values

Core values are the fundamental beliefs of an organization. Core values are also shared with personal values. This is why core values are so important. A core value is the intersection between what the organization treasures and believes, and what you feel is personally important.

Some core values should be very apparent and fundamental.

- Integrity and ethics are important core values. You want the organization to be honest and want yourself to be honest. You want people to be aboveboard and do the right thing, even if that means doing things that are difficult.
- Respect is another important core value. You want respect. And you should respect others. It is about as simple as that.
- Innovation is a top core value of many advertising industry companies. Looking for innovation and not imitation is an important core value in the advertising industry.

The importance of core values is to establish the parameters of how everyone should work. While, sometimes, core values seem like common sense, it is important for every organization to spell them out so that employees will internalize them.

For example, the following are some of the key core values for Google employees.

- Do the right thing. Don't be evil.
- Earn customer trust and respect every day.
- Technology innovation is our lifeblood.

If you were a manager at Google, these three core values would be what is expected of you and, in turn, what you would expect from your employees. For a company like Google, sometimes, core values can lead to conflict. For example, the first is, "do the right thing and don't be evil." This seems pretty straightforward. Some Google employees had a difficult time with Google working with the US government on defense cybersecurity projects. Some saw it as a conflict with this core value. The same goes for customer trust where Google is not as transparent as some customers would like to see when collecting their private information from their search history.

Core values are thus a guiding light for organizational and personal behavior. In advertising, there are times when core values are severely tested. We will discuss this in greater detail when we dig deeper into the area of ethics and social responsibility.

The point here is that establishing a culture and setting core values are a very important part of a manager's duties. It is one thing to establish a culture and set core values, and it is another thing to have everyone live by that framework. It is one of the daily tasks that any manager faces, that is, to reinforce that culture and core values.

## Administration and management

Culture and core values are a big picture item on the manager's to-do list. Management is challenging because it has such a range of activities. One day you may be on a senior management task force to craft core values and the next day you may have to do and approve company expense reports.

The range of activity for a manager is threefold. There is administration work. There is management work. And there is leadership. While a manager may do all the three all the time, let's take a look at each of these areas of responsibility. They do require different skill sets.

"Administrators make the trains run on time. Managers decide where they are going." This quote comes from Michael A. Loduha of the Advocates Network. It helps us understand the difference between administration and management.

Administration is a subset of management duties. It is important. If you plot the right course but don't clear the path, then your direction is worthless.

Administration gets a "bad rap" for being just mindless and senseless bureaucracy. Or it is those who just follow the rules.

Administration is focused on making sure that criteria are followed and the necessary paperwork is completed. For example, a project manager typically fills out some form of project brief to initiate work from a department. This project brief gives the media, creative or planning team the necessary information such as objectives, timelines and budgets necessary to do their job.

A project manager could just send some of the people involved a text. Or they might walk by and talk to them. Or they may just send a quick email. So why do a formal project brief? In this case, the project brief may be the only formal document that is used to track time, bill the client and determine if the task has been properly managed. Without the paperwork, there would be more time wasted, possible misunderstanding and no ability to track progress.

It is the same situation as just giving your accountant a shoebox full of receipts and asking them to do your taxes. Do you think that is more efficient than you actually organizing the right information and providing a detailed record of all your activity? We would advise you to do the latter.

Administration functions are not the glamorous part of a manager's job. But without doing proper administration, the manager's department or area of responsibility quickly can become chaotic and riddled with errors.

## Management and leadership

If administration is the floor for a manager, leadership becomes the ceiling. Together, they help build the management house.

A lot is said about management and leadership. Sometimes, it is very fuzzy if there is really a difference. There is a big difference, in fact. One way to visualize the difference is to consider the viewpoint of the manager. On the one hand, you have people who you are responsible for. To this group of people, you must be the leader. On the other hand, you have a senior level boss, who wants you to properly manage your area of responsibility. Exhibit 2.1 shows the contrast between the two activities.

**Exhibit 2.1 Differences between leaders and managers**

| *Managers focus on …* | *Leaders focus on …* |
|---|---|
| Goals and objectives | Vision |
| Short range | Long range |
| Organization and structure | People |
| Restraining | Enabling |
| Conforming | Challenging |
| Imitating | Originating |
| Consistency | Flexibility |
| Risk avoidance | Risk opportunity |
| Bottom line | Top line |
| Maintaining | Developing |

For example, as a manager, you have specific goals and objectives to achieve. You must hit them. On the leadership side, you have a vision that you want to see get executed. Thus, the manager is the one responsible for making that vision into a reality. They must translate the vision into specific objectives and goals and tasks for their team to complete.

That is the tricky thing about being a manager. It is that constant push and pull between working at a philosophical level and then working at a very tangible and specific level makes management hard.

As you review Exhibit 2.1, you will see those contrasts. Management is all about helping your team do the task to meet the goal that ultimately fulfills the mission. As you work in advertising, you will have to rapidly move from one to the other.

For example, you are the media director for Nike. Nike's brand is all about authentic athletic performance. Knowing that this is the overall Nike brand mission, for every new product Nike introduces, you are working with your team to secure media opportunities that match this mission. Authentic performance becomes your credo. That will translate to what media properties you have your team review, or what types of sponsorships you arrange. It may lead the team to develop real contests that anyone can participate in. This could lead to seminars on how to compete after you get out of school. One central idea then can lead to a number of tactics that support it. You, as the manager, must ensure that the idea connects to the tactics. To do that, you must help motivate your team to be looking for those opportunities.

There is an insightful quote from a Chinese philosopher 2,500 years ago regarding being an effective ruler.

> When the best rulers achieve their purpose, their subjects claim the achievement as their own.

As an advertising manager, you are not a ruler; you must be a leader of your team. The best leaders are those who get the team to believe in the mission and make that mission their own achievement.

## Leadership communication

Everything we do communicates. What we wear, how we look and how we walk and talk all say something about you. Every time you speak, text, email, tweet or publish you communicate something. And when you are the leader, all of your communication is magnified.

Any small thing you say or do may have ramifications. Your employees will notice if you are suddenly wearing a suit when you have only worn casual clothes for the past month. They may consider it as a sign. Is the company becoming more formal? Is there a big client coming today? Is our company being sold? Just a simple wardrobe change may have people buzzing.

Compounding this scrutiny is the sheer size and scope of leadership communication. Studies have shown that the average manager has at least 40 emails, 60 text messages and hundreds of personal interactions every day.

No wonder that both management and employees indicate that communication is the number one source of frustration as well as number one problem within the organization.

Let's start our discussion on leadership communication with effective internal communication. As a leader, your job is to inform others of what they need to do to achieve the objective. Your job is to get people to deliver their best work to achieve that objective. That may be developing a media plan or a piece of creative. It could be developing a long-term strategic plan or it could be reacting to some change in the marketplace.

Regardless of the goal, an advertising manager must do three things very well.

1 Empathize with their employees.
2 Facilitate the work.
3 Inspire the best work.

Often, empathy is an underrated trait in internal communication. It does seem ironic since advertising is all about understanding human beliefs and behaviors. By understanding human insights, advertisers craft compelling messages. Many times, advertising managers forget about this when dealing with their own employees.

For example, the CEO has just told you that he needs to increase advertising spending on a key brand immediately to blunt a competitor. This is exciting since he is trusting you to get it done. Yet you know this means that the team must work overtime to get it done. Plus one of your team members has asked to take some time off. Now that won't be possible.

Before you rush in and lay down the law, it would be wise for you to take a step back and think through the reaction that your team may have. Show empathy. Listen to what your team has to say. Engage them in how best to achieve this objective. Maybe, they will have some good ideas.

This example demonstrates the need for any manager to have a couple of core traits when communicating. The first is authenticity. You need to be authentic. That means true to yourself. Just because you are in a position of relative power, don't act differently than you have in the past. Be yourself. People will respond favorably to someone who is authentic.

The second trait is to be consistent. Have a plan; don't say one thing one minute and something else the next. People love consistency. The business world is very volatile. Things change and people in advertising know that. They hope that you can remain consistent even when change is swirling around.

The next stage of communication is facilitating the work. After you have listened to your team, you have prepared a plan. Now, it is time to make it happen. To facilitate the work, you are likely the one on your team with the most technical competence. This is likely why you were promoted to being a manager in the first place. You were doing a good job. Thus, if you are a creative director, you likely have the most experience in formulating campaign ideas. If you are a media director, you have the most experience in developing media plans.

Most early stages of management are marked largely by technical experience. This means that you have the role of showing others how to do it. You move from being the doer to the mentor and instructor. You need to communicate so that others can learn from your experience. The communication challenge is to help others along while understanding that they may not know as much as you do. Thus, you need to be clear. Communicate effectively. And do not talk down to your team. You want to "coach them up" and help them succeed.

The other part of getting the job done is to work with others. This likely means that you are working with members of a team with similar experience but different levels of technical experience. To get a website built, you may need copywriters, digital designers, coders and information architects. These roles encompass very different skill sets. Your role is to lead the team to build the website. That requires you to help everyone understand the complementary skill sets needed to complete the task. Here your role in communication is to ensure that a decision made by one person doesn't negatively impact someone else. For example, if the designer of your website wants to use lots of pictures on the front page without any copy, the media team may indicate that without the keywords, no one will be able to find the website. Thus, the design may need to be modified.

The next stage of leadership communication is inspiration. As you move up in management, inspiration will become increasingly important. Technical expertise will become less important. You need to provide the vision and mission. Your team wants to be inspired to work. They likely want to win awards. Advertising people are very competitive and innovative. They are looking for permission to do things that are unique.

## Understand cultural nuances

In today's workplace, one of the greatest challenges is to respect and recognize workers that have different beliefs and backgrounds from your own. This is especially true in the advertising industry. As we will discuss further in managing the creative class, creative people are different. Yet, as an advertising manager, you must work with creative people as well as accounting people. Thus, you are dealing with a range of backgrounds and personal beliefs or viewpoints.

These differences are magnified when you are dealing with intercultural communication. People from different cultures bring unique perspectives and background to communication. Two major aspects of these cultural differences are context and time.

There are high-context and low-context cultures. In a high-context culture, the message is somewhat unspecific. The communication style of a high-context culture relies on the understanding of the message largely through context.

Context refers to nonverbal cues. It is reading between the lines. The oral message may be subtle. The meaning of the message requires the receiver to infer the full context of what is being said. People from Latin American, Asian and African countries are high-context communicators.

On the other hand, low-context communicators are very direct and specific. People from countries that are English and Germanic are typically low-context communicators.

The message from a low-context communicator relies on direct verbal language with not as much regard for nonverbal cues.

As a result, if you have an employee from the United States working with an employee from Brazil, there could be moments of misunderstanding. The US employee may be left wondering what the other is communicating since the verbal expression is subtle and not explicit. And the employee from Brazil may be frustrated trying to read nonverbal cues that are nonexistent.

Communication issues among cultures can be exacerbated by using digital communication methods such as video conferencing or just texting to communicate. It is up to you, as the manager, to understand that differences exist. It is your role to ensure that everyone communicates effectively.

The concept of time is the other key difference in how various cultures behave. For example, English and Germanic countries treat time as sequential moments. This is why you see a lot of "to-do" lists and agendas in a meeting in the United States.

On the other hand, Latin American, Asian and African countries treat time from a synchronic perspective. This means that they view time in a circular rather than linear manner. The past, present and future are seen as a continuum rather than as a linear timeline.

A person from the United States may want to move step-by-step when completing a project. Each part of the project is detailed. You can't move from one step to the other until the former is complete. On the other hand, a person from an Asian country may view the project more as holistic, where as long as the project is completed, the order of the steps doesn't matter.

This can be a difficult situation for an advertising manager. And it can be even more frustrating for your project manager, as they try to complete a task within a certain time and budget. They may have to work with people who come at the problem from very different cultural perspectives.

As you look back at the TBWA culture of Disruption, TBWA has done an excellent job of having a simple process that is consistent yet flexible. The TBWA process is *convention*, *vision* and *disruption*. The *convention* is understanding the status quo from a communication perspective. The *vision* is the big idea. The *disruption* is the expression of the idea. By connecting those three elements, you have accomplished the Disruption.

Obviously, there is a lot of work that goes into the TBWA process. The framework of the process is something that can work no matter what the cultural context.

As you manage and develop systems, it is crucial that you take into account the types of people and backgrounds you must manage. Craft your systems for processes to ensure that it helps rather than hinders success.

## Effective written communication

Working with your team or your organization requires care on how you deal with people. Internal communication is all about understanding your team and how best to communicate and motivate them to achieve the objective.

As a leader, you will be expected to do more formal communication either internally or externally. This may be writing an email, expressing a point of view to a client or drafting a strategic document or plan. Or, maybe, it is a thought document for the organization's blog. Regardless of the type of communication, a leader must be able to effectively write.

There is just no substitute for clearly written communication. Writing is thinking. In a business setting, the enemy of effective written communication is a lack of time and attention by the receiver.

Employees, clients or other stakeholders have a finite amount of time to deal with their workload. But some managers communicate like there is an infinite amount of time in their day. It is important to understand that your management communication competes for attention with many other pieces of communication. The message and method must be well-thought-out.

Before you send a message, you should analyze the following.

- What is the purpose of the message?
- What is the best media channel to communicate the message?
- Is this a one-time message or is it a part of an ongoing series of messages?

Just thinking about the purpose of your message will likely increase your ability to communicate effectively. In fact, to avoid ambiguity, some organizations have a written style guide outlining specific formats for various kinds of communication that all employees use. Many memorandums have a purpose statement, such as, "The purpose of this memo is to provide strategic direction for the new product advertising campaign."

Just 20 years ago, business communication consisted largely of either face-to-face discussions, team meetings or a typewritten memorandum. Even when email replaced typewritten communication, business communication remained pretty much the same.

In the past five years, a variety of other communication platforms have emerged which allow instant messaging, video conferencing and workflow sharing that have altered how business is done.

The message platform strategy is nearly as important as the purpose of the communication. Choosing it is a crucial part of being a leader. For example, it would be inappropriate to send an important company-wide message via Slack, a popular social media business platform. Slack is great for instant messages regarding workflow but is too casual for very critical messages.

In the case of a company-wide communication, a leader sends out an email that details the message. Many company leaders send out an email and then follow up by holding a "town hall" meeting either in person or virtually, where they can answer questions and/or provide greater clarity about the topic.

The same is true for external communication. Whether you are an advertising executive at an advertising agency responding to a client or a media sales manager responding to an agency executive, a well-crafted email followed up with either an in-person meeting or phone call is a standard method for effective communication.

With any external communication, one size does not fit all. In this case, the receiver of the communication wants to know what is in it for them. Sometimes, the communication must be relevant to that specific situation.

When writing to any external audience, it is important to remember that there is potential for that communication to be forwarded to someone else. Hence, while being relevant is key, being discreet is equally as important. Do not put in writing something that you will later regret. Think about the implications of what you are going to say before you say it.

What you say is important. The language you use is very important. Advertising campaigns reflect a specific message with a specific tone of voice for a specific brand's personality. So it is crucial that you understand this prior to external communication. For example, if you indicate that a piece of copy reflects an upscale tone despite the client having specifically indicated that the copy needs to reflect a luxurious tone, you may have a disconnect. Upscale may not be definitive enough for the client. This is especially true if the client has already given you detailed instructions.

Keeping your message consistent is another big challenge when you are communicating to external audiences. If you are the advertising manager for a brand with a new advertising campaign, you may need to field questions from the media. If you tell one reporter one thing and another reporter another thing, you will have a problem. Or if you say one thing and your boss says another, you may have an even bigger problem. It is always important to get your "story straight."

There is nothing worse than having to retract or amend some communication. The other consistency challenge is to ensure that everyone in the organization is on the same page. Your organization is constantly communicating to outside audiences whether it is one-on-one, in meetings or through stakeholder communication. Keeping a simple, direct message is very important. It will help keep the entire organization message focused.

## Summary

Setting the right culture is a key aspect of becoming a good manager. This means that you must know the culture, communicate the culture and, most importantly, live the culture. Your personal values should be in line with the organization's values. You need to constantly reinforce the culture and values on a daily basis.

Being a manager means setting the course, making things work and motivating people to be inspired to achieve the objective. As a manager, you will do administration, which is crucial to making things work; management, which is setting the course; and leadership, which is inspiring others to take action.

Being a leader requires being effective at interpersonal communication. Understanding and empathizing with different people's beliefs and backgrounds is fundamental to being an effective manager.

Being a leader also requires being an effective written communicator. Writing is thinking. Thus, written communication shows your thought leadership. Keeping the communication clear and consistent is the hallmark of an effective leader.

## Review questions

1 What is an organization's culture? Why is it important?
2 How are values an important part of culture?
3 What is the manager's role in the organization's culture?
4 What is the key to effective interpersonal communication?
5 What are the key attributes of high- and low-context communicators?
6 What makes effective leadership communication?

### Case 2.1 Prime Media

#### *Issue: global expansion*

Bill Meade looked out his window and pondered, "The world is getting closer and closer day by day, yet our company is only looking at the United States." He turned back to his laptop and resumed his silent contemplation, looking at the screen and shaking his head.

Bill was the CEO of the publicly traded Prime Media Corporation. Prime Media was one of the leading media companies in the United States. They had holdings in television stations, newspapers, and some magazines. They had been a real growth story in the early 1990s but lately the growth had stalled. The newspaper industry was shrinking and the magazine industry was not growing either. The television stations were in strong markets such as Denver, San Antonio, and Phoenix, but that wasn't enough to offset the slower growth in the print division.

The board of directors of Prime Media wanted more growth out of the company. They were pushing Bill and his management team to consider moving into higher growth markets that were digital. While Bill agreed that digital media were a growth platform, he also believed that international growth should be considered.

On his desk, he fumbled for the article that had started his thinking. It was an economic trends article that detailed the GDP (gross domestic product) growth in various world economies. The forecast for the US advertising growth was at 2.3%, while other key industrial markets were running nearly twice that level—from Australia at 4.6% to Germany at 5.7%.

If these industrial nations weren't enough, there were also the emerging economies of China and India, which were rocketing along in double-digit growth. It seemed that anything that was in these markets was turning to gold. Through his media connections, he had friends in the governments of both Asian countries. Perhaps there was something that he could find that might be attractive for his company in these huge untapped markets.

He also had been approached by a group of German newspapers, who wanted to sell to a larger company. He had brushed them aside, since his board had made their feelings known that they were a US-only company.

"What do we really know about the rest of the world," said one of the elder board members. "There is plenty of growth in the United States before we go abroad," he added.

Bill continued to stare at the screen. There was a board meeting in a few weeks. He must put together a presentation that would open their eyes to consider a broader range of growth opportunities.

He thought out loud, *How should I tackle this one?*

### *Questions*

1 Do you think that the information Bill Meade has is enough to go to the board of directors with?
2 What other information should he get to strengthen his case?
3 What are the other considerations for a company deciding between domestic and international growth?
4 Are there examples of other companies that have faced similar circumstances that Bill could use as support for his premise?

Chapter 3

# Advertising ethics and social responsibility across cultures

## LEARNING OBJECTIVES

This chapter is intended to help you:

- Understand the establishment of organizational ethics.
- Learn how personal, business and organizational ethics tie together.
- Understand the social impact of advertising.
- Understand the ethical impact of advertising.

At its simplest, ethics is a system of moral principles. Within an organization, ethics relate to how you treat your employees, vendors and stakeholders. Advertising also has an ethic responsibility to society, since many advertising campaigns are consumer focused.

Working in an advertising organization has its own unique set of ethical challenges. Ethics relates to what is good or bad, as defined by moral duties and obligations. Ethics establish a set of rules for the organization and individuals within that organization that address industry, company and personal integrity standards.

In advertising, ethical problems often arise when dealing with human resources and personnel issues, or with the confidence of customers and vendors. Issues can also arise regarding the use of company resources and with potential conflicts of interest.

Personnel issues usually involve such things as safety, harassment, discrimination and hiring and firing of staff members. Personnel issues also involve the area of promotions or the lack of promotions as well as salary and benefits.

Confidence of customers and vendors often relates to telling the truth whether it is in dealing with a business situation or in the actual advertising message itself. This area also involves maintaining confidence information, answering accounting and financial questions and maintaining the safety and effective use of goods, services and ideas being promoted.

Use of company resources involves providing truthful information, correctly using corporate physical or financial resources and dealing with issues that involve the organization's reputation and standing within the industry.

Conflicts of interest may include using privileged or confidential information for personal gain. A conflict of interest can also exist in hiring or contracting with firms on the basis of personal interest. A conflict of interest can involve the area of bribery or payment for services outside the organization.

All of these areas are why every organization needs to have a comprehensive ethics program. By establishing an organizational ethics program, it can help avoid prosecution for criminal acts. Such a program can also be essential when questions are raised in public about an organization's behavior that may have a negative impact on its reputation, even if no laws were violated.

An organization's ethics program should interact with the overall strategic plan of the organization. Within this program, areas such as diversity and community service plus many others should be considered as an aspect of the overall corporate plan.

Ethics programs help the firm to project a strong public image and may help the advertising manager function more effectively and efficiently. If a strong ethics program is in place, the advertising manager doesn't have to guess on what is appropriate; it is spelled out. Since ethics ultimately gets down to doing the right thing, having the right thing spelled out is vitally important.

A strong ethical profile helps the firm present the organization to its internal and external publics. Many times, an advertising firm's ethical profile becomes one of its core differentiating points. Ethical core values translate to how an organization may approach its advertising. The process of establishing an ethical practice is ever evolving. It is something that is continually monitored and enhanced.

Good ethical practices also help build continuity in the organization. Those ethical practices also build continuity as a manager. Your performance, your employees' performance, customer loyalty, investor acceptance and public acceptance are all increased when good ethical standards are in place. Following good ethical practices will make you shine and give you a source of personal and professional pride.

Therefore, an effective advertising manager will integrate ethics into other management practices. This is particularly true when you must deal with situations where there are mistakes. They will inevitably happen. Without a strong ethical code, it is easy to take a different path when mistakes arise.

Setting up an ethical program is an ongoing process. It leads to preferred behavior and, more importantly, roots out unwanted behavior.

## Ethical dilemmas in advertising: personal and organizational

By now, you are likely nodding your head and thinking, *Isn't ethics pretty much common sense?*

*Why do we really have to devote a lot of time to it?*

This is very true. Since you were raised, you learn what is right and what it wrong. The basics of honesty, fairness and transparency are foundational principles of any person or business. You understand that you need to operate your own life with strong ethical standards. That translates to those whom you manage and the company you work for. It isn't always easy. Right and wrong aren't always clear cut.

Advertising does have some special nuances that can cause ethical dilemmas. You, as the advertising manager, are likely to be in the middle of it. Either your organization hasn't clearly spelled out what is ethical and what isn't or you may find that different people in the organization have different moral compasses or you may find yourself in a situation that goes against your own personal beliefs.

This is when personal, professional and organizational ethics collide. As a manager, you have those three ethical areas to consider. The first is what you believe in. The second is what is right as an advertising manager for your management area of responsibility. The third is for the organization itself.

Let's discuss one situation that can cause a conflict in either the brand or company you work for or the account you work on.

Imagine that you are an account supervisor at an advertising agency. Your agency has been asked to present for a cigarette account. Big tobacco. The agency principals hold an agency meeting to discuss this. On the one hand, there are people who are morally opposed to smoking. On the other hand, it is a personal choice. From a business standpoint, it would be a very lucrative account for the advertising agency. On the downside, by handling the account, other businesses that have strong anti-tobacco beliefs may not consider the agency. For example, a healthcare client would likely not be interested in an agency that willingly promotes the use of tobacco. This is a dilemma.

Now, if your agency's culture is to do no harm, that could solve the impasse. Having a tobacco account clearly goes against the culture. If the agency is about free will and choice, then it may not care. You can see where having a clear culture, values and ethics has a practical side. Let's assume the agency decides to pass on pitching this account. It reinforces its culture and values. Perhaps it was an easier decision than it appeared.

Now, what about applying these principles to alcohol. Is handling a beer account fine? What about wine? How about spirits? What if your state has legalized marijuana? Is promoting this fit within your ethical beliefs? What about gambling?

Would you work for an agency that handled one of those accounts? Or would you move to an agency that handled one of those accounts if you were offered a new position as account director that included a 30% raise?

These are real situations. You may be working for or on or with products and services that make you personally feel uneasy. In that case, you have to look at your own moral compass. And as a manager, you will need to understand if someone on your team may not want to work on a piece of business due to ethical reasons. It happens.

Another business situation may be where a brand you work on or for does something you feel is morally wrong. Nike was accused of sourcing their product using sweatshop child labor overseas. Wells Fargo had their bankers create accounts for their clients without authorization to increase their fees. The former may be morally repugnant. The latter was actually illegal. If you work for or on those two brands, would you resign? How strongly would you feel about the situation? And how would you counsel your team?

In all of these business situations, you have to assess the company's ethical point of view. As a manager, your job is to support the organization. It is to toe the company line. Doing so can, sometimes, make you feel a bit uneasy. That comes with the territory of being an advertising manager.

## Relationship dilemmas

Advertising is a relationship business. If you are an advertising agency, you try to establish a great relationship with your clients. If you are a media company, you try to establish relationships with media buyers, agency management and advertisers. If you are an advertiser, you want to have strong relationships with any of your external partners.

Success in advertising means collaboration. That requires internal collaboration. It also requires external collaboration. Sometimes, in building those relationships, you run into ethical questions.

For example, as the advertising manager for a major automotive firm, you are managing an internal group of advertising professionals plus various external specialists. It could be a media-only agency. Or it could be a research firm, or perhaps a production company. Any and all of these vendors want to have a strong relationship with you. It just makes good business sense.

That said, you may think nothing of having lunch with people from one of these companies. After all, a working lunch is no big deal. You work. You eat. No problem. As you get more comfortable in your relationship, perhaps you really enjoy one of your vendors' company. They have tickets to a high-profile sporting event. Do you go? Or they send you a gift on your birthday. It is a very nice travel suitcase. Can you accept it?

Having breakfast, lunch or dinner is a staple of business life. If you have a client, you may want to ask them to eat with you to break down some barriers. That is sometimes considered a business perk. So are tickets. The media often has access to tickets because they help promote those events. Companies buy stadium suites so that they can entertain clients. And who doesn't like getting a gift?

You do see where this is going. If you don't establish boundaries, things can get out of hand. Today, it is a lunch. Tomorrow, it is taking in a game. The next time, it may be a trip to the Bahamas.

Some companies simply set dollar limits to business perks. Some set it at $50, others at $100. Others will not allow any vendor to provide anything, including bringing in doughnuts for the team. There is no right answer here. The key aspect to this is consistency and transparency. The last thing you want to do as the manager is to accept a large gift but then chastise one of your employees for doing the same. That sends the wrong message.

The other aspect to relationships is awarding business to people you like. This is a sensitive and very tricky area. Let's say you are a creative director. You have had great success working with a certain film production company. In the course of business, you have gotten to be friendly with the owner of the company. You are friends. Your friendship has gotten to be social.

You don't think much about it. His company does a great job. All of a sudden, you realize that nearly all the agency's film production is being done by this one company. Were you ethically wrong in doing that?

This is where a tight set of company protocols come into place. In this case, the agency may have failed to take competing bids for film production. Your friend's film company may have won them all, but now you will never know. The cloud of possible unethical practices appears.

As a manager, you need to make sure that you as well as your team and your organization don't get into those situations. The creative director isn't a good manager. He needs to make sure that there are always alternatives considered before selecting a specific vendor. That is just good business. Plus it eliminates any question of ethical practices.

Advertising is also a very social industry. It is very common for people who work in advertising to date and marry others within the industry. This can raise some ethical issues. Advertising attracts young, single, talented people. Should they be allowed to date within the company? Many companies forbid dating among employees. Others discourage it but don't outright ban it. That is a policy issue that will face any advertising manager.

Another relationship issue regards having your spouse work at the same company as you. Some companies put that in the same category as dating. And it is forbidden. Others allow it but only if the two spouses don't directly work in the same department. Where two working spouses can become a contentious issue is when one spouse works for a competing company. Obviously, a company can't bar a non-employed spouse from working. They can put pressure on the working spouse to encourage the other to find employment at a non-competing company. Is this something to worry about? Are there ethical issues or do you assume that the two spouses can maintain confidentiality of important information? This is an ethical area for the advertising manager.

The same is true of hiring friends, sons or daughters, or even sons, daughters or spouses of your client. All of these hiring practices have ethical considerations.

The most sensitive ethical area is salary. Depending on the marketplace, there is sometimes pressure to hire a new person at a higher salary level than that of an existing employee. If demand for talent is high, then to acquire talent may take more money. The ethical question is, do you pay your existing person more, given that you just hired someone at the same level for a higher salary? Now that is a tough question. Some companies do work in good faith to bring others up to that salary level. Other companies view this as a free market situation.

The most sensitive area regarding salary is to ensure that salary levels for the same position are comparable based on gender, race and religious background. It is totally unethical to pay someone more or less just based on any of these personal attributes.

## Social media ethics

One place where personal, business and organizational worlds collide is social media. As an advertising manager, you are likely responsible for either managing or having a large role in your company's social media program.

Social media is the only media category where all three aspects of marketing communication take place. Marketing communication has a paid, owned and earned model. Paid refers to paid advertising. Owned means that the brand controls the channel, and earned refers to others promoting your brand.

For example, Allstate Insurance uses a character named Mayhem in some of their advertising messages. Mayhem is an antihero. He creates havoc. Having Allstate means that you don't have to worry about him. Allstate makes media purchases on social media platforms to promote their brand. The Mayhem character has his own social media platforms including an extensive Facebook page and Twitter page where he is actively promoting his character plus Allstate. Others help promote Mayhem and Allstate by retweeting or forwarding Mayhem's messages.

This seems like a very controlled universe of communication; it is to a large degree. However, let's take an example using Allstate's Mayhem. There are a number of writers who are the voice of Mayhem on social media. They post items and interact with fans. What happens if one of those writers says something in poor taste? Perhaps, it is a swear word or something that comes off as racially insensitive. Now, you have a big problem. As the advertising manager, it is your job to ensure that all communication remains on brand.

A more difficult situation arises when someone on your team does something inappropriate on social media—What if they posted Mayhem dressed as a KKK clan member, or put Mayhem toppling a building in downtown Manhattan or posted that they really don't like the actor who plays Mayhem?

Since this is their personal account, what recourse do you have? And what recourse do you have for them just posting items that you are uncomfortable with? Perhaps, they are a member of an organization you disagree with, or are with a religious group that you find offensive.

There is so much content on social media. As a manager, it is something to take very seriously. That is why many companies are developing social media ethics for their employees. These policies are established to protect the company's reputation as well as any other business or personal reputations.

As the advertising manager, it is your role to set the example on social media. You should review all your social media platforms for past content and eliminate the "drunken college party pictures" and anything else that is not professional.

Hold your employees to a high ethical standard. Since messaging is your craft, it is incumbent on anyone in the advertising industry to be sensitive to your social media profile. A "snarky tweet" that you may find hilarious may be very offensive to someone else in your organization. It is crucial to think before you post on social media. Most advertising firms view social media ethics as an extension of internal ethics. Since social media plays such an important role in brand communication, it is important to view your personal role as an extension of the brand. It may not be as much fun as having a "twitter war" with someone, but it is an important part of being in the advertising industry.

## Global differences

While there is universal ethics, there certainly exist differences in how different cultures and countries do business. These differences can bring up thorny management issues.

For example, in the United States, there is an ethical standard of an advertising agency not having more than one of a certain business type. It is called a client conflict. You can't handle two banks. Or two different automotive companies. Or two different pharmaceutical companies. The reason is that you have proprietary information that should not be shared with a competing organization. As a result, unless the two brands compete in very different markets, the ethical rule of thumb is that there is a conflict.

In Japan, the opposite is true. Many Japanese advertising agencies handle multiple automotive brands or appliance makers. The Japanese culture encourages the agency to specialize in an area so that they can effectively distinguish one brand from another.

While the United States sees having multiple brands of the same category as a conflict, Japan sees it as a true benefit. Therefore, being the head of a global advertising agency is a potential issue.

The same is true of vendor relationships. In some countries, it is common for payment to be made to secure a contact. In the United States, some may look at this as "payola" or a "pay off." In some countries, this is just the way that business is conducted; it is no big deal.

Hiring practices are different in different countries. Some countries are much looser on hiring of family to work at an organization. In fact, some encourage having multiple family members in the fold; they feel it provides a more stable work environment.

As a company sets up its ethical practices on a global basis, it is important to build an overall framework first, then tailor details to each country so that the ethical standards match with the expectation of the respective culture.

## Social impact of advertising

It is clear that advertising can impact how we think. Advertising can be powerful and persuasive communication. Because of this, there is a constant debate over whether advertising shapes or reflects our societal values.

One of the most highlighted issues for advertising revolves around the portrayal of our society and how a company fits into people's lives. There are two elements to this issue: one is diversity and the other is stereotypes.

Both diversity and stereotypes are quite sensitive topics. For example, if the consumer target market for your brand is largely made up of Caucasian men, should that be the only type of people featured in your advertising? Or if you find a concentration of a minority group that represents a disproportionate amount of a brand's user base, should you reflect this group in your advertising? And if you feature either of these groups, how might that be viewed by people outside these groups?

These are difficult questions. As the advertising manager, it is your job to help deliver the right message to the right audience. You need to do it in a socially responsible manner. While you may have a personal viewpoint about the topic, there are business and financial implications to consider.

Cheerios was one of the first advertisers to show an interracial couple eating breakfast together with their daughter. When the advertisement first aired in the 2013 Super Bowl, it generated much positive publicity. It also generated a large racist backlash. In fact, YouTube had to shut down their comment section for this advertisement since many of the posts were extremely racist.

The question for the brand was, "Was it worth the risk?" On the one hand, there was critical acclaim, and on the other, harsh negative feedback. At the end of the campaign, the actual business performance of Cheerios was status quo. The campaign didn't help the brand's sales nor did it significantly hurt its sales.

Since the United States is becoming much more ethnically diverse, more advertising campaigns are reflecting this societal norm. Some may say that this is "forced diversity." Others may just see it as "the way America is."

Diversity typically occurs on a natural course. As a brand gets a more diverse customer base, it reflects that in its advertising. As an advertising manager, it is your job to stay abreast of cultural trends so that you help create communication that is culturally relevant.

Stereotyping can be a much more sensitive area than diversity. In fact, the United Kingdom's Advertising Standards Authority (ASA) has advocated for strict guidelines regarding the display of social stereotypes. Stereotypes such as women seen only as homemakers or Caucasian men only seen as businessmen are examples of cultural stereotypes.

Some brands, such as Dove's Campaign for Real Beauty, directly confront stereotypes. Dove featured women who were not professional models in their award-winning campaign to break with female beauty stereotypes.

Body image stereotyping is prominent in our media culture. Establishing physical ideas is something that advertisers must take into account when developing messages.

There are obviously lots of stereotypes that go largely unnoticed. Put glasses on someone and the thought is that they make them look smarter. Tattoos denote a sense of counterculture. Baggy pants indicates that you are a "gangster." Having a Southern accent in the United States indicates that you are a bit slow. How people look, what they wear and what they say are all part of how society views them.

Moving past gender, body types, clothing and regional dialects is the more sensitive area of ethnic stereotypes. Are Asians always smart? Are African Americans great dancers? Are rural white people rednecks? This can go on and on. If you look at ethnic stereotypes from the early 1900s, you will find that Irish Americans were portrayed as either policemen or drunks, and Italian Americans as gangsters or sexy singers. Every era has ethnic population stereotypes.

The latter examples are from the United States. Every country has their own version of stereotypes. Some are highly regional in nature, while others are ethnic.

It is the job of the advertising manager to ensure that stereotypes are not used in a condescending or insensitive way. Just as Dove illustrated, by playing against the stereotype, you can help elevate the brand and the societal conversation.

## Social and ethical advertising considerations

Along with being socially responsible, advertising must adhere to high ethical standards. Advertising messages must be honest. False, misleading or deceptive advertising is considered unethical. As the advertising manager, it is your responsibility to uphold those ethical standards.

Advertising is governed in the United States by the Federal Trade Commission (FTC). This government agency alongside the industry has strict standards for advertising. The following are some of the key items.

- False advertising is a type of misleading communication where the message is simply not true. For example, if you advertise a car for $5,000 when it really costs $20,000, that is false advertising.
- Misleading claims are those that lack substantiation. Misleading claims can also arise from wording that is deceptive. For example, if a diet drink claims that you will lose 10 pounds a month if you drink it daily when in reality only one person out of 10,000 has experienced this type of loss, then the claim is considered misleading.
- Comparative advertising is a popular way to make a point. It can also lead to misleading claims. Under the law, any type of comparative claim must be evidence based. If not, then the claim can be considered misleading and you are legally liable for damages.
- Puffery is an exaggerated claim. It is not misleading, nor is it illegal. Puffery is usually characterized by superlative words or phrases. For example, it is puffery to say that the product is the "best" or provides "instant relief" or offers "maximum payloads." The only question surrounding puffery is an ethical one. The industry standard is that if a reasonable person does not regard the claim to be a

fact, then it is considered to be ethical. If it is meant to be deceptive, then it is considered unethical.

- Endorsers, celebrity spokespeople and influencers are all popular ways to promote a brand. Using any of these people is perfectly acceptable. That is so unless the endorser of the product does not actually use the product; then, it is considered misleading. Paid influencers on social media must identify themselves as paid spokespeople for a brand so as to not be misleading.

As the advertising manager, you may help establish the company's ethical standards and guidelines to be used by all parties that communicate on behalf of the brand.

Nearly every company and advertising agency uses legal counsel to review all advertising prior to its release. This helps avoid any potential ethical and legal liabilities. Industry groups such as the Adverting Review Council and the Better Business Bureau also serve as watchdogs for possible ethical violations.

The media themselves also screen all advertising prior to its running in their particular media property. If the media believes that an advertisement does not meet ethical standards, they have the right to not schedule the ad.

Specific industry groups such as liquor, tobacco and pharma all have very stringent guidelines for advertising content that go well beyond the traditional ethical guidelines. The same is said for any advertising that is directed at children. There are special rules and regulations when advertising to this category of audience.

Aside from the ethical considerations of the industry and your own company, you have to use your own personal experience. As we have said all along in this chapter, ethics boils down to "doing the right thing." Every person has their own moral compass. While ethical issues may come down from the industry or corporate level, ethics always begins with the individual. It is up to you to make the right decisions and do the right thing. That is the mark of a good advertising manager.

## Summary

In summary, it is crucial to hold yourself, the company and your employees to the highest ethical standards. The same is true for having a good social compass. Ethical behavior and being socially conscious are personal traits that all good advertising managers must have. It is the responsibility of the advertising manager to be a role model for this behavior and to ensure that it is translated into ethical and socially responsible advertising campaigns.

## Review questions

1 What is the advertising manager's role in organizational ethics?
2 What are common pitfalls regarding ethical behavior in the advertising industry?
3 What role does ethics play in developing an advertising campaign?
4 How should you treat the role of social media from an ethical perspective?
5 What role does advertising play in reflecting social mores?
6 How should advertisers approach the use of diversity and stereotypes within an advertising campaign?

## Case 3.1 KMF Agency

### *Issue: ethical issue of when to change jobs*

Sarah Habib felt like she had it made. Her hard work as an undergrad was paying off: she recently graduated from a top-tier advertising program, maintaining a 3.5 GPA and being actively involved in extracurricular activities. She had been the account director of her NSAC campaign team and was proud that her school finished in the top two of their district and went to nationals.

One of her professors, Dena Jacobs encouraged her to apply for a scholarship that was awarded by a large advertising agency in Chicago. Not only did the scholarship help defray her school costs, but it came with a paid internship at the advertising agency. The agency, KMF, was a large independent agency in the Midwest, and had successfully embraced the industry's move to digital campaigns. KMF management hoped that this scholarship would help to attract new talent with digital skills.

Sarah won the scholarship, beating out 20 other candidates. KMF flew Sarah and Dena to Chicago, where her scholarship was announced at an Ad Club function. Both Sarah and Dena were impressed with the first class treatment that KMF offered.

During her internship, Sarah was assigned to one of KMF's largest accounts: a large computer manufacturer. Sarah met the clients and sat in on strategy sessions. KMF also trained her in the way the agency operated. At the end of the internship, Sara was offered a full-time position with the agency, working with the same account group as her internship.

"Sarah, this is a great opportunity for you to contribute to the agency. We are excited about having you as one of the new generation of KMF associates to help us expand our digital offerings," said the KFM account director, Marcus Washington.

Sarah really liked KMF. They were professional yet family oriented, which matched her background. The agency's accounts reflected the agency's personality. They handled a number of large corporations and did professional yet somewhat conservative work. Sarah saw the only downside of KMF as this: there weren't a lot of people her age in the agency. Most of the associates had been with the company for years, and most were at least ten years older than she was. She missed having people to socialize with after work.

At the same time, several of her friends from college had also moved to Chicago, so it wasn't hard to find people to do things with. Her parents were only a five-hour drive away in St. Louis.

Sarah had been at her job for six months when she got a call from another NSAC team member, Greg Patrick. Greg was working for a very hot creative agency in Miami called InspirAd. Sarah had caught up with Greg when she and her parents were in Miami over Christmas. At that time, Greg gave her a tour of InspirAd and arranged for a courtesy interview with Elena Martinez, one of the founders of InspirAd. Elena told her that InspirAd was all about creativity and pushing the envelope. Most of the accounts were youth-oriented brands including shoes, soft drinks, beer, and ski equipment. Everyone who worked there was young and excited. It seemed like 180 degrees from KFM.

When Greg called, he said, "Elena Martinez wanted me to tell you that she has a job for you at InspirAd. It's on Silver, the new cosmetics brand that is coming to the United States from France." Greg went on to tell Sarah that she would have to go to Paris every few months to meet with the client's marketing director. He continued,

> Elena remembered that you can speak French and asked me to call you right away. I have a friend looking for a roommate—she lives right on the beach. We can be a team again, just like in college. The work is awesome and the people here are great.

Sarah paused. "I don't know, Greg. I have a good job and I've only been here for six months. InspirAd sounds great but I don't know if it would be right to leave here."

Greg replied,

> Sarah, get real! InspirAd is nominated for creative agency of the year. You get to go to Paris for free! You can live right on the beach. Isn't that a lot better than that stodgy agency in Chicago? Why don't you at least call Elena and talk to her about it?

"I guess it doesn't hurt to talk," said Sarah.

Somewhat reluctantly, Sarah called Elena, who quickly began to convince Sara that this was the job of a lifetime.

> Look, Sarah, this job was meant for you. Your background is perfect for this account. I think this will be the next great cosmetics company in the US. The client wants to do cutting-edge work that will win awards.

At the end of the call, Elena mentioned a salary that was 20% more than Sarah's current salary, and asked Sarah to let her know by Friday.

Sarah hung up, somewhat stunned. *What should I do?* she asked herself.

### Questions

1 Should Sarah take the job at InspirAd?
2 Should Sarah discuss the job offer with KMF?
3 If Sarah decides to leave, should she give back the scholarship money?
4 If Sarah stays, should she ask for a 20% raise?
5 How long should you stay at your first job?

Chapter 4

# Understanding the role of finance and budgeting

## LEARNING OBJECTIVES

This chapter is intended to help you:

- Understand the budget responsibility of an advertising manager.
- Understand how advertising is budgeted.
- Understand the basics of accounting procedures.
- Learn how management uses accounting.
- Understand the role that finance plays in advertising.

Budgeting is at the heart of advertising management. Managing a budget is one of the key roles of any manager. It is especially complex for an advertising manager.

An advertising manager deals with a variety of budget items. This requires the advertising manager to know something about budgeting, accounting and finance. You don't have to be an expert in these areas. You do need to know enough to be conversant.

In your role as an advertising manager, you will likely interact internally with the chief financial officer and human resource director regarding personnel budgets and resource budgets.

The advertising manager manages a department of people. They must be paid. That requires some understanding of how the company makes money and allocates dollars for salary and benefits.

To do the work in the advertising department requires resources. This means simple items such as computers. It also means items such as syndicated research for marketing and media. It may mean acquiring consumer behavior research. And it can mean attending conferences or training sessions. All of these items must be budgeted.

Internally, the advertising manager will have a variety of meetings with other department heads and the CFO regarding how to budget for their respective areas. We will discuss this in more detail later in this chapter.

The big budget line item for the advertising manager is the advertising budget. For some companies, this can be millions and sometimes billions of dollars. It can cost a significant amount of money to advertise to consumers on national media.

For some companies, advertising is one of their largest expenses. As a result, it is not uncommon for the advertising manager to have meetings with the CEO or other top management to understand how to budget for advertising.

The key management questions to answer include the following.

1 What are we getting for our advertising investment?
2 If we increased that investment, what would be the impact?
3 If we decreased that investment, what would be the impact?

These three questions are the big picture tough questions to answer. Yet, as an advertising manager, it is likely that someone will ask them. So you need to be prepared. As we will discuss in the measurement chapter, this is why you put into place research to understand the impact of your advertising program. That way you can answer the question, "What should we spend on advertising?"

Depending on the level of sophistication of the organization, there will be a variety of budgeting methods for advertising.

## Popular advertising budget methods

There are many types of advertising budgeting methods. Many are brand or situation specific. Exhibit 4.1 provides a list of many of those methods. We will focus on two of the most common methods for determining an advertising budget.

### Exhibit 4.1 Advertising budgeting

1 Percentage of past year's sales
2 Percentage of past year's profits
3 Percentage of anticipated sales
4 Percentage of anticipated profits
5 Match the competition
6 "All you can afford"
7 Allocation per unit sold
8 Allocation per outlet
9 Objective-and-task ("Task" or "Reverse")
10 Share point
11 Zero-based
12 Incremental
13 "Scientific"
14 Percentage of sales mission (for firm alone or vs. competition)
15 Industry norm
16 Formula
17 Reserve fund
18 Marketing task
19 Percentage of corporate mission (alone or vs. competition)
20 Contingency plan
21 Minimum effective level
22 Investment spending
23 Remainder
24 Top-down
25 Arbitrary
26 Situational

For now, let's assume that the purpose of your advertising is to increase sales of a good or service. There is a body of research that indicates that there is a relationship between advertising and sales. That means that more advertising brings in more sales.

There is also a body of research that indicates that there are threshold levels of advertising support. Below these threshold levels, advertising will have little or no impact on sales. Conversely, there may be a point of diminishing returns where more advertising is not generating more sales.

If you are working in this type of advertising budget situation, it is likely that you have strong information on which to budget.

One common budget approach to determine advertising budgets focuses on a percentage of the past or future year's sales. Since we are assuming that advertising helps bring about sales, setting an advertising budget as a percentage is widely used. For example, the automotive industry typically allocates around 6% of their revenue towards advertising. The grocery store food brands you see on your shopping trips allocate around 12% of their revenue to advertising and cosmetic brands can allocate upwards of 30% of their revenue to advertising.

Another way to look at this is that the car you buy for $20,000 has $1,200 built into the price to cover advertising. That can of baked beans you buy has 12 cents of the dollar allocated to advertising. And nearly one-third of the cost of the lipstick is advertising.

This method is also used from a comparative perspective with other brands. An advertising manager can use syndicated research to analyze the competitive advertising spending of other brands and determine the percentage they spend on advertising. This way, the advertising manager can provide context for the advertising recommendation. Is it on par with industry averages? Or are we spending more or less aggressively than our competition? This is a popular method of budgeting among categories where many brands are competing for the same consumer.

Another popular method of budgeting is called the objective-and-task method. This is widely used for advertising tasks where the objective may be to generate a lead or drive people to a website or just change the perception of the organization.

This method sets up communication goals and then works to determine the appropriate advertising spend necessary to achieve those goals. As with the prior method, the key to any sophisticated advertising budget allocation is to have a strong set of data on which to base your decision.

## Advertising budget allocation

Once the advertising budget is determined, it is up to the advertising manager to best allocate that budget among its various possible uses. Now comes the time when the advertising manager determines how much and where to best allocate those precious dollars.

The allocation process occurs in two phases.

1 Phase one is the overall allocation to different activity categories.
2 Phase two addresses different target segments and timing.

There are some overall advertising budget categories that begin to define how the dollars will be allocated. The following is an example for an advertising campaign.

| *Category* | % |
|---|---|
| Paid media | 75 |
| Production | 15 |
| Research | 5 |
| Contingency | 5 |

For any advertising program, the lion's share of the dollars usually go towards paid media. This can be broadcast, digital, audio, print or other types of media.

Producing the content for the paid media is also a significant line item. Much of this area depends on the media support. If the media plan calls for a series of television commercials, you may need a considerable amount of money. If it is focused largely around just digital display, it may not require as many dollars.

Research is usually a line item in most advertising budgets. Sometimes, research is a separate item outside of the advertising campaign budget.

Advertisers can allocate dollars to a contingency budget. Contingency dollars are used for a variety of items. If you are unsure about the cost of an area such as production, setting up a contingency fund can be useful if costs are higher than you project. Or dollars can be used for opportunistic areas. Perhaps your media team runs across a "great deal," or there is a new media channel you want to try. Contingency funds should be allocated with a purpose in mind.

Some other budget items to consider are the following.

- Agency fees
- Internal personnel
- Resources

If you are an advertising manager at a major corporation, you may be hiring advertising agency partners to help you with content development, media placement, public relations, events and promotions and many other activities. Some advertisers budget their agency fees outside of their advertising campaign budget. Others make it a line item within the budget. Some advertisers pay their agencies based on a fee. Others pay based on a commission of media. Regardless of how compensation is negotiated, it can be a significant cost. It will be an item within the overall advertising manager's budget.

Internal personnel and resources are usually not applied to the actual advertising campaign budget. They are a part of the overall advertising manager's budget. There are instances when advertisers apply all associated costs to a single budget item so that senior management has a sense of size and scope of the budget.

## Applying the budget

Once the overall advertising budget framework is established, then it is time to develop the details. That means developing a media plan that includes how the dollars allocated to paid media will be invested. The media plan is developed in concert with other aspects of the complete advertising plan.

This may include a public relations plan or social media plan that works to generate earned media. The plan likely includes internal resources that may work on anything from website to sales promotion activity.

As the plan gains traction, the advertising manager may also ask the media planning team to consider how they allocate dollars to different market segments. This could be demographic markets such as the Hispanic market. Or it could be to selective geographic markets based on sales development information.

The other area that may warrant a dollar allocation is to test markets. Perhaps the advertiser may want to develop some test situations where advertising is significantly increased or decreased. This may be requested by senior management so that they can better gauge the impact of advertising.

When the plan is being solidified, the content elements of the plan can be put into production. Production costs can then be detailed.

Even after the budget has been determined and allocated, the advertising manager's work is not done yet. As the plan is executed, the advertising manager will constantly monitor its impact and make adjustments accordingly.

## Working with accounting

Every manager needs to know something about accounting and finance. You don't need to know every detail, but you do need to understand the basic accounting reports.

Accounting involves gathering, measuring and stating financial information that is used by managers, investors, government tax authorities and other decision makers. Management uses these reports to allocate resources and to help determine the monetary success of the company.

An advertising manager is unlikely to prepare accounting reports. However, an advertising manager is likely to prepare budget reports that will be used by accounting.

The budget reports we have previously discussed, personnel, resources and advertising spending, will all be needed by accounting. Within this group of reports, any contracts will need to be considered and any financial commitments made from a long-term standpoint. All of this needs to be accounted for.

There are some key terms that every advertising manager needs to understand. They include fiscal year, profit and loss statement, balance sheet and cash flow statements. Let's review each of these and how it impacts the advertising manager.

## Fiscal year

One key aspect to both managing a staff and planning an advertising program is to understand that many businesses operate on a fiscal year.

A fiscal year may or may not coincide with a calendar year. Businesses establish their own fiscal year for a variety of reasons. For example, many retailers have a February-to-January fiscal year. This means that their new budgets begin in February of the current year and go through the following January. The reason for this is to account for the Christmas sales season. Retailers use January to liquidate the inventory for that holiday season. By setting up their fiscal year so that December is in the middle of the last quarter of the year, companies can adjust costs in January depending on the holiday sales cycle.

Many food companies establish a July-to-June fiscal year. Sometimes, this is called a crop year. By beginning in July, food manufacturers will have a good handle on crop commodity prices so that they can properly price and market their brands for the year.

Understanding and planning for the proper fiscal year is important from both a personnel and an advertising campaign perspective. Companies use the final quarter of the year to adjust their annual profits. This can be a time when companies look to reduce costs. That may mean advertising. Advertising is not a fixed expense. And it can be large. Thus, if a company is looking to boost short-term profits, there can be pressure to reduce advertising expenses for that quarter. Or the CEO may elect to push advertising into the new fiscal year.

On the upside, there can be a lag effect of sales impact in relation to advertising support. A fiscal year adjustment can help smooth that out. Companies look to have quarters that are relatively stable in terms of profit rather than large swings. By adjusting their calendar, companies can smooth the sales and expense costs out.

From a personnel perspective, employers sometimes stagger personnel reviews and/or salary adjustments. That way, a salary increase doesn't impact the company all at once. It can be staggered throughout the year. As a manager, understanding that timing is important for adding or reducing costs for the business is a key concept. Adjusting either personnel or advertising expenses based on their impact for the fiscal year is one part of the advertising manager's job.

## Profit and loss statement

All organizations are in business to make a profit. Firms produce a monthly profit and loss statement. This statement shows earnings, expenses and profit or loss for that time period.

Typically, profit and loss statements are done so that managers can review the same period from a year ago to understand if there have been any changes to either revenue or costs. Profit and Loss statements also may be rolling. They may show the current month but also provide a rolling year-to-date analysis so that management can see the immediate month plus the year-to-date information.

The monthly profit and loss statement gives managers a view of the business so that they can adjust their thinking. For example, if the company historically lost money during the first half of the year, yet made most of their money in the latter half of the year, they may look to be conservative on adding costs to the business until they felt comfortable that the latter half of the year would be strong.

This, again, impacts the advertising manager from both a timing of personnel activity as well as advertising campaign timing. Profit and loss statements can become very detailed. For example, a retailer may have a profit and loss analysis for every item sold. The same may be true for an automotive company. Each car model has its own P&L.

For an advertising agency, each client served has a P&L. Advertising agencies, sometimes, track the hours applied to each client from various agency personnel. If they find that an account is losing money, management may want to review if the reason is an inefficiency in staffing or if the client compensation is not adequate for the amount of work involved.

From an advertising campaign perspective, management may review a rolling P&L statement and decide to make adjustments to the advertising schedule by either reducing or adding to a schedule.

## Balance sheet

A company's balance sheet shows the financial position of a business at a particular time or date. The balance sheet shows the assets and liabilities of the company. Exhibit 4.2 provides a detailed review of how to analyze a balance sheet for a corporation.

## Exhibit 4.2 Analyzing corporate annual reports and financial reports

A corporate annual report is a critical document because it contains information about the company's performance, including its financial performance. This is presented in the report's financial statements such as the balance sheet, the profit and loss statement, and the cash flow statement.

A balance sheet indicates how strong the company's financial situation is in assets, liabilities, and shareholder equity.

Inventories (look under "Assets" on sample balance sheet illustration) normally grow at about the same rate as sales, meaning that the company is selling most of the items that it produces. Inventories rising faster than sales means that not everything being made is being sold, which might cause the company to sell off those items at reduced prices.

Total liabilities are debts. Compare the current year's liabilities with those of the preceding year, and look at both short-term and long-term borrowing (again, see the balance sheet illustration). Strong companies have steady or decreasing debt. Recent legal cases involving misleading bookkeeping often had debt rising when sales were also strong. Sharp increases in short-term debt are of more concern than increases in long-term debt because short-term debt must be paid off sooner.

Deferred tax liability (again, see the balance sheet example) that increases rapidly may be a sign of problems, because it represents taxes that the company has not yet paid but will need to pay soon.

Many corporations keep two sets of accounting records, one reported to shareholders and the other reported to the Internal Revenue Service.

Retained earnings (see balance sheet example) consist of profits that are reinvested in the business instead of distributed to shareholders.

Not in the balance sheet is information on cash flow from operations. Another section of the corporate annual report should include a consolidated statement of cash flows, which indicates all cash that the business took in, not just profits.

Balance sheet, ΩΣΛ Corp
As of Dec. 31 (in $ millions)

| | *Year 2XXX* | *Previous year* |
|---|---|---|
| Assets | | |
| Cash and equivalents | $16.1 | $13.6 |
| Investment securities | $35.4 | $30.0 |
| Current receivables | $14.4 | $13.3 |
| Inventories | $9.9 | $9.1 |
| Properties, plans, and equipment | $60.4 | $55.9 |
| **Total assets** | **$136.2** | **$121.9** |
| Liabilities and equity | | |
| Short-term borrowing | $58.6 | $57.2 |
| Accounts payable | $22.2 | $11.7 |
| Dividends payable | $2.1 | $1.9 |
| Long-term borrowing | $22.7 | $13.9 |
| Deferred income taxes | $13.9 | $11.8 |
| **Total liabilities** | **$119.5** | **$96.5** |
| Common stock (shares outstanding at end of year) | $5.9 | $5.9 |
| Retained earnings | $11.0 | $12.0 |
| **Total shareholder's equity** | **$16.9** | **$17.9** |
| **Total liabilities and equity** | **$136.4** | **$114.4** |

On the left side of the balance sheet are the assets. Assets represent the value of everything the company owns. Liquid items that can be quickly turned to cash are called current assets. Current liabilities are the debts due to be paid within the coming year. The difference between current assets and current liabilities is the net working capital.

From an advertising perspective, the balance sheet shows advertising expenses as a current liability. As a company reviews its balance sheet, management discusses the impact of costs relative to its working capital. Decisions that impact the amount of dollars allocated to advertising may be made.

## Cash flow statement

The cash flow statement provides information on the liquidity of the firm. Liquidity means how readily available funds are if needed for purchases or investments or other needs. It includes figures that reflect financing, investing and operating costs.

Expect yourself to be involved in a variety of budget meetings with the accounting group. The advertising manager will compare accounting results with the original budget plan, and use this information to manage resources, and to highlight changes or shifts that need attention or adjustments.

Accounting is a form of record keeping that helps with planning and cost controls within the company. Accounting information is used in making decisions about a wide variety of activities. It is central to making decisions that impact the advertising manager from both a personnel as well as an advertising program perspective.

## Understanding finance

In any business, there are many competing needs. The advertising manager may be competing with a host of other managers to fund their projects. As an advertising manager, you may find yourself in a meeting with someone from operations who wants to build more stores, or someone from the IT department who needs more equipment and software, or someone from the human resources department for a new employee benefit.

Usually, the costs for all these needs and wants will far outnumber the amount of money available for them. Thus, senior management must decide carefully on which projects monies will be spent. Part of this task involves budgeting and accounting, which we just discussed.

Finance involves how the firm raises money and allocates funds. Finance does this with an eye on the risks involved. The chief financial officer or CFO and other senior managers are concerned with managing risks and taking actions to provide funds for business operations.

The sound management on monetary resources depends on finance and financial decisions that work to support the firm's goals. The purpose of the firm's operation is to make money, to provide a profitable return on investment and possibly provide cash for dividends to be shared with stockholders.

Capital is money. Capital costs and capital management are a prime part of the financial task. Equity is involved when you want someone to invest in your business. Debt occurs when you borrow money for your business.

Revenue is a function of several factors. It includes the price charged for goods and services, the volume sold and the mix of items sold and possibly currency trading if the operation is international in scope.

## Financing growth

Establishing a new firm, buying a new acquisition and expanding your current operation all require money. So, where do you get it?

First, you can put up your own money. Maybe you have a savings account, other funds. Or you can borrow the money using your home or other assets as collateral.

Most of us simply do not have enough personal money to provide some significant business financing. So you review how much money your business may have on hand and determine if that is enough or whether you have to borrow.

Banks prefer to work with businesses that have a proven track record. So, for many businesses, getting a bank loan may not be possible.

Other lenders will lend money in return for partial ownership of the business. This could be some employees. Or it could be outside investors. Outside investors are usually in it to make a large return on their investment. Thus, this may not be a path to take.

If you are a private company and want to remain a private company, then your options for raising capital are yourself, your company, a bank loan or selling a portion of your company to investors.

From an advertising management perspective, working for or on a privately held company advertising account is pretty straightforward. The company reviews the same accounting information and makes a decision in the best interest of the company. In this case, that company may be owned by an individual or a group of people. Because a privately held company is relatively small in terms of ownership, the owners have flexibility in how they manage their capital.

If an owner wants to borrow a lot of money in the hopes of getting a big return, they can do so. If an owner thinks that better days are ahead, they may be fine with losing money in the short run to make more in the long run.

Other privately owned businesses pay the partners through profit sharing. The bigger the profits, the more they make. In this case, the partners may be less flexible in how they view the business since their personal wealth is largely dependent on the profits of the company.

## Publicly traded company

Another way to raise money is to form a corporation and sell stock, letting other people buy portions of the firm and letting you use that money in return for anticipated increases in stock price or in stock dividends.

You have likely heard of publicly traded companies. They are typically the largest and best known companies in the world. Companies such as Alphabet (parent company of Google), Apple, Amazon and Facebook are examples for large publicly traded technology companies. This group plus Microsoft are among the top ten largest companies in terms of market capitalization.

Market capitalization is the amount of capital these companies have at their disposal to either expand their current business or buy other businesses. Companies such as these have sometimes over a trillion dollars of market capitalization.

With that kind of access to capital, it is no wonder that these companies aggressively acquire other companies to help them accelerate their own growth. These companies think nothing of allocating millions of dollars towards reach and development for new products that lead to new revenue sources.

Who wouldn't want to have a trillion dollars to allocate? While this may seem like the world's easiest job, it comes with a lot of responsibility. Publicly traded companies are highly regulated. They must disclose their financial statements to the public. They usually report to their stockholders and analysts on a quarterly basis. The latter group provides third-party analysis of these companies which is used by others to determine if they should buy or sell their stock.

The high degree of regulation means a significant amount of work for publicly traded companies to have the highest degree of ethics and accountability. That is needed since many people put their trust in these companies with their money.

Stock price tends to be a reflection of earnings per share. EBITDA stands for "earning before interest, taxes, depreciations and amortization." Interest is the cost for borrowing money. Depreciation involves recording the expense of a tangible asset to cover its useful life. For example, an advertising agency might depreciate the value of a computer over the life of the machine. Amortization is similar to depreciation, but for intangible assets. And taxes are money paid to the government.

EBITDA is useful because it allows comparing profitability among various firms by eliminating accounting decisions and the impact of financing. It is a key measure that investors use when determining to buy a stock.

There are a number of key measures that an advertising manager needs to understand when working with a publicly traded company.

## SG&A

Advertising is a company expense. It is accounted for under the category of SG&A. This stands for selling, general and administrative. This is a key measure that stock analysts look at to measure the efficiency of a company. If the company you work for has a high percentage of its revenue devoted to SG&A, the CFO and CEO will have to answer pointed questions about this from analysts and shareholders.

As the advertising manager, you may be asked to prepare documents that detail why you are spending the amount of advertising dollars relative to other companies in this category. There may be a good reason for it. Perhaps the company is introducing a number of new products that requires a considerable amount of advertising. If so, that is fine. The analysts then will want to see how that investment pays off the next time they talk to the CFO or CEO.

However, if there is not a good reason for the spending, it could lead to analysts downgrading their recommendation to buy the company's stock. This could lead to the company losing millions and sometimes billions of dollars of value.

You can begin to see that the advertising manager dealing with a publicly traded company is subjected to a tremendous amount of scrutiny. The advertising program can have big ramifications on the value of the company.

## Goodwill

Advertising produces more than sales. Advertising can play an important role in building a brand. The brand's reputation is called goodwill. It is the intangible value of the company. For example, if you have bought the assets of a milk company, that means you buy the farm, cows, manufacturing plant and so on. Those are the tangible assets of the company. If the brand is Bordon Milk, there is a value to that brand name that is above those tangible assets. That is the goodwill.

Goodwill then becomes a financial asset that companies look to grow. Advertising can play a big role in this. Building brand value or goodwill is another way to justify investing in advertising for the long term.

## Margin

A key element in generating EBITDA is the profit margin. Profit margin is a company's profit (sales minus all expenses) divided by its revenue. The profit margin ratio compares the profit to sales and tells you how the company is handling its finances.

There are high and low margin industries. For example, the grocery store industry is a very low margin industry. For every dollar spent on sales, the grocery company may get two cents in profit. Thus, the profit margin is 2%. To make money, a grocery chain such as Kroger needs to maintain a high volume of sales.

On the other hand, a technology company such as Facebook has a high profit margin. It runs in the 40%–50% range. That is because the company is largely just people and technology. It doesn't have lots of tangible assets.

One of the key elements that stock analysts identify when determining if they should recommend a stock is the profit margin. If the profit margin is going up, that is a good sign. If the profit margin is going down, that is a bad sign. If the profit margin is not as strong as that of other comparable companies, that is also a bad sign.

The good news is that advertising can play a big role in helping maximize profit by creating a strong brand that offers greater opportunity to raise prices in the market. For example, Apple has an incredible brand and has a very loyal customer base. As a result, it can raise prices on its products without much pushback from customers.

On the other hand, it would be very difficult for a grocery store chain such as Kroger to raise prices that would be significantly higher than Walmart. Do consumers believe that a can of peas should cost more at Kroger than at Walmart? The answer is not really. So, in such a case, Kroger looks to sell items that Walmart may not carry.

The ability to raise prices or increase margin is a key financial aspect for the advertising manager to consider when developing a campaign. Getting people to buy a product is one thing, while getting people to spend more for the product is another. By impacting margin, advertising can have a significant impact on the company's financial standing.

## Global currency

One aspect of the advertising manager's job is to understand not only different cultures but different monetary and currency policies.

Imagine you are working on a global advertising campaign. You have scheduled advertising in a variety of countries. Each have their own currency. Yet you need to report a common figure to your company regarding advertising spending.

You will need to be able to convert one currency to another. Depending on the strength of a country's economy, its currency or monetary value rises or falls. This currency exchange rate changes every day.

If you are based in the United States, you would peg foreign currency to the US dollar. The dollar is a very desirable currency to own since the US economy is relatively stable compared to other economies around the world.

When assessing a global campaign, you may want to understand what that dollar might buy. Here is a brief rundown of top foreign currency exchange rates pegged to the US dollar as of 11 January 2020.

| *Currency* | *Exchange rate* |
|---|---|
| British Pound | 0.77 |
| Euro | 0.84 |
| Canadian | 1.31 |
| Mexican Peso | 20.89 |

What this chart tells you is that the dollar is worth about 77 cents in the UK. So, it is discounted 23%. It is a bit under in the rest of Europe as well. Thus, that means you may need to spend relatively more to get the same equivalent value in Europe than the United States.

On the other hand, the Canadian currency trades at 1.31 per dollar. That means for every dollar, you can get 1.31 Canadian dollars. Thus, Canada is relatively inexpensive than the United States. When you get to more emerging economies such as Mexico, the difference can become very great. For every dollar, you can get almost 21 pesos. That is quite a big difference.

The other thing to remember when dealing in a global environment is that sales is the same situation. A dollar of sales in the UK is really worth only 77 cents. Therefore, you may need to work with your financial team to understand the implications of currency regarding your global advertising program.

## Summary

Budgeting, accounting and finance are all important items for an advertising manager to understand. Budgeting is the key task that an advertising manager does for the personnel, resources and the actual advertising campaign.

Accounting and finance are related areas but not identical. Accounting is a reporting of cost and revenue. Some key reports include a profit and loss statement, balance sheet and cash flow analysis.

Finance is the management of capital. Knowledge of finance helps a manager do a better job so that they can contribute to the success of the firm. It is important to understand that capital is the key ingredient for growth whether that is through expansion of current business or by acquiring another company.

Budgeting, accounting and finance are impacted by global markets and currency evaluations. It is up to the advertising manager to understand the dynamics of global markets to ensure financial success of any global advertising programs.

## Review questions

1 What are key budget areas for advertising?
2 What are important aspects of accounting that impacts the advertising manager?
3 What role does advertising play in finance?
4 What are tangible and intangible assets?
5 How does advertising impact the balance sheet? How does it impact a publicly traded company?
6 What value can advertising bring to the balance sheet?

## Case 4.1 The Southern Rice Company

### *Issue: advertising spending*

The Southern Rice Company is one of the country's leading rice brands. The Southern Rice Company's distribution area is generally equivalent to the territory south of the Mason-Dixon Line with some distribution into western states. The Southern Rice brand is the leading seller among premium-priced brands of rice. The brand costs the consumer approximately 10 cents per pound more than the other leading brands in the market and 20 cents per pound more than private label or store brands.

For more than 50 years, the Southern Rice brand has based its entire marketing and advertising strategy on the sale of a quality brand, which management states costs more due to the natural harvesting technique that they use to cull their rice from the fields. The Southern Rice approach has been a hit with consumers, since a large segment of the population in the southern states indicated that they are willing to pay a bit more to get the type of quality that they enjoy in a rice brand commodity. Price increases for rice in recent times have begun to impact Southern Rice's ability to continue to price its brand at a premium cost. Consumers have been less willing to pay more for rice as overall food prices continue to increase.

The initial distribution for Southern Rice began in Atlanta where the company was able to obtain a good distribution and acceptance within a short period of time. Management believed that this success was largely due to the association that the brand had with white-tablecloth restaurants that served the product. In fact, Southern Rice was seen as a part of the old southern genteel restaurant scene in Atlanta. Southern Rice used its Atlanta strength to expand to other markets in the south.

The original Southern Rice was a natural long grain rice and was slow-cooked. However, the overall market for slow-cooking rice was dwindling as convenience products entered the picture. Eventually, Southern Rice realized that its next logical next step was to enter the instant rice market.

At the present time, instant rice is available in a wide variety of physical forms and compositions. The most successful instant rice is made by National Rice, which has national distribution and a strong advertising budget. Instant in a Second by Genfoods is also a strong competitor. Tennessee Tom's rice is another regional competitor and a family-operated business just like Southern Rice. Tennessee Tom's is owned by a colorful character, Tom Trager, who is featured in their commercials (Exhibits 4.3–4.5).

### Exhibit 4.3 Southern rice marketing formula

2 × SOV = 1 × SOM

*Note*: SOV = share of voice; SOM = share of market. Spend at least two times the category advertising spending to achieve one share point by the second year.

### Exhibit 4.4 Rice consumption trends (lbs per HH per month)

| *Year* | *Regular rice* | *Instant rice* |
|---|---|---|
| YTD—current year | 2.70 | 2.39 |
| Past year | 2.75 | 2.34 |
| Two years ago | 2.85 | 2.30 |
| Three years ago | 2.90 | 2.25 |
| Four years ago | 3.00 | 2.20 |

*Note*: Regular rice equals 80¢ per lb. While instant rice equals $1.50 per lb. Total: 110 million HH.

**Exhibit 4.5 Geographic analysis**

| *Area* | *Natural rice CDI* | *Instant rice CDI* |
|---|---|---|
| New England | 40 | 50 |
| Metro New York | 75 | 95 |
| Middle Atlantic | 110 | 120 |
| East Central | 65 | 70 |
| West Central | 90 | 85 |
| Southeast | 185 | 120 |
| Southwest | 125 | 135 |
| Pacific | 115 | 140 |

*Note*: CDI = category development index.

Instant rice household consumption varies from region to region. A recent article stated that instant rice represented 46% of K-Store overall rice sales, in contrast to its overall 30% share of the rice category. Another trade release stated that nearly 40% of rice sales in the Publix's grocery chain was now instant rice. This was a big trend for Southern Rice since Publix's was the leading grocery chain in the South. K-Store was also important since it was the leading national grocery chain.

Although there are some areas that are strong natural rice areas and weak instant rice areas, the South is strong in all forms of rice consumption. This was a concern for Southern Rice since they did not want to introduce an instant rice that might hurt their own natural rice brand (Exhibit 4.6).

**Exhibit 4.6 Instant rice goal**

| *Year* | *% instant rice share* |
|---|---|
| First year | 5 |
| Second year | 10 |
| Third year | 13 |

There were significant differences in who purchased natural rice and instant rice. Natural rice was purchased by large families and it had a distinctive ethnic bias. On the other hand, instant rice attracted singles and small families, and had a more upscale consumer base than natural rice.

The bulk of instant rice advertising funds of the leading brands was allocated for advertising in television.

The two national brands, National Rice and Instant in a Second, used national television and some magazines. Tennessee Tom's used only spot television in the key southern markets. However, both the national brands also used spot television in the South to add incremental advertising support in this key region.

### Exhibit 4.7 Advertising media expenditures (past year current dollars, in millions)

| *Brand* | *Magazine* | *Net TV* | *Net cable* | *Spot TV* | *FSI* | *Total* |
|---|---|---|---|---|---|---|
| Southern Rice | 1.0 | – | – | 3.0 | 1.0 | 5.0 |
| National Rice | 2.0 | 8.0 | 2.0 | 3.0 | 5.0 | 20.0 |
| Instant in a Second | 3.0 | 1.0 | 3.0 | 1.0 | 3.0 | 11.0 |
| Tennessee Tom's | – | – | – | 3.5 | – | 3.5 |

The Southern Rice Company is planning on entering the instant rice market in a big way. The markets that they plan on expanding into include Tampa/St. Petersburg, Charlotte, and Washington, D.C. The plan is to obtain a 10% market share in sales in these markets within the next two years.

Southern Rice management recognizes that to realize these objectives, it is necessary to allocate a substantial amount of advertising dollars. But they are unclear on how to determine what the appropriate spending level should be.

As a guide to its first efforts in these markets, the company plans a test market program. Results from this test are expected to be in by the end of next year. Southern Rice management expects to launch their marketing program right after assessing the test market results.

The key question for Southern Rice management has been the level of spending required to make their market share goals. They turned to their advertising firm, Barkley and Peachtree, to help them determine the number of markets and the level of spending that would be required (Exhibit 4.7).

Your challenge at the Barkley and Peachtree advertising agency is to determine the advertising spending for each of the two-year periods in the plan and to justify that spending level.

### Questions

1. How would you approach determining the advertising spending levels?
2. What types of analysis would be some of the best methods for determining advertising spending levels?
3. Should you consider developing a test market approach? If so, how would you construct a test market scenario?
4. What methods would you consider to justify the spending?
5. What primary research would you consider to aid in determining the advertising spending or the outcome of the advertising?

## Case 4.2 Vineyard Agency

### *Issue: new business profitability*

Founded in 1990, the Vineyard Agency had emerged as one of the South's most successful advertising agencies. With a staff that totaled over 200 people in 2001, the agency was seen as a creative powerhouse. All of this great work was based on the strategic thinking of Beryl Vineyard, the founder of the firm.

In fact, the agency was a contender for "Agency of the Year," which was a prestigious award given out by *Advertising Age*. Beryl Vineyard was a driven person who built the agency on what she perceived to be a gap in the market. That gap was tourism. She focused on this sector and it served her well, as the agency had won national accounts that represented airlines, tourism boards, hotels, and rental cars.

Beryl Vineyard had been a renowned speaker on the tourism circuit until the global coronavirus pandemic hit. With the pandemic, the travel and tourism business tanked. Hotel and resort bookings moved to historic lows. Clients began to reduce ad spending and she began to reduce her staff.

The biggest blow to the agency came when her head account management person and her top creative team left to form their own agency. The agency's creative product began to suffer and Beryl's usually reliable new business pipeline began to run dry. Normally, she would get a call nearly every month to pitch a new piece of business. Now, the phone was silent. She needed to restart the agency and gain some momentum.

### *Enter the new business savior*

Tony Wright was a slick New Yorker who had recently turned around two agencies in Manhattan. The most recent was Mariner, which he doubled in size within three years. The agency had just been sold to WPP. After a transition period in the buyout, WPP dismissed Tony from the agency, saying that they wanted more of a traditional CEO. So Tony was looking for a new adventure.

A New York-based recruiter called Beryl Vineyard to introduce Tony's credentials to her. "If you want a proven new business rainmaker, this is your guy," said the recruiter to Beryl (Exhibit 4.8).

Beryl wondered why Tony would leave New York. She was a bit skeptical that a hard-charging New Yorker would like the slower pace of the South. But the recruiter said that Tony was ready to leave New York and wanted to show the New Yorkers that he could energize an agency regardless of the location.

Tony and Beryl met in a neutral setting of Washington, D.C. Although Beryl was not comfortable with Tony, she recognized that Tony would be a new business machine. "With my contacts, I will be able to double your business within a year," said Tony to Beryl. "All I ask is that you give me control of the new business process and some resources to get the job done. It takes some money to get some money," he added.

## Exhibit 4.8 Vineyard Agency: income statement (March)

| *Item* | *YTD actual (000)* | *YTD budget (000)* | *Prior year (000)* |
|---|---|---|---|
| Gross income | | | |
| Production commission | 162 | 200 | 117 |
| Media commission | 893 | 738 | 550 |
| Fees | 36 | 36 | 32 |
| Total gross income | 1,091 | 1,174 | 699 |
| Loss of revenue | 786 | 809 | 387 |
| Gross profit | 305 | 365 | 312 |
| Operating expenses | | | |
| Salaries | 170 | 150 | 130 |
| Rent | 19 | 19 | 19 |
| Travel | 3 | 3 | 2 |
| Entertainment | 15 | 2 | 1 |
| Computer, phone | 3 | 3 | 3 |
| Legal | 5 | 2 | 1 |
| Depreciation | 6 | 6 | 6 |
| New business | 16 | 12 | 11 |
| Misc. | 1 | 1 | 1 |
| Total expenses | 238 | 198 | 174 |
| Other income interest | 5 | 5 | 3 |
| Net income before extra items | 72 | 172 | 141 |
| Agency write-off | 20 | – | – |
| Net income | 52 | 172 | 141 |

Beryl was in no position to say no. She needed new business and here was a proven big-league new business guru. She thought that it was best for the business if she hired him, whether she liked his style or not. So Beryl hired Tony, who immediately went to work.

### *Financial impact of Tony Wright*

As Beryl and her CFO looked over the March income statement, Beryl began to see the impact that Tony Wright was making on the agency. On the positive side, Tony had been a great new business guy. Gross income was up by over 50% from a year ago. Tony had brought in different accounts from the ones the agency traditionally had handled. Instead of just tourism-related accounts, Tony had expanded the list to include luxury retail accounts and even some upper-end packaged goods accounts. This had certainly been a breath of fresh air to the agency. Even *Advertising Age* was giving the agency kudos for new business.

However, to get this new business, Beryl and her CFO had budgeted for greater expenses. There were increased salaries to add more creative staff to the fold and there was a significantly larger amount of money devoted to new business. While the March numbers were a bit higher than they had budgeted, Beryl wasn't too worried about it.

"We need the creative horsepower to get more business and we should be increasing our expenditures on new business," she told her CFO.

"I understand that, Beryl, but I do worry that the new business Tony is picking up has a lower margin than our current accounts," said the CFO.

However, the numbers that concerned the CFO were not the salaries or the new business expense. The CFO pointed out the extremely high entertainment number. "Tony's entertainment number is higher in one quarter than we have had in the last three years combined," said the CFO to Beryl. He went on to say that at this rate, the agency would spend a huge amount on entertainment.

"Is this guy just buying accounts?" questioned the CFO.

The other number that the CFO brought to Beryl's attention was the agency write-offs. The agency had been very good about not writing off any items in the past. They had made their fair share of mistakes but rarely did they have to eat any outstanding costs. Now, they had write-offs that they had never seen before.

"Beryl, you must find out what is behind these write-offs," said the CFO. He went on to say that this type of write-off level was just unacceptable. "I know that we need new business, but while we have increased our top line income, our bottom line is less than half that of last year," said the CFO. The CFO voiced more concerns about the bottom line of the company. He was concerned that all the focus on the new business efforts was not going to help the overall financial health of the agency.

### *Beryl's decisions*

After meeting with the CFO, Beryl walked back slowly to her office. Her mind was racing. On the one side, she knew that hiring Tony Wright had been a gamble. But the gamble seemed to be paying off with the rapid growth of new business. The agency was getting mentioned again in the trade publications as a "hot shop" and the people in the office were much more excited about the work.

On the other hand, she shared some of her CFO's concerns over Tony's lack of controls over spending. She wasn't sure if all the entertaining that Tony did was necessary. She had heard that Tony lived an extravagant lifestyle, but she had hoped that this was just a Manhattan circumstance that would go away after he moved to the South.

The one thing that she couldn't overlook was the large agency write-offs. That was just like flushing money down the drain.

Beryl also thought about the different accounts that Tony was bringing in. If they have a lower margin, she wondered if they were really worth it.

Beryl had a number of decisions to make about the agency's future. Should she continue on this course with Tony Wright or not? Should she require that Tony get a certain margin on the new accounts, or else not take them? Should she rein in Tony's entertainment expenses? Should she penalize those involved in the write-offs to set an example for the rest of the staff?

Beryl wanted her CFO to take another pass at giving her an analysis of the March income statement so that she could better understand the relationship of the top line income and the bottom line. She hoped that by getting a bit more detail she could better understand what she should do.

She closed her door and hoped that she had made a good decision by bringing in Tony Wright. The consequences of changing again were not appealing.

### Questions

1. Look at each question that Beryl identified. What are the pros and cons of each possibility?
2. What further questions would you ask yourself?
3. How would you pursue each of the above questions?
4. What types of analyses would you do to get a better handle on the financial picture of the agency?
5. Do you feel that the short-term expense is worth it in the long run for the agency?
6. What would you do to solve the problem?

Chapter 5

# Managing means measuring

## What and how to measure

### LEARNING OBJECTIVES

This chapter is intended to help you:

- Understand the key areas of advertising measurement.
- Understand message and creative measurement.
- Understand tracking perception and reputation.
- Understand how to develop return on investment.
- Understand media measurement and impact.

If you can't measure it, you can't manage it. This saying has been attributed to Peter Drucker, a prominent management thought leader. Mr. Drucker published extensively in the area of management productivity and organizational efficiency. No matter what the topic, Mr. Drucker's first step was to determine how best to measure the process. Otherwise, how would you know if you are successful?

An advertising manager needs to think through what to measure and how to measure it. If you don't properly define success, you can believe that someone will define it for you.

In this chapter, we will focus our attention on the measurement of the advertising process and campaign. As an advertising manager, this is not your only item to measure. We just talked about budgeting. That is certainly one aspect to measure. We will devote future chapters to personnel management. That is another crucial area to develop a measurement strategy.

Unless your advertising program is successful, properly managing a budget and your staff isn't going to keep you on the management track for long. Much of your career success will be determined by the success of the advertising programs that you manage. You need to develop the key performance indicators (KPIs) for your advertising campaign.

Advertising measurement should be put into place to help answer the following questions.

1 Message: Is the message compelling? Is it built on a compelling insight? Is the message idea executed in an equally compelling manner?
2 Communication Impact: What is the communication impact of the advertising? Do people recall the advertising? Did it change the awareness level of the product? Did it have a positive change on the attitudes towards or the reputation of the brand? Did it help persuade people to consider taking action, which could be buying the product or some other form of it?

3 Media Impact: What was the media impact of the program? What was the overall delivery? What was the reach and frequency? What was the level of engagement or action on digital media platforms? What was the earned media?
4 Business Impact: What was the business impact of the advertising? Did it get more people to buy the product? Did the program generate incremental sales? Were there other business impact benefits that can be measured (employee performance, stock purchase or multiple, etc.)?

Answering these questions is crucial to the success of your advertising program. You can't win in one area and lose in another area and still consider your advertising program a success. Everyone must work together for your advertising program to generate the results you plan on.

As you develop a measurement plan, it is very important that you understand that advertising is not done in a vacuum. You need to account for variables that may not be in your control.

For example, you may develop the most compelling message carried by an innovative media plan to motivate consumers to seek your product. However, if you drive them to a website that keeps on crashing, no orders would be fulfilled. You might claim that the advertising is awesome but that the operations are bad, which may be true. The CEO of the advertised brand, however, will say that the program is a failure because no one has ordered the product.

Or you have a compelling advertising campaign for a delivery company to drive more business. Business does increase, but not significantly. However, on-time shipments increase significantly because the frontline employees are positively impacted by the message. This ultimately leads to greater customer retention, followed by new customer acquisition.

The point of these examples is that you must understand the entire situation. Try to develop a measurement plan that not only measures advertising communication impact but other areas that may be impacted as well. It is in your best interest to isolate the impact of advertising so that senior management knows exactly the benefit of your advertising program.

The first place to start is with the message and execution.

## Message and creative execution measurement

It is easy to get distracted by a creative execution of the strategy and miss the key point of the communication. Advertising content creation is viewed many times as the "fun and exciting" part of advertising. And it can be.

However, it is important to remember that no matter how interesting or intrusive the creative execution, if the strategy is not right, you will not have success.

As an advertising manager, one of the most important things you can do in the advertising process is to separate the message from the execution of the message. If you don't take control of that aspect of the advertising campaign, you can have a bad outcome. That won't be good for you as well as the brand.

Message strategy for an advertising campaign follows from broader company or brand strategies. There is the overall vision and mission of the company. The advertising campaign must take that into account. There is the specific brand strategy. This is called brand positioning. How the brand is positioned in the market must be considered.

When you look at Coca-Cola's mission and vision, it states that "refresh the world in mind, body and spirit, to inspire moments of optimism and happiness through our brands and our actions." Is it any wonder that the flagship brand of the corporation, Coke, has had advertising campaigns such as, "Share a Coke and a smile" or "Open Happiness"? Coke has introduced memorable songs such as, "I would like to teach the world to sing." And Coke has introduced characters such as polar bears and even Santa. This is one positive brand. Thus, the history of Coke's advertising falls in line with the overall corporate mission of the company. Now, other brands of Coca-Cola are positioned differently and take on different brand positions and personalities. Their advertising reflects that as well.

Let's say that you are the advertising manager for Walmart. The new CEO comes to you and says, "I want to show the world that Walmart is a fashion oriented brand. We aren't just selling cheap goods."

After you have picked yourself up off the floor realizing that Walmart has a legacy of "Save Money. Live Better" as a tagline and actually as a corporate edict from its founder, Sam Walton, many years ago, you might advise the new CEO to do some message testing.

Will consumers believe that Walmart would offer fashionable items? Even if Walmart radically changes its product mix, would those who seek fashionable items come to Walmart buy the same?

As an advertising manager, you need to be very sensitive to how any communication fits within the overall company's mission, vision and brand position.

Just because a brand has a long legacy it doesn't mean you can't make the brand position and/or communication more contemporary. In fact, that is the purpose of advertising. Consumer tastes and values change. You need to make sure that the message resonates with a new consumer.

For example, Tide laundry detergent had for long remained the market leader, positioned as the "one consumers trusted the most." However, Tide was losing some market share to less expensive brands. Over time, consumers believed that nearly any brand of laundry detergent could clean their clothes. So, Tide was still in the mix but not considered the only choice.

Through research, Tide learned that their target market of mothers with two or more kids in the household were more concerned about clothes wearing out than keeping them clean. Tide's formula actually helped prevent clothes from wearing out more than other laundry detergents. Tide had just not talked about it. So Tide positioned itself around the idea of "not wearing out" versus "keeping clothes clean." This propelled Tide back into a "must have" brand among those who were cost conscious. Tide has subsequently had many other product improvements and campaigns. This shift from clean to not wearing out was a crucial repositioning effort.

The other overarching message is called the "big idea." The big idea is the message behind the message; it is the overarching idea for all future communication. For example, Dove's classic "Campaign for Real Beauty" was based on the big idea that "All women are naturally beautiful." The execution of that idea was to break the mold of the beauty industry and use "real women" in all of their advertising. The idea was to help build self-esteem among all women. By addressing the stereotypes of the beauty industry, Dove broke through.

One of the first steps before developing the campaign is to determine if the overall message will resonate with target consumers. This can be done in a variety of ways. You may have a simple value proposition testing where you test different ways to look at the brand. For example, going back to the Tide example, Tide could have tested these three benefits.

- Tide is the most trusted brand of laundry detergent.
- Tide's formula cleans clothes and keeps them fresher than any other brand can.
- Tide's formula cleans clothes and keeps them from wearing out.

These simple statements could be tested. There are many other methods to test value propositions or key messages that involve various sophisticated statistical techniques.

Other methods to test messages involve having the creative department develop videos that highlight the central message in a more emotional way. These messages can also be tested with your target market to determine how a particular type of message may resonate with target consumers.

## Execution of message: copy testing

Once you have the overall message, it is time to determine the best way to express it. You may want to evaluate some alternatives. At this stage of the process, it is important to challenge the creative team to find different ways to express the idea. This is the time to experiment.

Even if it is a simple project such as communicating that a retailer offers zero interest for 60 months, there are lots of ways to communicate it. Here are just three we found.

- Opera singer with a parody of Verdi's Rigoletto. No.no.no.noooo.
- A "no" machine.
- Series of zeroes done to the music of The Fixx's "Saved by Zero."

There are many, many more. In this experimental process, it is important to agree on a method that is agreed on by the creative team and yourself. You want to understand how alternatives may work. The creative team doesn't want to be stifled.

The "how to say it" part of message testing has spawned an entire industry devoted to this area. The industry is advertising pre-testing. It is typically known as copy testing.

Copy testing has been around for a long time. It is traced back to the 1930s. The Advertising Research Council formalized the process in 1939 with the first published guide to copy testing.

Copy testing really took off in the 1960s with the acceleration of television commercials. The cost to produce a commercial plus the cost of the airtime made many advertisers turn to copy testing to mitigate the dollar risk associated in a television-driven campaign.

Today, there is a wide range of copy testing solutions in the market. What was once confined to a single medium such as television has now been expanded to include a variety of media including print, digital, radio and others.

The main purpose of copy testing is to determine if the message is memorable, engaging and persuasive. In most copy testing situations, a message is shown to a sample of the target market to gauge their response. The respondents are asked questions about what they have seen or heard, and if they understood the message, liked the message and would consider taking action based on the message. Some copy testing companies use sophisticated measuring devices such as facial coding, eye tracking or galvanic skin response. Some use MRI technology to understand a consumer's brain response to the advertising message.

Some copy testing research companies focus on specific industries such as consumer packaged goods, restaurants or automotive. This allows the research company to build a databank of knowledge by business category. These research companies then develop normative data based on the aggregation of these measures. It allows the advertiser to compare their execution to hundreds of previous examples.

This normative data is controversial. On the one hand, it aids the advertiser in understanding what has worked in the past. On the other hand, many creative communicators believe that it provides a formulaic method for communication. It does not reward communication that markedly deviates from the norm.

Copy testing has its pros and cons. On the one hand, copy testing can improve the chances an ad will benefit the advertiser. On the other hand, some feel that a good idea can get lost in the development process. It forces a "beat the test" mentality among the creative team.

Copy testing is done extensively in the United States. Copy testing is not as extensively used in the rest of the world. There are a number of reasons for it. The United States is by far the largest advertising market in the world. As a result, there is an extensive amount of data on creative. The costs for advertising put pressure on the advertising manager to "prove that it works" before putting a campaign into the marketplace through a multimillion paid media purchase.

## Tracking perception and reputation

Once the campaign message and creative executions have been approved, it is now time to place the creative content in the marketplace. This means you have to measure the impact of the campaign.

One of the key ways that an advertising manager measures the impact of the campaign is by doing research to measure if there are changes in awareness of the brand and the advertising, perceptual change in attitude towards the brand, a change in the reputation of the brand and ultimately a change in behavior.

Most companies and brands have some form of ongoing research to understand the communication impact of the advertising campaign. Those studies are typically called tracking studies, since they track a variety of measures over time. Some are called AAU, which stands for awareness, attitude and usage. Others are called brand health studies. Some are called brand reputation studies.

These studies are done in a variety of manners. Most are large surveys with hundreds or thousands of respondents. Historically, these studies were done via telephone, but they have largely migrated to some form of online survey. The goal is to get a large enough sample so that you can measure statistically significant changes in the dimensions that are important to the advertiser.

The AAU study is a standard piece of research that many brands employ. The reason is that the key measures fit into what is called the brand purchase funnel.

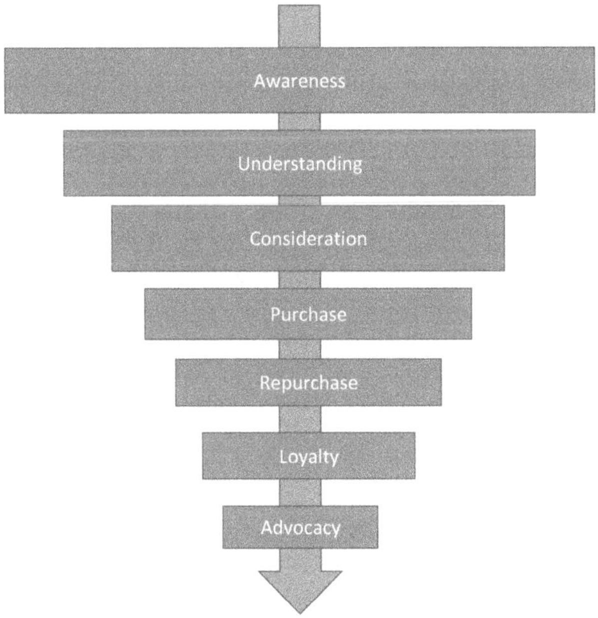


## Exhibit 5.1

Exhibit 5.1 shows an example of a brand purchase funnel. The top of the funnel is awareness. The thought is that if people don't know your brand, they won't buy it. The second stage is understanding. This is a deeper level of awareness. The third stage is consideration, that is, if the consumer would consider purchasing the brand. The next stage is purchase. Following purchase is a series of other stages for current customers such as the likeliness to buy again, loyalty to the brand and advocacy for the brand.

All of these are metrics that can be measured and analyzed to determine if there are communication gaps to be filled. For example, if the advertising campaign generated a high degree of awareness but low levels of consideration, perhaps there is a message problem that the consumer doesn't believe the brand is worthy of purchase. This may require more inquiry. These studies are cornerstones for the industry to tie directly into the business of the campaign.

Other measures in tracking studies address advertising or reputation issues. Do people like the message? Does it make them like the brand? Does it make them think more highly of the brand? All of these are possible areas to devote some questions to.

The advertising manager will likely work with other stakeholders on this piece of research. It may be a brand manager or marketing manager. It could be a CEO. It can be the advertising agency. All stakeholders are impacted by the success or failure of the advertising campaign.

When developing a global advertising campaign measurement plan, it is important to note that there is a great deal of variance in the quality and quantity of research partners across the globe. Some countries like the United States are very research heavy, while other countries are not. Thus, while it is ideal to use the same research measurement method and vendor across all audiences, it is likely not a practical solution.

Just like communication needs to be tailored to different markets and audiences, so too do the wording of questions and research approaches. This is also why having global themes or ideas is so important. That way, regardless of the way an idea is executed on a local basis, there can be a measure put into place that tracks the overall theme across countries and then offers specific measures on local market creative execution.

Beyond the metrics to track should be a consideration of the audiences to track. Obviously, the audience for the advertising is the key focus of the study. However, advertising may impact other stakeholders. For example, a retail campaign may increase customer satisfaction since the employees are excited to see the advertising and work more diligently as a result. Or perhaps current shareholders of the company's stock could like the advertising and as a result are more favorably predisposed to the company. As the advertising manager, it is your role to think through what audiences could be impacted by the message and to design research aimed at assessing its impact.

## Marketing impact: ROI

Developing measures that track the marketing impact, and ultimately the return on investment, is central to just about any advertising campaign. After all, an advertising campaign usually is designed to change awareness or perception of the brand that leads to some form of action.

That action can be to go to a retail store and buy a product. It can be to go to an online retailer and buy a product. It can be to sign up for more information so that a sales person can follow up. The action is the behavioral change that you are attempting to impact.

The great majority of advertising is used to impact a company or brand's sales. The basic components of sales are fundamentally the same. Sales is a function of the number of buyers multiplied by the number of items and amount that they buy. This could be 12 tubes of toothpaste over a year at $1.50 per tube. Or it could be one car purchased at $40,000. Or it could be signing up for insurance which costs $50 per month. While every industry has its own nuances on generating sales, advertising is one of the key ingredients to get someone to purchase a product and/or to keep them buying the product.

Advertising is used quite often to bring in new customers to a store, whether it is a physical location or an online retailer. In today's global and digital age, it is likely that the company you are working for may have both a physical and online presence.

Getting new customers to your brand is called trial. This means that they are trying the product for the first time. Trail is crucial to a brand since the goal is to always expand a brand's customer base.

Another marketing approach is to accelerate the repeat purchase of a brand. Once you have a customer, you have the ability to persuade them to continue to use your brand more often. This is a frequency of use strategy.

Another aspect to this strategy of growing the customer is to market other items to that customer. For example, if you have sold someone an auto insurance policy, you may want to market life insurance or home insurance. The idea is that if the customer likes you for one purchase, they are already familiar with you and more likely to buy other items from you.

This same concept is true when you eat out. You buy a main course and the waiter offers you dessert or an after-dinner drink. This is adding to the order or increasing your ticket. You may be caught in a weak moment and go for it. That action raises the value that you are to this restaurant as a customer.

The latter is a good jumping off point for the other key business metric, that is, margin or profit margin. This is the percentage a brand makes on its sales. Comparative profit margin within industries is a key metric among financial analysts as to the strength of the company.

Advertising is sometimes used to help impact profit margin by making it easier for a brand to raise its prices. The ability to raise prices is another important financial metric.

The trick for the advertising manager is to understand how advertising played a role in the business. Sometimes that is clear. Driving people to a website is a function largely of communication. Selling a car might be more difficult to determine the exact role advertising played. If you are marketing a business-to-business product such as an oil field pipeline, it gets even more difficult.

With the increasing amount of data available, particularly driven by digital media, more and more marketers are able to isolate advertising as a variable in the marketing mix. Through the use of sophisticated multivariate statistical models, an advertising manager can begin to understand more precisely the role that advertising alone may have played in the increased business of a brand. For example, the World Advertising Research Council (WARC) has awards for the best advertising campaigns that are based on return on investment or ROI.

To be considered for a WARC advertising award, the advertiser must submit a case study that includes an analysis of how the advertising alone performed for the campaign. This means assessing whether for every dollar spent on advertising there was an incremental two or three or more dollars in return generated for the brand.

Econometric modeling is used by many companies to better understand how each touchpoint of a brand's communication and selling efforts impacts the ultimate sale. For example, Adobe Experience Cloud is one of many companies that provide this type of tracking and analysis. Through Adobe's software platform, business-to-business advertisers can understand the return of specific elements such as a sales person's phone call, a digital advertisement or a print ad. The level of granularity is amazing. None of this would be possible without robust data. Whether you like it or not, big data is here to stay. It is being harnessed to understand a myriad of issues.

As an advertising manager, it is important that you understand the increasing role such models play in the field of advertising and marketing. It provides the level of detail that the CEO and other senior managers need to see to understand the importance of advertising for their company.

## Media measurement

One of the key measurement areas for any advertising campaign is the media impact of the campaign. This includes KPIs for paid, owned and earned media. All of these areas have specific metrics to gauge success.

The fundamental measures for paid media are delivery and cost efficiency. The delivery metrics of the campaign tell you how many people have been potentially exposed to the advertising message. The key metrics include the following.

- Impressions: the total number of exposures for the campaign. This is a very good benchmark measure to compare to past year's plans, competitive brands and future alternatives.
- Reach and frequency: This is the percent of your target market that is potentially exposed to your message and the average number of times they have been exposed. This adds another layer of dimension to impressions.
- Effective exposure: This is the percentage of the audience who has been effectively reached by your campaign. You may define effectiveness by a specific frequency of exposure. The industry default is 3+ times.

These three metrics should be analyzed based on a comparison of the planned delivery to the actual delivery. This tells you the effectiveness of the plan with regard to the actual media purchase.

Cost efficiency is the other core paid media metric. Cost per thousand analysis is the common measure of cost efficiency. The cost per thousand or CPM analysis is calculated by dividing the cost of the plan by the number of impressions, and then multiplying by 1,000. This analysis tells you how much you are investing to reach 1,000 of your target audience. Like impressions, CPM is a good benchmark to measure the plan with regard to the purchase as well as to compare plans to others.

In measuring digital media, you can have a much more detailed view of costs beyond CPM.

It is important to note that the details of paid, owned and earned media may be used in various economic models used to isolate and analyze the impact of advertising. Thus, it is crucial to keep monitoring these areas for model input.

Owned media consists of media that you control. This is typically a company's website. It can also include social media platforms. Some brands have an extensive amount of owned media including their own events, television programs and/or publications.

Digital advertising has many of its own metrics. Many advertising campaigns direct traffic to the website as a key action item. Here are some common digital measures.

- CPC or CPA: Cost per click or cost per action is the cost for each time someone clicks on a website or landing page, or takes action such as filling out a form.
- Click through rate or CTR: This is a measure in which a percentage is assigned to how many people click an organization's ad versus the total audience impressions.
- Website page views: the number of times your website has been visited. Keep in mind that page views don't discern how many times a particular person has visited the website. It is just a total amount.
- Unique visitors: This metric counts only the unique users who visit the website. It nets out duplicate visits.
- Time spent: This measures how much time a user spends on the website.
- Bounce rate: This is the percent of visitors to a website who only view the landing page and then navigate away from the site.
- Page views: the metric that shows how many pages a viewer visits during a session on the website.

These measures can tell you a lot about your campaign. For example, a high bounce rate may indicate that your message is driving them to the site but they don't see what they came for. It means that there could be a message-to-content issue. If a person doesn't go far into the site, then it may have a navigation issue. The same is true if someone doesn't spend much time on the site; it may indicate that your content doesn't meet their needs.

Tied into the website are metrics around any aspect of search engine marketing. From an owned perspective, your goal is to organically have your website at the top of key categories so that consumers will quickly find your brand. Pay-per-click or paid search uses large search platforms such as Google to help promote your brand or website. These two areas will tie directly into your website measures.

The other big aspect of most digital campaigns is the use of social media. Social media is the only media category that has a paid, owned and earned component. From a paid standpoint, measuring CPM, cost per click and impressions is very similar to other media categories.

From an owned perspective, the idea for having a company or brand social media channel is to engage with your audience. Social media engagement includes a variety of metrics that indicate the quality and frequency of interactions between the audience and the campaign.

These actions can be graded into high and low effort categories. High effort means that the audience is spending time crafting a response to the brand. This can be items such as leaving a comment. Low effort categories include items such as "likes."

The key measures range across these categories. They include comments, "likes" and "shares." The latter "shares" metric is a key one. By sharing something, the audience is amplifying the campaign. This is the key to generating earned media. That is the number of people who are reached without spending advertising dollars on paid media.

Engagement is pretty straightforward for most large social media platforms. For example, Facebook engagement focuses on the number of likes, shares and comments as well as link clicks and page likes from promoted posts, ads or videos. Twitter reports on retweets, favorites and replies to tweets.

Beyond the action of engagement, there are research companies that provide metrics on sentiment from social media. This is the aggregate amount of positive versus negative comments the brand may be receiving across a variety of platforms. That way, you can determine if your social media presence is helping or possibly hurting the brand's reputation.

You may need to have a variety of partners help you assemble the entirety of your media program. This may include a media planning and buying firm, a social media or public relations firm and your internal resources for website and other owned media. It is a complex task.

The task becomes even greater with a global campaign. Media measurement is not always uniform across countries. There are different media audience research companies that serve various countries. Of course, there are different media outlets that serve specific countries and local communities. That is why it is a good idea to have some core metrics such as impressions and CPM to provide an overall view of media efficiency. Those two metrics are universal. They can form the foundation for more sophisticated media analyses.

## Summary

In summary, measurement impacts every aspect of an advertising campaign from message to market impact. As you develop a measurement plan, it is important to view the approach in two ways: One is to measure success. The other is to provide insights for improvement.

It is crucial to review each step of the process. Message should proceed execution of the message. Each should be tested separately. Market measures should include communication impact such as awareness, perception and attitudinal change along with business metrics such as sales.

Media metrics should also be detailed for paid, owned and earned media. Each aspect of the media plan should be analyzed based on delivery and cost efficiency. Work should be done to determine the value of the advertising campaign from a return on investment perspective. This may require conducting a sophisticated econometric modeling exercise to isolate advertising from the rest of the marketing mix.

Global measures should be put into place to allow for the advertising manager the ability to understand global impact as well as individual country issues. Measurement is one of the key areas of accountability for an advertising manager. It is a key responsibility as a part of crafting an effective campaign.

## Review questions

1 What are the key components to measure an advertising campaign?
2 What is the difference between message and creative execution testing?
3 What are the core measures for advertising campaign output?
4 What are the key business measures that should be analyzed? What role does econometric modeling play in analyzing an advertising campaign?
5 What are key media plan metrics?
6 What are specific metrics around digital media including website and social media?
7 What makes measurement difficult in a global environment?

### Case 5.1 Randall White Dog Food

#### *Issue: advertising planning*

The Randall White Feed and Milling Company is an old-line regional marketer of farm feeds, grits, and corn meal. It was established in 1929 in Berry, Georgia, by Robert White.

Berry, Georgia has been dubbed the "bird dog capital of the world" by *Popular Hunting* magazine. Robert White was a hunting enthusiast. His favorite avocations were hunting quail and raising bird dogs. He and his son, Randall, had been recognized as a top father/son hunting duo by *Popular Hunting*.

Robert White soon turned his passion into profits. He used his money and the resources from his milling operation to develop and market a dry dog food formula specially made for hunting dogs. He named the brand after his son, Randall, and launched the Randall White Complete Dog Ration brand.

Today, Randall White Complete Dog Ration is the company's largest volume and highest profit margin product. It is also the number one brand of dog food in its limited distribution area.

### The product

Randall White Complete Dog Ration is a high-energy, high-protein, complete and nutritionally balanced dry dog food in concentrated form. The brand has historically been positioned as a high-performance dog food for dog owners who desire superior nutrition. This positioning was designed specifically for hunting dogs and for working farm dogs. It is a premium priced product and appeals to the hunting enthusiast and to dog owners who have large, active dogs.

### The dog food market

The dry dog food market is big and growing fast. Sales for the last year nationally and in the Southeast (Randall White's marketing area) were both very strong. From a distribution perspective, grocery stores are the dominant outlets, closely followed by pet food stores and by feed and farm implement stores. Randall White has sales disproportionately weighted to the feed and farm implement stores in its region. The brand also has strong grocery sales in the Southeast but has yet to crack the national pet food distribution market. All of Randall White's pet food sales are to local mom-and-pop retailers and dog kennels (Exhibits 5.2 and 5.3).

**Exhibit 5.2 Dry dog food sales and five-year CAGR**

| | *Total sales millions $* | *% CAGR* |
|---|---|---|
| National | 2,000 | 8.6 |
| Southeast | 750 | 13.3 |

*Note*: CAGR = compounded annual growth rate.

**Exhibit 5.3 Sales distribution of dry dog food sales and Randall White brand (% distribution)**

| | *Grocery* | *National pet stores* | *Farm/feed* | *Kennels/local* |
|---|---|---|---|---|
| National | 55 | 30 | 5 | 10 |
| Southeast | 50 | 25 | 10 | 15 |
| Randall White | 50 | 0 | 30 | 20 |

Dry dog food is categorized into two overall product groups, ration—or meal type—brands such as Randall White, and expanded products such as Checkerboard Chow, Gravy Boat, and Puppy Puff, all made by the national marketer, Ralston Dog Food.

Ration-type brands are composed of separate ingredients mixed together in particle form, providing higher-protein energy levels in a highly concentrated form. They are generally priced at lower levels than expanded products and are most indigenous to the Southeast and Midwest where outdoors activities, including hunting, are the strongest.

Expanded products are homogeneous in appearance with all ingredients ground and blended together. They are often "puffed" with air to have a larger-than-life appearance. Usually, they are in "nugget" or simulated "hamburger" form and priced at premium levels. Expanded products are the mainstay of house pets and smaller dogs. Most nationally advertised brands are of the expanded product variety.

In the Southeast, the ration-type brands account for about 40% of the market, yet nationally, they account for only about 20% of the market. Even within the Southeast, the ration-type brands vary markedly by state.

### *The consumer profile*

There are three basic markets for dry dog food: The first and largest is the pet dog owner. The second is the hunting/working dog owner. The third is the show dog or pure breed market. The last one is a very specialized market with specific niche dog food products tailored to each breed (Exhibit 5.4).

**Exhibit 5.4 Ration-type vs. expanded formula sales: geographic analysis (in %)**

| *Geography* | *% Ration-type* | *% Expanded* |
|---|---|---|
| National | 20 | 80 |
| Southeast | 40 | 60 |
| Tennessee | 40 | 60 |
| Mississippi/Alabama | 45 | 55 |
| Georgia | 50 | 50 |
| Florida | 25 | 75 |
| Virginia/North Carolina | 20 | 80 |
| South Carolina | 30 | 70 |

Of the two larger markets, each has a distinctive consumer profile. Nationally syndicated research shows the consumer profile for the *pet dog owner* dog food market to be as follows.

- Women, age 25–49
- Married with children age 5–17
- Attended or graduated college
- Living in suburban areas of highly populated DMAs (designated marketing areas)
- Household income levels of $75,000+
- Own a single dog

This is contrasted to the dog food consumer market for the *hunting/working dog* category, which breaks down as follows.

- Men, age 35–64
- Married with either teenage children or no children
- High school education
- Living in C and D counties
- Household income level of less than $75,000
- Own multiple dogs

On a per capita basis, the hunting/working dog owner is the heaviest consumer of dog food due to their multiple dog ownership. Because he is an extremely heavy user of dog food, the hunting/working dog owner is extremely price conscious.

### *Randall White challenge*

Within Randall White's marketing area, Randall White has been the number one brand for many years. However, its market share has been consistently eroding over time (Exhibits 5.5–5.7).

**Exhibit 5.5 Dry dog food: sales by county size (in %)**

| *Southeast county size* | *% population* | *% category sales* | *% Randall White sales* |
|---|---|---|---|
| A | 22 | 18 | 11 |
| B | 36 | 45 | 31 |
| C | 23 | 21 | 28 |
| D | 19 | 16 | 29 |
| | 100 | 100 | 100 |

**Exhibit 5.6 Randall White sales and distribution by state (in %)**

| *State* | *% sales* | *% ACV* |
|---|---|---|
| Alabama | 20 | 100 |
| Georgia | 18 | 100 |
| Florida | 6 | 40 |
| South Carolina | 13 | 100 |
| Mississippi | 13 | 100 |
| North Carolina | 8 | 70 |
| Tennessee | 14 | 100 |
| Virginia | 8 | 60 |

*Note*: ACV = all commodity volume.

## Exhibit 5.7 Randall White five-year market share trends (in %)

| | *Year 5* | *Year 4* | *Year 3* | *Year 2* | *Current year* |
|---|---|---|---|---|---|
| Randall White | 40 | 38 | 33 | 31 | 29 |
| Ralston brands | 35 | 34 | 34 | 33 | 31 |
| Private label/other | 25 | 28 | 33 | 36 | 40 |

Randall White's losses are primarily traceable to the dynamic growth of private label brands of dry dog food that are priced 30% less than Randall White brand. There are other factors that compound this problem. The first is the urbanization of the Southeast. Fewer and fewer farms are being worked, and with fewer working dogs. The growth of the Southeast has been in large cities and Randall White has been and continues to be more of a rural brand.

The largest factor is that Ralston has begun a specific campaign in the South to launch its new high-protein dry dog food mix targeted at large dogs. It is made with 20% more protein than Randall White and is sold at a price point 10% less than the Randall White brand.

The other day, Randall White sat in his office and thought about his father's legacy and pondered over what he might have done in a situation like this. With his father's death three years ago, Randall had assumed the head of the company. He knew that he had to not only arrest the declining share of his market but find ways to increase his brand volume (Exhibit 5.8).

## Exhibit 5.8 Advertising media competitive spending (000)

| *Brand* | *Spending ($000)* | *Media mix* |
|---|---|---|
| Ralston Checkerboard Chow | 15,000 | 80% network TV, 20% magazine |
| Gravy Boat | 12,500 | 60% network TV, 40% magazine |
| Puppy Puff | 3,000 | 100% magazine |
| Kennel Club | 6,500 | 100% spot TV (Pacific, Northeast) |
| Randall White | 1,500 | 100% spot TV (Southeast) |
| Others | 7,500 | Various |
| Total | 46,000 | |

His marketing people had been hounding him to spend more money on advertising, but he had felt that he couldn't compete with Ralston in that arena. His product people had begged him to expand his line into the pet owners' market. His salespeople had felt that if he expanded his geographical distribution to other feed stores, and even other grocery chains, he might not be so vulnerable. His neighbor had said that he had just switched to a private label brand since it was so much cheaper. That really got to Randall. He began to wonder if his product was out of touch with the market.

He knew that he must take some action. So he asked all of his key management to develop a plan of attack. The question was, What course of action should he take?

### Questions

1. What analysis do you think that Randall White should ask for to determine his proper course of action?
2. How would you construct a SWOT analysis based on the 4Ps (product, price, place, and promotion) of marketing?
3. Is there any missing information that you would need to make a decision?
4. What decision could you make to have an immediate impact on sales?
5. If Randall White decides to introduce a new product, what would you recommend?
6. What role should advertising play in Randall White's future plans?

## Case 5.2 Tinsdale Agency and Design

### *Issue: agency profitability*

As the president of Tinsdale Agency and Design, LuLu Tinsdale had always been lax in her management approach. Perhaps it was her design background that made her a pretty laid-back manager. The creative capability of her graphics design firm had led to more advertising work. Soon, she found himself the president of one of the largest advertising agencies in Nashville.

LuLu had just hired a new CFO, Marta Chavez, who had a big agency pedigree. Marta had been with large agencies in New York and Chicago. She recently was with JWT until they closed their Nashville office after losing their largest account. LuLu was excited to get someone of Marta's magnitude and hoped that Marta's influence would help the Tinsdale Agency become more sophisticated. However, she was worried that Marta would not fit into the laid-back culture that she had cultivated.

That day, Marta had stormed into Lulu's office waving a cost accounting report. Marta said, "LuLu, this is crazy. Do you realize that we could be making at least 15% more money if everyone filled out their time sheets? We need to change this right now."

Marta went on to say that not everyone was keeping a time sheet. Camille and Jason, the receptionist and mailroom guy/runner, had *never* kept a time sheet. Jim, one of the old-time copywriters, was three months behind in his time sheet. Carol put her travel time as a nonbillable agency expense. Yet, as Marta pointed out correctly, she traveled on client business.

When LuLu asked why Camille and Jason needed to do time sheets, Marta was quick to point out that even though a high percentage of their time could be reported against the general office, there are times when they can legitimately report direct client time.

"Didn't both Camille and Jason deliver agency proofs to a client last week?" questioned Marta indignantly. "That is an example of billable time," she added. Then Marta went on a tirade on how lax the agency was on keeping time. She said that was one of the reasons they were barely making a profit.

"You've got to stop giving away the farm," said Marta to LuLu.

Marta went on to outline a detailed plan to have everyone keep a time sheet by the quarter hour and have it done by every Monday. She also said that if they failed to turn in their time sheets on time, she would withhold their paychecks.

"Together, let's make this agency into something," said Marta. She added, "I have no trouble being the bad guy on this. We need more discipline on this issue. Withholding their paychecks will send a message that we are serious."

LuLu closed his door and began to think about what Marta had said. She wanted to be more sophisticated—and profitable—but she wanted to retain her culture. She needed to do something; but what could she do?

### Questions

1 What should LuLu do to ensure that her employees had better keep track of their time?
2 Should every employee be required to record their time?
3 How should she distinguish between client billable and nonbillable time?
4 How should she treat travel time?
5 What should LuLu do with chronically late time sheets?
6 How should she communicate with people at the agency on this issue?

Chapter 6

# An overview of advertising personnel management

## LEARNING OBJECTIVES

This chapter is intended to help you:

- Learn about the fundamentals of advertising personnel management.
- Learn how to manage people that report to you.
- Understand how to encourage and manage diversity within the organization.
- Learn how to manage teams and conflict.
- Learn how to manage up within the organization.

People are the essence of the advertising business. As David Ogilvy, founder of the famous advertising agency Ogilvy & Mather, once said, "My inventory goes up and down the elevator every day."

Hiring the right people, supervising, evaluating, promoting and paying them are all essential personnel functions. Most advertising managers indicate that they spend as much as two-thirds of their time and attention on their job. Solving personnel problems may represent approximately 70% of all the problems solved at an advertising company.

While the human resource manager may have a hand in helping you with these fundamentals, the majority of personnel issues will start in your office. Let's review the core aspects of personnel management.

## Employee/management job perceptions

While it does seem simple to hire the right people, motivate them to do their job and then promote and pay them a good wage, there are differing views of an advertising job depending on your position in the company.

People get into advertising because they feel it is creative, exciting and fun. Those who are writers or art directors want to work on projects that are interesting. In fact, working on interesting projects is the number one thing that an advertising employee wants from their job. The second is to be fully appreciated for the type of work that they are doing. Employees are looking for interesting work that can build a personal portfolio and recognition for a job well done.

At the bottom of the list for advertising employees is security and pay. What employees are saying is that they will trade off doing some exciting work for les pay. Exciting is more important than boring and secure.

Contrast this to what employers feel that employees want. Employers feel that pay and security are the top two attributes for a new employee. Doing interesting work and providing continual feedback are low on the list.

The reason that there is such a divide between potential employee and employer in advertising is the fundamental needs for each. If you are beginning your advertising career, it is personally important to find work that helps build your portfolio and resume. Having interesting and possibly award-winning work is what you want.

From an employer perspective, there are tasks to be done in any job that are pretty routine. That includes advertising. As a copywriter, you may be asked to write daily copy to promote various sale items for a retailer. Or you may be doing copy for a corporate brochure. These are necessary communication tasks but they may not be "too sexy." The employer expects you to do them. That is just a part of the job.

As an advertising manager, it is important that you understand where the associate is coming from versus what the company is asking.

## Personnel evaluations

Hiring, evaluating talent and promoting may be the most important tasks that a manager does. Getting the right talent that fit your culture is one of the most difficult tasks for a manager.

You are trying to determine what a person may do based on their past. If you are hiring for entry-level positions, then that past is a limited sample size. Most advertising firms have a hiring practice. The first rule of hiring is to ensure that you are reviewing candidates in a legal and ethical manner, which means following government guidelines in terms of asking personal questions. For example, you can't ask someone if they have children. You can't assume someone's ethnic background based on their name. This is also why you partner with the human resource manager to ensure that you are compliant with any legal issues. If you are unsure about any personnel issues or procedures, it is vital that you confer with a human resource specialist.

Many advertising firms have a variety of methods for assessing talent and cultural fit. Some firms use personality tests or aptitude tests to better understand a potential employee. Some firms give a potential employee an assignment to see how they think. A media planning and buying firm asks potential entry-level candidates to do simple math equations in their head. One large advertising agency asks all job candidates to see how many different things they can do with a paperclip within two minutes. If the candidate can provide more than twelve things, they are considered for the job. If they do not reach twelve, they are automatically rejected.

There are lots of ways to get at a candidate. Basically, you are trying to see if the candidate can think beyond the obvious and is curious about life. Exhibit 6.1 provides a review of the late William Masteller's questions for interviewing prospective creative people for his advertising agency. You can see by the questions that he was interested in how curious someone was and if they had a handle on pop culture. The latter is a key part of the advertiser's tool kit. Making your brand relevant to pop culture is one of the core items for advertising.

### Exhibit 6.1 Bosco Hot Sauce

| *Market* | *# of HH* | *% United States* | *Hot Sauce CDI* | *Total category $ volume millions* | *Volume dollars per HH* | *% category volume three markets* | *Advertising budget allocation* |
|---|---|---|---|---|---|---|---|
| Nashville | 880,700 | 0.83 | 110 | | | | |
| Birmingham | 750,000 | 0.72 | 140 | | | | |
| New Orleans | 650,000 | 0.59 | 210 | | | | |
| Three market total | 228,700 | 2.14 | | | | | $1,000,000 |
| Total United States | | 100 | 100 | $700.0 | | N/A | |

*Note*: HH = households; CDI = category development index.

## Managing those who report to you

Managers must provide direction, encourage, motivate and monitor work of those who report to them. It is much like coaching. A good coach provides a clear game plan and motivates his or her team to execute that plan. In the course of the execution, he or she monitors to make adjustments or to help those who need extra help. Managers who are successful as coaches believe in their employees and recognize that employees want to contribute and work, and be recognized and be put in a position to succeed.

Beyond the day-to-day management, one of the big roles a manager plays is to periodically evaluate an employee. Ideally, evaluation and performance critiques should be done continually. That way, there is no surprise when the performance review is conducted.

Performance reviews are a sensitive topic. Most companies perform annual performance evaluations. These evaluations are meant to evaluate progress in the employee's career. They should be constructive and productive.

Few employees or managers like annual performance reviews. One big reason is the annual review period. A year between evaluations leaves too much time to judge whether an employee is improving. It can also lead to recency bias, that is, putting more weight on the most recent timeframe. If an employee makes a mistake a few weeks before the annual performance review, that mistake may get magnified. Conversely, a great job done by the employee nine months ago would soon be forgotten.

Another problematic area for performance reviews is the actual review diagnostics. This is particularly true in advertising where jobs require very different skill sets yet performance reviews tend to be very generic. For example, if being very detail oriented and analytical is a criterion for performance, that is a great criterion for a media planner or buyer. Yet it is not as relevant for a creative director.

The best reviews happen when the criteria are agreed on by both parties and they are career oriented and not a list of meaningless items. If you are reviewing a copywriter, you want to give them feedback on their work. If that work includes research results or, even better, business results, that is much more meaningful than just an opinion. The same is true for a media buyer. There is a number of metrics that a media buyer must deliver on, impressions, costs and extra value. These are much more meaningful than just an opinion of their ability.

Even though advertising can be subjective, it is important to make performance reviews as objective as possible. Part of the performance review should address the specific tasks of the job. Other parts of the review should address areas such as how well they get along with others, personal judgment and attitude. A great writer with a very poor attitude may actually harm the performance of the team, even though they may have great writing skills.

As you enter a performance review, it is important to know that there are three outcomes. The first is that the employee does well and gets promoted or gets a raise. The second is that the employee does a good job but will not get promoted, nor will they get much of a raise, if any. The third is that the employee is a poor performer. If you have a performer with a poor performance, it is important to be specific and provide steps and a timeline to correct that performance.

There can be a myriad of reasons for poor performance. Sometimes, it has nothing to do with you or the employer. It could be as a result of an outside issue. If the employee brings up an outside issue, then it is your responsibility to work with the human resource department to see what resources would be available to help.

Sometimes, an employee is a poor fit. They just can't perform the task like you had hoped they could. You have given them training, mentoring and coaching. Nothing seems to work. When you have exhausted all avenues for improvement, you may be put in a position to fire them.

Nobody likes to be fired. And nobody likes to fire anyone. It is emotionally tough for both parties. And it is tough on the rest of the staff. Firings affect everyone in the company. There is a lot of tension in a firing.

It is always important to fire someone in a humane and respectful manner. You should not be evasive. You should be simple and direct. Beyond the emotional toll of the meeting, you need to be extremely careful to ensure that the company is protected from any wrongful firing. That means having another person witness the event and take notes. It means putting everything in writing. This is a business matter. You may elect to offer the terminated employee personnel services or other benefits to help them through the transition.

The responsibility for hiring, evaluating, coaching and, sometimes, firing is a huge responsibility. It forces any manager to think through their own behavior. Managing means that you are constantly interacting with your employees. Setting the right tone and being a thoughtful leader is what everyone wants.

## Managing diversity in the workplace

One of the biggest challenges and opportunities for an advertising manager is to build a diverse staff. Advertising is built on ideas. As the old saying goes, "If all you have is a hammer, every solution looks like a nail."

The same is true with your staff. If you hire only people like you, you will get a limited range of thinking. Having common thought is great for the accounting department. But the same is not good from an advertising perspective. Thus, a big part of your job is hiring people who can do the job and bring in new perspectives to the team.

When most people think of diversity, they might think of ethnic diversity. Others might think of gender. Others may think of age or generational diversity. Ethnicity and gender get the most attention for good reason. There is an underrepresentation of African American, Asian and Hispanic senior management in the advertising industry, particularly in the United States.

In fact, this underrepresentation has led to opportunity. There are advertising agencies that specialize in specific cultures. There are agencies that just focus on a single culture such as African American or Hispanic. There are others such as multicultural agencies that address a broader array of cultures. And there are agencies that focus solely on women.

One part of diversity is to take a look at your team from a demographic standpoint. Do you have a diverse workforce? Are you missing a big part of the population? These are questions to ask as you build out your team. Strategies for doing this will be discussed in Chapters 9 and 13.

There is also the area of age diversity. Advertising tends to be a young person's industry. If all you have is a 20-year-old viewpoint, you may miss some other viewpoints regarding advertising.

The same is true of geographical diversity. Is your staff from the same area of the country? Did they go to the same college or university? Are they all from large cities? Where you grew up will color your views.

As you review your staff, consider gender identity such as LGBT. The LGBT audience is a key part of cultural expression in the arts. Think broadly about your staff. Are there parents represented? How about different religions and cultures.

From a legal perspective, you cannot ask your staff their age, gender identity or religious affiliation. You should be observant. Make mental notes.

The goal of diversity is to have a broad array of people on your staff so that you can get a broad array of thought. Ultimately, diversity of thought is what drives great thinking.

Many studies show that having just a demographically diverse team will increase the performance level. That is why there is a push for diversity in all aspects of the advertising industry.

Assuming that you buy into the need for diversity, now you have to manage diversity. That is not always easy. For starters, you are likely comfortable with a certain type or set of people. Most people are. That is pretty common. So, as a manager, you may need to hire people who are outside your comfort zone. That can be very tough for some. It is important to focus on building a team of diverse thinkers even if that team may have moments of conflict.

When you are managing a global advertising department, you have built-in diversity. You are dealing with people from around the globe. This brings with it many different challenges.

A major challenge is language. The default global business language is English. That means that the majority of the world has English as a second language. So, even if your global teammates are fluent in English, there are obviously nuances that can be missed. This is why some managers are fond of hiring people who speak more than one language. Thus, if you are managing a global organization from the United States, and have a large office in Brazil, it would be great if you had someone in the United States that spoke Spanish. That way, you can ensure that communication doesn't miss a beat. It also allows you to learn how different cultures interpret different words or phrases. Busting through the language barrier is an ongoing exercise in management. It may require you to consider building into your process methods to ensure that communication flows quickly and accurately.

Knowing that you will manage a diverse staff means that you have to acknowledge and accept differences. That may be easier for you to do than it'd be for other members of your staff.

For example, there are cultures where women are not accepted as authority figures. That said, if you are a female manager or have women in management roles working with you, it is important to understand that. You may have to find a way to manage or get the outcome you need by adjusting how you do it.

The same tension is true for a younger manager having to manage an older employee. Different generations are comfortable with different types of communication methods and styles. A millennial may be very comfortable using various internal texting to communicate with the staff. A baby boomer may not like texting and prefers email.

There may be some on your team that really have ingrained biases or prejudices. This can be particularly true when dealing with global workforces. There can be deep-rooted biases that you are likely not going to overcome.

As a manager, it is your job to get the job done. It is also your job to put your staff in a position of success. From a practical standpoint, if you know that there will be conflict between people based on ingrained bias, you should head it off before it begins. While conflict avoidance is not an optimal strategy, conflict prevention can be a prudent measure.

When dealing with these sensitive issues, you should make sure that you are not the only mediator of conflict. When there is bias in the workplace that hinders work progress, it is your job to manage it. That may mean bringing in your human resource manager to help associates work through the issues.

This is also why it is important to have a strong corporate culture and values. Typically, most issues of cultural bias can be resolved by bringing back the agreement of company and employee around these shared values.

This leads to defining the issue. The more the manager can define the issue as one of work productivity, the better. This helps avoid getting into personality or other more sensitive areas that are more difficult to resolve. By keeping things focused on the task, it is much more likely you can resolve the short-term issue of getting the job done.

Longer-term issues regarding cultural bias and sensitivity need to be a part of the overall corporate mission. Many companies offer cultural training to educate others about the need for diversity and how to be more accepting of differing viewpoints. With a more diverse workplace, you will ultimately have more conflicts. Managing conflict is a key part of the advertising manager's job.

## Managing conflict in the workplace

Every organization has conflict. It happens in every industry. It does seem to happen more so in advertising. In advertising, conflict is just inevitable. There is a built-in tension between departments such as media and creative. Media people look for efficiency, while creative people look for impact. Account people need to keep a project on task, yet both media and creative people always feel like they are being rushed.

Advertising is a *create on demand* industry. Just because you don't feel "creative" today doesn't mean you get an extension on your work. You find a way to get it done. Thus, conflict is inevitable as there are a wide range of stakeholders with differing short- and long-term goals for any advertising project or campaign.

You, as the advertising manager, sit in the eye of the storm. If conflict is not controlled, it can be extremely detrimental to the organization. On the other hand, sometimes, conflict can lead to better ideas and thinking. Conflicting thoughts may spur new and better ideas. In fact, there are a number of advertising agencies that actually pit creative teams against one another to see if that will spark a creative edge.

Then, there are the "run of the mill" conflicts that happen on a daily basis. Someone doesn't turn in their time sheet on time and accounting is screaming. The creative team have an idea for a long-form video that the media department thinks is a waste of money. Someone is talking too loud on a video chat. Or two associates have a disagreement regarding politics. The list goes on and on.

Conflicts cover a wide variety of social areas including social disagreement, conflicts of interest and fights between departments or organizations. There are five common reasons for conflicts.

- Need based: Conflicts occur when our needs differ from someone else's or a group's needs in the organization or when we ignore the needs of others.
- Perception based: Conflicts often occur when there is a difference in perception about an action. Everyone has a different version of reality. Thus, one person's "innocent comment or joke" is the next person's "public offense."
- Power based: Conflicts readily occur when someone wants to assert authority over someone else.
- Values based: Conflicts occur when people's values are different from that of others in the organization. Most value-based conflicts arise by not accepting someone else's values.
- Feeling based: Conflicts occur when people have very strong feelings about a subject that is different from others. It can also occur when people ignore the feelings of others.

As you can see from this list, many of these five areas have significant overlap. Someone who may hold liberal views on politics may be adamant that conservatives are not worth listening to. This covers values, feelings and part of perception-based conflicts. Conflicts rarely fit into neat boxes. Most conflicts come from some mix of the above.

As a manager, it is important to manage conflicts so that they don't negatively impact productivity. Keep in mind that solutions for conflicts usually involve finding the root issue and then proposing solutions that deal with those causes. Conflicts over structure usually require solutions that involve structure, just as conflicts over authority usually involve solutions that deal with authority.

When the issue is a personnel issue that is not impacting the advertising campaign, the best approach is to help people find common ground. As a manager, you can facilitate compromise, which should defuse the situation.

When the issue is about the advertising campaign, the best approach is to help people collaborate. Work together to find a mutually beneficial solution is the key. This may be frustrating if two associates hold opposite views on a topic. The idea is to use conflict to make the campaign better. As a manager, you should encourage a healthy exchange of ideas. When it comes to advertising, compromise is not usually the best approach, since it tends to "water down" the campaign. Advertising, by its nature, should be memorable and persuasive; compromise can lead to not achieving those goals.

At times, every manager must deal with office politics. These matters include things like power struggles, unsubstantiated fears and rumors and half-truths.

There is plenty of office gossip any time you get more than two people together. Gossip forms an unofficial communication between employees. While you may want to think that you are above petty gossip, it is your job to make sure that rumors and other half-truths don't get out of hand.

As a manager, you want to make sure that gossip is dealt with directly and firmly. The first step in this process is to not be a gossip yourself. Your team looks to you to set the tone. If you are talking behind people's backs or in a power struggle, your team will pick up on it. The other big area is transparency. If you do hear something that is not right, feel free to say so. Be an open communicator. And be a good listener. Many times, you will find that people just want to vent. It is OK to let people do some venting as long as it's not harmful to anyone else.

## Managing up in the organization

A manager by its organizational structure means that you report to someone. It may be the CEO or the president or the COO. Regardless of who you report to, it is important to have a good relationship with that person.

It is likely that if you are reporting to senior management, there are other departments reporting to that person as well. In any organization, there could be an accounting manager or human resource manager. If you work for a media company, you have sales management and editorial management. If you work in an advertising agency, there are various departments such as media, creative and account management who are all managers.

Having a good rapport with your other managers plus your senior manager is crucial to your personal success. To be effective as a manager requires you to be an excellent communicator (not just a good communicator, but an excellent one at that).

Seventy percent of an adult's waking hours are spent communicating: writing, speaking, reading and listening. A manager must be able to write, speak, read and listen at an excellent level.

The higher you go in management, the more information you need to be able to process. That means that senior management is dependent on you to deliver crisp and clear communication. They don't have time to sort it out. They don't want communication that is ambiguous or muddled. One of the quickest ways to exit management is by not being a strong communicator. It is a necessity.

As you communicate upward in the organization, you need to try to put yourself in your boss's position. Your boss's goal is to look out for the welfare of the company. They review financial information, overall personnel information and corporate strategy. They are big picture thinkers and doers.

That is their context. They have hired you to do a job, that is, to manage the advertising program. When you communicate to senior management about the advertising program, you should frame your communication in terms that support the overall corporate strategy. That is what your boss is looking for.

There are some basics in managing upward. The first is that your work is a reflection on his or her management just as your staff's is a reflection of you. Thus, the better you do, the better he or she looks. Giving your boss positive information about the strength of the advertising program will help both of you.

It is also important to ensure your boss is "in the know" regarding new areas you may be considering; this may be a new technology or a new media platform that is gaining popularity. Or it could be a new consumer insight. A big part of the senior management job is to constantly be looking ahead. By being proactive and innovative, you can help both of you succeed.

The other key area for managing up is to anticipate problems before they occur. A senior-level manager has to deal with a lot of "crisis" situations. Some are larger than others. Crisis in this context means the manager has to deal with it now. There is not much time to think. They have to react to the situation.

If a manager has time to think through a potential problem before it happens, it leads to a much more thoughtful solution. It takes pressure off your boss since they have some time to think about alternatives rather than just having to react at that moment.

The other benefit of giving your boss a "heads up" about a possible problem is that they don't get blindsided. There is nothing worse for a boss than to be blindsided by a problem that they should have known about. For example, if your advertising campaign had to be pushed back a week, that has ramifications for many other organizational things. It could impact inventory, merchandising, staffing and so on. If you knew there was a potential problem and didn't give your boss a "heads up," imagine how foolish they would look when someone else tells them about it. You don't want to be caught in that situation.

Managing upward is certainly an art in and of itself. By understanding your boss's needs, you can deliver effective communication. Communication is the key element to your own personal growth in the organization. Take steps to ensure that you are the best communicator you can be.

## Summary

Advertising managers must be able to manage people. It is the core aspect of being a manager. Advertising management is all about communication. You must be an excellent communicator with written, oral, listening and reading skills.

Building a strong and innovative staff means finding people with diverse backgrounds and skills. That will lead to better diversity of thought which leads to better advertising. Diversity will lead to conflicts. Conflicts, if properly managed, can, in turn, lead to good outcomes. It is important to manage conflicts so that they don't contribute to a lack of performance.

One other aspect of management is managing upward. This means understanding the expectations of your boss and delivering on those expectations. Always keep your boss appraised of positive news about your team's work, keep innovation information flowing and ensure that you are quick to identify potential problems before they happen.

## Review questions

1 What are the fundamentals of personnel management?
2 What is the best approach for motivating those who report to you?
3 What role does the manager play in developing a diverse workforce?
4 What are typical conflicts a manager faces?
5 How should a manager manage upward?

## Case 6.1 IPortal Media Company

### *Issue: employee/supervisor review*

It was the day of a personnel review meeting between Melissa Chan and Bill Hinojosa. Melissa was Bill's supervisor, and she had hired Bill in her group at IPortal Media Company two years ago. Melissa was worried that the meeting was likely to be contentious, as the two had very different views on Bill's work.

Melissa considered Bill to be a very competent worker. His work, in general, was better than most of the other people at his level. Melissa had given him appropriate raises and did her best, in her view, to reinforce his good work.

However, Melissa felt that Bill had two very undesirable characteristics. First, she found him terribly verbose. This affected both his writing and also, particularly, his talking. She felt it took Bill twice as much time or space to say things as it should. Listening to Bill took a lot of her time, and she felt that supervisors in the country felt his written work was subpar. A few coworkers joke about his verbosity behind his back.

Bill tended to do his work quickly, and often had "down time" at the office. This was the second undesirable characteristic. He tended to clown around with other employees in his down time, to the extent of telling jokes and stories that were borderline inappropriate and what some people considered "off color.: Recently, a few other employees have gone to Melissa about Bill and his jokes; one of them asked, "Can't you find ways to keep him busy?"

Melissa had hoped that these two characteristics would have been corrected naturally, but they seem to be getting worse and they were hurting Bill's image. As a result, Melissa's image was hurt as well. She planned to discuss both of these at her meeting with Bill, and she dreaded it.

From Bill's perspective, Melissa appreciated his work and thought he did very well, since he had received good raises and never had to redo his work. However, Bill had one issue with Melissa—he didn't think she was a good communicator. He found she gave him insufficient information and details on projects, both verbally and in writing. Bill prided himself in taking the time necessary to say what he means clearly and precisely, not boiling things down to "sound bites" like others in the agency. He also likes to be sure that people understand his points by repeating explanations. He thought that although Melissa hadn't commented directly, she appreciated and respected the quality of his work. He planned to discuss this with her at the meeting.

Bill also wanted to check in on his relationship with Melissa. He thought she had used to be more open and relaxed with him, enjoying his jokes. Now he was sensing tension. She didn't spend as much time with him and his colleagues—in fact, Bill thought Melissa was avoiding them. This was particularly concerning as Bill thought one of the strengths of the company was that people really liked one another. They enjoyed socializing after work, and Bill thought his coworkers enjoyed his sense of humor. As Bill saw Melissa tense up often, he started telling even more jokes to loosen everyone up.

Bill wanted to move up in the company and hoped Melissa can help him. She was well regarded in the company and he thought she could help him grow and develop. He was looking forward to the meeting and discussing how he could move up.

### *The meeting*

Bill entered Melissa's office for the meeting with a real sense of accomplishment. He was ready to take his career to the next level. Melissa greeted Billy with some sense of dread, thinking to herself, *How could I tell him that he has a couple of serious flaws?*

### *Questions*

1 Who do you think has the most valid viewpoint, Melissa or Bill?
2 Why are they so far apart on their views?
3 What could each of them do to gain perspective?
4 Who is responsible for making it right?
5 What should they have done before so that they wouldn't be in this situation now?
6 How do you think this meeting will go?
7 What do you feel will be the outcome of this meeting?

Chapter 7

# Adjusting to being a new manager in advertising

## LEARNING OBJECTIVES

This chapter is intended to help you:

- Understand the difference between personal performance and management.
- Learn about the skills needed to be a manager.
- Learn how to deal with ambiguity/stress.
- Understand the value of being a coach/player.
- Learn how to plan for your future.

Congratulations! You have been promoted to be a manager. Now what?!

Adjusting to being a new manager can be difficult. Perhaps, you have been promoted to be a media supervisor with either media planners or media buyers plus assistants reporting to you. Or, perhaps, you have been promoted to an account supervisor. You now have a number of account executives reporting to you. Or, perhaps, you were a copywriter and now you have been promoted to be an associate creative director with a number of copywriters plus art directors reporting to you.

You have just moved from being a doer to a manager. Unfortunately, what got you promoted is a totally different skill set than that you need to be a manager. You likely got promoted because you were a good media planner, project manager, copywriter or art director. In fact, you were likely the best in that role in your company and hence the promotion.

Advertising is a unique business. It is very talent driven. Just because you have a lot of talent doing your task doesn't mean you have talent for managing. It is like a great actor becoming a director or producer, or a football player becoming a general manager of a team. They are different skills and different worlds.

Consider the following traits that advertising departments look for when hiring a copywriter.

- Nontraditional
- Questioning/challenging
- Unique
- Individualistic
- Creative

Now consider the following traits that make a great manager.

- Traditional
- Open-minded
- Diplomatic
- Analytical/organized
- Charismatic

Can you see some differences?! The copywriter is graded on talent. Being a nonconformist is a good thing. Being a bit egotistical is fine. You are asking a copywriter to provide unique and interesting ideas. Their ideas.

Now consider the manager in the creative department. They have to be diplomatic and not egotistical. They need to listen to others and not get focused on only their work. They have to be organized and analytical.

Wow. It sounds like two totally different people. And that is one of the big problems in advertising management. Senior leadership wants to reward people for doing a great job. The typical award is through some form of promotion to management. The problem is very clear. It can be like taking Michael Jordon off the court and putting him on the bench to lead the team. That may not be the best use of his talents.

Advertising organizations wrestle with this problem. A media company may be better off with an average sales person becoming the sales manager versus the star sales person. An advertising agency may be better off with a star art director not being a manager so that they can continue to actually do the work.

The same is true of very technical areas such as search engine marketing or informational architecture. The people that are great at these specific skills may make the worst managers.

In fact, some advertising organizations hire professional managers to be a buffer between the people who do the daily work and those in more senior positions. The role of these managers is to be the one who listens to problems, figures out how to make things work well and deals with a variety of personnel issues. Senior managers are then freed up to focus on helping guide the advertising process without becoming burdened with a lot of what managers do.

## Becoming a manager

The bottom line is that being a manager will require you to stretch your skill set. This is a new job even if you have been at the same company for some time. You need to treat it as if it was new.

The basic skill set for being a manager in advertising is similar to what you may have learned in grade school. You need to be a good listener. You must be able to speak and write clearly. And you need to be empathetic.

You can learn a lot about management leadership by reading about situations where senior leaders are asked to come in and turn a company around. In nearly every case, the first step they took was to listen—listen to employees, vendors and other stakeholders—and then make a plan.

As a new manager, you can take that advice to heart. Make sure your first impression with your staff is a good one. That means listening. Understand where the team is coming from. How would they like to be managed? Usually, no one asks them what they would like. Staff is typically just asked to "do."

You cannot take listening for granted. Listening is a mental operation. Just like other skills, listening can be improved. Practice to be an active listener. We sometimes assume that listening is automatic. Although we may not need to practice to hear, we may need to do so to listen and comprehend. Just remember, if a verbal communication is to be successful, at least half the responsibility lies with the listener.

Have you ever been in a meeting where you are formulating a response or question while the speaker is about midway through their talk? That is because you can listen faster than someone can talk. Thus, many times, people will either formulate what they are going to say or just get distracted.

This is a tendency you must overcome. Listening is not about you. When you were not a manager, many times, you listened so that you could respond. That gets you noticed or you get to prove you are bright. As a manager, you listen to help. It takes concentration. You may want to take notes. That can be helpful.

Also pay attention to the speaker's nonverbal cues: how the speaker makes eye contact, what their facial expression is or their body motion. Pay attention to the tone of how something is said as well as what is being said. You may never have realized how important listening is. Being a good listener is the mark of being a good manager.

Another key trait of a manager is being able to speak well. Now this can be a real issue for those new managers who may have been promoted based on technical or special skill sets. They may be great at the task but are very nervous about speaking in front of people. Yet, as a manager, you will likely be speaking in front of your team often. Plus you will be representing your team in many meetings.

Just as listening, speaking is a skill that can be improved. You may want to ask your senior management to give you training on public speaking. There are a number of good programs that can help.

Over time, with practice, you can become a good speaker. You will find that your fears will subside. Practice speaking to make eye contact. Speak in complete sentences. Learn to speak without filling every pause with things like *um*, *er*, *like* and *you know*. Know what you want to say before you say it. And when you are not speaking, go into active listening mode.

The best speakers are the best writers. If you write well, then you can speak well. As a newly crowned manager, you will be asked to write more than advertising. You will be asked to write viewpoints to your boss. You may need to write direction for your team. How well you write is going to impact how people relate to you. If you write in a rambling fashion with poor grammar; your team and boss will think you don't know what you are doing. However, if you can make a clear and compelling point of view, those same associates will likely understand why you have been chosen to be promoted.

The final big tool is empathy. Empathy goes a long way to make a great manager. The more you give empathy, the more people will give you a break in your new management journey.

There are three types of empathy: cognitive, emotional and compassionate. Cognitive empathy is putting yourself in the other person's shoes. A good media buyer should do this when negotiating a media purchase with a sales person. If they understand what the sales person wants or needs (other than the greatest amount of money), then a buyer can craft a win/win situation.

As a manager, it is important to put yourself in the other person's shoes. For example, if you gain a new account, that is exciting and may mean more money. However, for some of your staff, it just means more work. So they may not be excited at all about the prospective of more business. You need to understand their point of view.

Emotional empathy is being able to feel what someone else feels. If someone has shamed someone else or made them angry, you feel the same way. You empathize with them on a very personal level. This can be good as well as bad. Emotional empathy lets the other party know you really get it. On the other hand, lots of emotional empathy can drain you. It is difficult to constantly be sharing others' feelings. You need to strike a balance.

Compassionate empathy is what most people think about when they talk about empathy. You can recognize and feel someone's pain but have control over your emotions so that you can provide comfort with appropriate response to their needs.

Given that you are a new manager, it is good for you to exercise cognitive and compassionate empathy. Try to see things from the other person's perspective. It goes a long way in helping you build a solid relationship.

## Dealing with ambiguity and stress

One of the biggest changes in your role as a manager is dealing with ambiguity. In your previous job, you relied on yourself. You got the job done. You were on top of it. And as a result, you got promoted. Now, your performance relies on the work of others.

The more you move up the management ranks, the more you will deal with ambiguity. That means that you won't always know what it happening. If you have a staff of twenty people, you can't possibly know what they are doing at any moment. Plus you don't want to micromanage them. So you have to learn to deal with ambiguity.

Because you are learning a new role and have to rely on others to perform their job well for you to be successful, that translates to a stressful situation. You have a lot of responsibility. With increased responsibility comes stress.

One of the biggest inhibitors of management success is the lack of ability to deal with stress. Stress is with us all the time. It comes from mental, emotional or physical activities. Each of us develops ways to deal with stress.

Stress can also be a positive. It can make you more in tune with your body. Stress moves in three stages: alarm to resistance to exhaustion. That is why not dealing with stress is a serious management issue. More than one executive has had mental breakdowns due to stress. It can cause exhaustion, which impacts your ability to think clearly.

Know your limits. If you have a problem that is beyond your control, instead of fighting it (resistance stage), learn to accept it, at least for the moment. As one advertising manager once said, "If you have a problem and cannot find a solution, then change the problem."

Some simple solutions for dealing with stress are to take a break. Try some physical activity. That can just be walking around the block. Clear your mind. Stand and stretch. Change locations. That helps break the pattern.

Eat better. The more stress we are under, the more we are likely to snack. So forget the snack machine. Make sure you are eating properly. It will pay dividends in the long run.

Many managers do things like having checklists or "to-do" lists for daily or weekly tasks. The benefit of doing this is that you get to physically check things off a list. That can add a sense of accomplishment.

Sometimes, things can get overwhelming. Feel free to share with a friend. If you need to seek professional help, don't feel that there is a stigma attached to it. Sometimes, counseling can really help managers get a handle on how to deal with things that are not always in their control.

Advertising is a stressful business. The more you move up in management, the greater the stress. On the other hand, advertising is an exciting business. So one person's stress may be another's pleasure.

Given the pace of business, many advertising companies do have programs on relaxation, enjoyment and overall good health.

## Being a player/coach

One of the biggest mistakes that a young manager makes is getting caught up in "being a manager." You may think that now that you are a manager, your job is to make others do the work while you sit back in your office and survey your domain.

Management does mean that you have power over others. You are in an authoritative position. Power can be intoxicating. People who may not have given you the time of day are suddenly your best friends. Many a young manager, as well as seasoned managers, can run afoul of the "being a manager" trap.

"Being a manager" is not the same as "doing management." Management moves from personal doing to shared doing. You are now helping a team work toward achieving a common goal.

One of the best transition strategies for a new advertising manager is the player/coach model. This offers a number of benefits.

- You were likely promoted based on your talent. By continuing to work on projects with the team, you can continue to demonstrate your ability. Your team will likely see you as a person they can go to with a specific advertising work problem.
- The player/coach model also makes you a part of the team. It is not a case of us and you, but a case of all of us. A good player/coach may take some workload off a team member if they are overloaded. By actively being engaged, you are seen as a more valuable leader.
- This allows you to more seamlessly share "the ball" with your staff. Rather than just giving people assignments, you may want to work with some of your team members on an assignment. This allows you to model the behavior you want to ultimately see from your team.

The transition from player to player/coach to ultimately coach is a natural one. By getting involved you can build confidence in yourself with the team. You can also learn about their needs in a more natural manner.

Coaching is most successful when managers find ways to inspire their team members at just the right moment for maximum impact. The ability to inspire people to reach great heights of performance and success is a skill that managers need.

Inspiration comes when passion for the organization's vision is clearly communicated. Thus, if you are excited about your company and the advertising work you are doing, it will rub off on your staff. Conversely, if you are always stressed and feel being put upon, your staff will pick up on that as well.

When your communication is genuine and is a two-way interaction that combines job purpose and meaning with the inclusion of your staff's ideas and goals, you have a winning playbook.

Just as you began, it is important to make sure that your staff gets to do some work that is challenging. As a player/coach, that may mean that you temporarily take on the mundane necessary tasks to free up your staff to grow.

As we have said before, advertising people are in the business to do great work. They want the opportunity to show what they can do. If you are providing them those opportunities along with feedback and insight to make their work even better, that is the mark of a good manager.

## Where to go from here

You made the leap from worker to manager. Where do you go from here? That is the big career question. By taking on a management role, you can learn a lot about yourself—things that you like and things that you dislike.

After experiencing life as a manager, it is time to reassess your career goals. You need to develop a plan. Your initial plan was to do a great job so that you could be promoted. Having reached that goal, you need to reflect on the next steps. That first promotion is a lot like having graduated from school. You had a clear goal. You finished up school. You celebrated. And then you wondered what is next? It seemed daunting. There is sometimes a clear path now. You need to develop a plan for the next stage of your career.

Perhaps, that means that you don't want to be a manager. That is great learning. There are many successful people in advertising who are not managers. They are experts in their respective fields. They may be great creative talents or media tacticians or strategists. They would prefer to work alone or in a very small team rather than manage others.

In the advertising world, that is common. You may end up being a freelancer. You work for a variety of companies who may need your talent. In essence, you become a "hired gun." You may be someone others call in for help on solving a problem or working on a new business presentation for an advertising agency.

Freelance work is a mixed bag. If you are working on your own, that can offer a lot of freedom. On the other hand, if you are working for yourself, you have to hustle and constantly sell yourself to others to make a living.

In many advertising organizations, there are senior advertising professionals that are not managers. Sometimes, an account executive really likes just working directly with the client and not having to supervise others. The same can be said for creative, media and strategy talent. Many advertising people just like doing the "work." The higher the level of management, usually the more removed you become from the day-to-day work. That is the trade-off.

If you feel that management is exciting and that you could be good at it, then continue to practice the traits that make a good manager. Make sure you can express your thoughts clearly on paper and to a group. If there are any traits in which you are not strong, practice on them. For example, to overcome speaking before a large group, you must do that very thing repeatedly; then you can master it.

Also, practice persuading others. That is the key to rising in the ranks of management. It is not enough to think that you can create great advertising. You must be able to convince your superiors or your clients about the wisdom of your plans, suggestions and direction.

Take advantage of your current situation. If you find yourself in an Uber with your boss, talk about some things you normally may not have time to address. Ask about what it takes to get to the next level. The same is true if you chance to have a quick elevator ride with the chairman of the board. Be curious. Ask about their challenges.

In advertising, you run across a wide variety of people. Always see what makes them tick. You never know what you might learn that could aid in your career development.

Stay on track. Do not let yourself get sidelined. Remember that most good managers are good students of management. Keep on reading and attending seminars and observe how others do it.

Motivate your team through communicating effectively. Encourage better ways of doing things. And encourage your team to like each other. That alone will produce superior work.

As one manager said, "The best thing that you can do in your career is to embrace change. Never get complacent with yourself both personally and professionally."

If you can't readily adapt to change, how do you expect your team or your client to do so? Look at every situation as a learning opportunity. No matter what path you take, you will be a success.

## Summary

Now that you are a manager, the challenge is to learn a new skill set. You are moving from individual performance to group performance. Your ability to motivate and inspire a team is what senior management is looking for you to do.

That means that you need to develop great listening, writing, speaking and empathy skills to successfully become a great manager. You will also need to learn how to deal with ambiguity. You will no longer be in control over every aspect of a project. As a result, that creates stress. It is important that you learn how to properly deal with stress so that it doesn't inhibit your and your team's performance.

Because you were likely promoted based on your personal talent, an effective management transition is to move from player to player/coach. This means that you work alongside your team rather than dictate to the team. This will aid in you being more readily accepted as a manager and it allows you to grow into that role.

After being a manager, you may either see that you want to move up more into management or that management isn't for you. Either path has its pros and cons. No matter what path you feel best meets your personal and professional goals, stay the course. Build your personal brand. Plan your career path.

## Review questions

1. What is the biggest trait differences between being a worker and being a manager?
2. What are the key skills that a manager must obtain?
3. What is the key to dealing with ambiguity?
4. How should a manager deal with stress?
5. What is the player/coach model of management?
6. What are the keys to planning your next career step?

## Case 7.1 Metropolitan Media Company

### *Issue: managing upward*

Ebony Johnson was so excited when she joined Metropolitan Media corporation right out of college. This was a dream come true. Ebony graduated with an advertising degree from a college in Boston. Through her studies, she had become intrigued with the rapidly changing media landscape and wanted to be part of it.

Metropolitan Media was a New York-based media conglomerate that owned magazines, cable properties, and numerous digital assets. They were an innovator in migrating their offline media properties to online properties, and some of the top visited websites on the web belonged to Metropolitan Media.

Ebony was an assistant in the magazine unit working for *Healthy Woman* magazine, one of the largest women's magazines in the country. Her boss was a 55-year-old woman named Donna Carbone. Ms. Carbone had spent the past 30 years at Metropolitan Media where she rose from a secretarial position to become a senior vice president and publisher of *Healthy Woman*. Ms. Carbone prided herself on the fact that she was the first woman in Metropolitan Media to become an officer of the company. She was a hard-charging and very blunt woman, who got things done but didn't make a lot of friends along the way.

"She is a real old-school woman. Be careful in dealing with her. She is particularly hard on young women starting out. She feels they should be toughened up," said one of Ebony's coworkers.

Ebony took it all in. She was anxious to set a good career course and get promoted within this exciting company. Her first task was to understand how to best utilize social media, in particular Instagram and Snapchat, to extend the reach of the magazine into the online world.

Ebony threw herself into the project, working 12-hour days for four consecutive weeks. When she wrote a report on her work, Ms. Carbone barely gave her any feedback. Later, Ebony learned that Ms. Carbone took Ebony's report to her management claiming full credit for it.

A few weeks later, Ms. Carbone appointed Ebony to chair a project committee. This was a great honor, as it was rare then for an assistant to chair this type of committee. Ebony was thrilled. However, after the committee's work was completed, Ebony learned that its recommendations and actions were not what Ms. Carbone wanted. Ms. Carbone had failed to tell her or the committee about a key management change that would impact the project. As a result, the outcome did not meet the new objectives. Not only was the project a bust, but Ms. Carbone was overheard making caustic remarks about Ebony and the committee. "Maybe a few failures will take the wind out of her sails," said Ms. Carbone to another publisher.

When Ebony started her job, she was promised a six-month review, where she would be considered for a step up in her job responsibilities and a raise. She had approached Ms. Carbone about the review for a week, with no response. Now, it was three months past the review period and Ebony was getting very frustrated.

Ebony liked her coworkers and loved the work itself, but she was continually frustrated by Ms. Carbone. Ebony wondered if others in the company knew of her good work, since Ms. Carbone constantly took credit for it. Ebony was also concerned that anytime Ms. Carbone didn't give proper direction, she blamed Ebony and others in the department. Finally, Ebony felt that she was being treated unfairly regarding her raise. She had been working 60-hour workweeks since she got to Metropolitan Media and was living on very low wages. She was ready for a bit more money so that she could take advantage of all Manhattan had to offer.

Ebony felt that she was at a crossroads with Ms. Carbone and Metropolitan Media. Although she had to take some action, she couldn't make up her mind about it.

### Questions

1 Should Ebony confront her boss, Ms. Carbone?
2 Should Ebony seek counsel from the human resources department regarding Ms. Carbone?
3 Do you feel that Ebony should go around Ms. Carbone and discuss these issues with a high-ranking officer in the company?
4 Should Ebony just wait it out until she has been at the company for a year?

## Case 7.2 Gotham Media

### *Issue: new job responsibilities*

Kyle Bennett had very high standards. He was a rising star in the media department of Gotham Media, one of the top media planning and buying companies in the United States.

Kyle joined the firm just two years ago, right out of college. Within that time, he was promoted twice from an assistant to a media planner and, most recently, to a media supervisor. This last promotion had been the hardest for Kyle: he was used to doing everything himself. As an assistant, he took on work that no one else wanted to do. He plowed through paperwork and learned all the software programs, becoming known as one of the few assistants who actually cared about his work.

Kyle knew that if he worked hard he would get ahead, and he was right. His promotion to media planner happened after six months on the job. As a media planner, he was responsible for helping his supervisor develop media plans and then coordinating the execution of those plans. Within three months, his supervisor had turned over the smaller accounts to Kyle to supervise. This suited Kyle's style, and while he periodically checked in with his supervisor, he ran the accounts himself. He loved seeing projects through.

His only frustration was in executing media planners, because he lost some control when he turned over media buying specifications to media buyers. Gotham Media was set up with specialists who purchased each medium, from network television to print to online. Kyle's job was to give them the purchase parameters and then follow up to make sure they did their job.

Kyle had a few run-ins with some of the buying supervisors, since he rejected some of the media buys as not meeting his purchase specifications. In fact, for one outdoor purchase, Kyle asked the out-of-home buying supervisor, Maia Barret, if he could do it himself. Maia told him to go ahead, and Kyle executed the buy.

While senior management at Gotham thought Kyle was a bit headstrong, they also thought he was a rapidly rising media star. "There aren't too many young people who throw themselves into a job with such as passion as Kyle," said senior manager Tessa Morgan.

Kyle's immediate supervisor, Marla Hanson, agreed and said, "Kyle is a quick study. He gets it done and done right. He is quite a perfectionist—which can be a good thing and a bad thing." Regardless, based on his performance, he was promoted to media supervisor. His promotion rankled some of the other media planners who had been at Gotham longer than Kyle had. One of the older associate media directors said, "It is one thing to be a great media planner and another to be a supervisor of people."

In his new role, Kyle was in charge of 12 accounts, three media planners, and two assistant planners. Two of the planners were close to Kyle in age and one was ten years older. Each planner worked on four accounts and the assistants supported the entire group.

Kyle felt the planners weren't as good as he was and he was concerned the quality of work would suffer as a result. He decided that he should be involved closely in every media plan that came out of the group. He started working with each planner but soon found himself doing the plans on his own, since it was easier to write them how he thought was best, as opposed to having to continually rewrite others' work.

However, being involved with 12 accounts was proving to be a difficult task. He was working 14-hour days and still had trouble getting his work done. He also saw that the media execution was slipping, since the media planners weren't familiar with the plans.

One of the planners, Jerry Jeffries, told Kyle, "I want to help you but you don't tell me what's going on. It's impossible for me to help the buying groups execute the plans."

Kyle was particularly frustrated with the Dave Edwards, a 34-year-old planner who had been in the position for ten years. Kyle had disdain for Dave because he couldn't believe someone could be in the same position for so long. However, Dave handled the tedious job of coordinating the Star Drugstore account, a retailer with many stores in multiple markets. Star Drugstore changed their print ads several times a week. Dave had been offered promotions but said he preferred to be a planner on Star Drugstore because it gave him flexibility in terms of working hours, and as a single parent he liked to be able to pick his kids up from school.

Kyle was trying to get Star Drugstore to embrace more online media, but they were stuck on using traditional newspaper ads. The client felt that newspaper ads drove people into the stores, and until they felt that it didn't work they would continue with newspapers. The meetings between the Star Drugstore client, Dave and Kyle were starting to get tense, as Kyle kept pushing for a transition to online media and the client kept resisting. Kyle felt Dave wasn't as up-to-date on digital media and wasn't helping convince the client to move in a new direction.

At 7:00 one evening, Kyle was just starting a new deck to convince the Star Drugstore client to move most of their budget to digital media. He was exhausted but he felt that his group was not serving its clients. Marla Hanson stuck her head into Kyle's office as she was leaving for the day. "Kyle, we need to talk," she said. "Nine am. Tomorrow. My office."

### Questions

1. What advice do you think Marla gave Kyle?
2. How can Kyle get more control over his time?
3. What sacrifices will Kyle have to make to become a better supervisor?
4. How do you deal with people like Dave, who have career goals that are different from your own?
5. What would you say to Kyle if you had been a media planner in his group?
6. Have you ever been on a team where the "star" tries to do too much? What happened?

Chapter 8

# Managing creative people

## LEARNING OBJECTIVES

This chapter is intended to help you:

- Understand the creative mindset.
- Understand how to manage processes focusing on creativity.
- Learn about the techniques for supporting creative colleagues.
- Understand how to assess creative work.

When it comes to working with colleagues in various departments in the agency or company, account managers face an interesting and sometimes challenging situation. Account managers are in charge of the entire process of creating advertising and developing brands. At the same time, account managers do not directly manage many of the people involved in the process, such as the people in the creative, media, planning and production departments internally at the agency, or people working for companies outside the agency on which the process relies (such as people working at production houses or media vehicles). The account manager must build strong relationships to manage the process, based on mutual respect and a desire to create the best brands.

Of all these relationships, one of the most delicate is the relationship between the account manager and those working in the creative department. As anyone who has ever tried to paint a picture or write a story knows, creativity does not happen "on demand." While it is very reasonable to set deadlines for the more objective parts of the advertising process—such as conducting consumer research or developing a media plan—it is particularly challenging to set a deadline for the creative work. One just never knows when that great creative idea will hit.

That said, the account manager has a responsibility to make sure that the process delivers the campaign on a timely basis, and as a result must learn to negotiate the tricky space of working with the creative department. This begins by understanding the creative mindset.

## The creative mindset

Let's begin by stating a huge strength of the advertising and marketing industry: These industries tend to attract interesting people who make the workday interesting. Regardless of the department to which they are assigned, most people working in the communications field are creative thinkers, popular culture mavens, and savvy businesspeople.

The best meetings are ones where colleagues from any department throw out ideas and the rest of the group runs with them.

A decade or so ago, many agencies used their physical safe to "silo" different departments: Creative people may have been on one floor and the media people on another. Today, though, agencies have moved away from a traditional "departmental" layout of the agency space into one that groups people by client, not by department. Today, you can walk into an agency and see a media buyer sitting next to an art director, both working on the same brand campaign. You may not even be able to tell which is the media buyer and which is the art director.

However, there is difference in the mindset between the creative person and others working on the brand.

- First, creative people are independent-minded, and, in general, don't like being told what to do. They may bristle at being managed by the account manager, perhaps because they think the account manager doesn't understand the creative mindset. This doesn't mean that they are being "divas," though—many highly creative people are also high in autonomy, or the freedom of thought and action. In other words, many creative people don't like to play by the rules. Thus, the fewer constraints someone puts on a creative person, the more creative they will be. The more you manage a creative person, the more likely you will be to come up with some uninspiring creative work.
- Second, highly creative people see the world differently than other people. Research has shown that they actively seek innovation, are adventurous and like pushing boundaries. In general, they like to think "outside the box" and like working with people who also think outside the box.
- Third, the process of creativity is unpredictable and risky. A creative person doesn't know when they will get a great idea—or sometimes even if they will get a great idea at all. At the same time, as an account manager, part of your job is to minimize risks (such as the campaign not getting finished on time) and to deliver predictable results (such as a campaign that really moves the needle on the goals that you have set). It's not that the creative don't understand this—they do. They also understand that they will never be able to commit to a timeline in a way that a media or account planner can do.
- Fourth, the work that creatives develop can be highly personal. Many see the work as an extension of themselves—which is par for the course for creative people in other industries. While a media planner might not get hurt feelings if the account manager doesn't like the media mix, a copywriter might fight to keep the account manager from changing the name of a character in a television ad from "Beth" to "Mia."
- Finally, no two creative people are alike—just like no two media people are alike or no two account managers are alike. Some creatives are motivated by competition—can their ideas be chosen over the ideas of other teams? Some creatives are motivated by tight deadlines. Some are motivated by taking long walks outside of the office. Traditional management "guidelines" of how to manage people may help you work with the copywriter working on the television campaign, but not with the art director doing the digital work.

As a result, the account manager has to figure out how to allow the creative team members a certain amount of creative freedom while at the same time keeping control of the outcome. One uncomfortable place for some new account managers will be to tolerate the risk of losing control of the account without letting the process get out of hand. To put it another way, how much rope should the creative teams have? Getting to know the creative team, understanding their creative processes, and seeing the results of the work will be key indicators to the appropriate level of your involvement. Talking to other account managers about the different creative teams can also help you manage your own expectations during the process.

## Managing responsibility

Building trust and shared responsibility is just as important for the creative team as it is for other members of the brand team. The account manager also has the responsibility to motivate the creative team—and this motivation for your team should come from the inside. What do we mean by this? Many people will be more creative when two things happen: First, they have to believe their work has value. Second, they have to have the space to pursue their creative ideas. As an account manager, you can address both of these.

### *Valuing the work*

When we talk about valuing the work, we don't mean getting excited or rapturous over the executions that the creative present to you; instead, we are referring to the overall ethos of a creative organization. This ethos is often known as a learning orientation.

In a learning orientation environment, managers recognize that creativity is a process, and that a certain number of iterations of an idea are going to be necessary to get a message that will meet the goals of the campaign. In a learning orientation, people make mistakes, but they don't get punished for mistakes that are in service to achieve the ultimate goal—great work.

### *Providing creative space*

In this case, space doesn't refer to the physical location of the creative team (although that can certainly help). Space refers to having the time to understand the brand, the competition, and the brand's consumers, and to develop ideas that will resonate with consumers and the client. In many cases, a brand will have an established team of a copywriter and an art director that are used to working together and complement one another's ideas. Sometimes, shaking up this partnership can be a spark to creativity, as new perspectives and outlooks can be generated.

Give your project team freedom to pitch unexpected and "weird" ideas without the fear of being "punished." Creativity is about changing things, and change is possible only when team members have the authority to experiment and try new ways of doing work.

## Supporting creative colleagues

There are many different ways that you can support your creative teams.

1 Understand creative team members as individuals. Take the time to get to know the creatives that you'll be working with and understand their unique talents and

contributions. Does this copywriter do well with "women's" products, but struggles when working on an automotive client? Does that art director prefer photographs to drawings, and do they like to contemplate hundreds of fonts before selecting one?

Aside from the fact that the creative people will appreciate that you see them more than a factory worker tasked with making creative things, having an understanding of the skills and traits that people have and how to connect them to accounts in order to put the best talent possible on the work really helps. When you make an objective assessment of each person's skills and outlooks, you can work to optimize those strengths by assembling the right skills and talents for projects.

You also will want to understand each person's pain points: What is standing in their way in their quest to deliver great work? A pain point is simply a problem that has to be solved: Some creative pain points might be working on too many clients or having to spend too much time traveling. Often, people don't want to share their pain points—they don't want to be seen as a complainer, or they might not want to be seen as not being able to handle the work. However, once a bond of trust is established, it may be easier for creatives to share their pain points with you, and you may be able to work with others in the agency to ease some of the pain points.

2 Be empathetic. So often, the account manager has the role at the agency of representing the client's viewpoints. They are trained to think like the client, which gives a valuable perspective to the work as it is produced. At the same time, a great account manager will see the creative's perspective as well. Once you understand who the creatives are as individuals, you will be able to better understand what they're going through and understand the better ways to motivate them.

3 Suggest, but don't dictate, the process. To put this another way, tell the creative team what you want done, not how to do it. This is the value of the creative brief—the document that sets the goals of the campaign and gives the creative information that will help them narrow down their creative choices.

One challenge that many account managers face is that they hear about the "right" answers to creative problems from a variety of people, including the client. Many clients are likely to have their own ideas on how to solve the problem at hand—this isn't surprising, since it is human nature to try to solve problems and clients are, of course, well acquainted with the brand.

However, it is important to remember that clients are clients because of their business acumen, not necessarily because of their creative skills. Client-driven solutions tend to be less nuanced and more heavy-handed than what an agency will develop. Thus, the account manager should work with the client to develop the general roadmap to the solution, and then let the creative team figure out the best way to proceed.

It's challenging to suggest rather than impose a process, as everyone in an agency knows that there is a flow of work that results in the work being produced—there's a client meeting, there's the strategy development, there's the briefing, and then there is an eventual presentation of work internally and then externally to the client. Make sure creatives know the timeline; sometimes, this simple knowledge can help the creative parts of their mind start to work on the problem.

4 Listen, ask questions, and listen some more. Be available to look at and listen to the creatives' ideas as they are in development—don't wait until the "big meeting" where the creative will pitch to the whole account team. The way this works best is if the account manager is positioned as a "coach" of the process, which means a willingness to put aside one's own ideas about the "right answer," and to ask questions to get other's ideas. Questions are also a powerful way to influence people without telling them what to do—and help open up new ideas for solutions. It also removes the perception that the account manager is telling the creative team what to do. This should foster commitment and give a greater sense of ownership to the creative team.

5 Expect greatness. Having a positive attitude and expecting the work to be great can be a powerful motivator. How can an account manager do this? To put it simply, an account manager has to be enthusiastic. They have to truly believe that their client is terrific, and that the work being done for the client is also going to be terrific. At the same time, they need to be enthusiastic about the role that the creative team plays and use this enthusiasm to let the creative team know that the account manager will always have their back should any issue arise with the client.

Enthusiasm is the deep-seated belief that any project can be great. Help create an environment where the problem you're solving for the client has as few constraints as possible. And help the client share in the idea that every project is a chance for their brand to show greatness.

6 Be inspirational. An inspirational account manager is an individual who is a mix of a cheerleader and a proud parent. The account manager who understands the process, who is sympathetic to the realities of the creative job, and who is an advocate for the client's vision will gain the support of the creative team. Be open to debate while having everyone know you are on their side.

## Assessing creative work

A mix of praise and thoughtful guidance is always welcome as a highly motivated team searches for the optimal solution. Now the one caveat here is that, whatever the business, this is never "art for art's sake," but art for commerce's sake. When a project is going off the strategic track—when you can see it is straying from a fundamental business objective—it needs to be reeled in.

1 Use the creative brief and the advertising strategy as an assessment tool. In your career, you are likely going to have to tell that the work that someone came up with is amazing—but it doesn't address the brief and it won't be able to be used on the campaign. The brief, then, can be positioned as the "bad guy" in the scenario, which sometimes makes the conversation a bit easier.

You may someday hear a creative suggest, "Well, let's just change the brief." It is important to remember that the brief is a living document, but it is also an agreement between the agency and the client regarding the direction of the advertising campaign. As a result, an "in the moment" revision of major aspects of the brief is likely to be a challenge. However, this type of statement may open the door to have a close examination, discussion, and debate on how aspects of the brief can be interpreted.

This type of discussion and debate can be extremely valuable to push creative to a better place.

2 Remember, this is both business and personal. The creative team is likely to be highly invested in their work, as it is something that they personally "birthed." Be careful not to make a comment about the work that may be accurate but unconstructive. Instead of saying, "that image is ugly" think about saying, "that image seems to use colors that don't reflect the current brand palette" or "that image may be a bit avant-garde for our target."
3 Look for the platform idea. Look deeply at the work to see if there is a platform idea that is original, that can be part of a bigger campaign, and that can be extended into a variety of executions and channels. There may be a clear one, but there also may be a nugget of one that needs to be pulled out.
4 See the insight come to life. The entire account team knows the insight from the brief—after all, you had a hand in crafting it. Examine whether the insight comes across clearly and/or determine whether it will resonate strongly with the target audience. You may wish to show the work to agency or brand personnel who aren't working on the campaign to see how they react.
5 Evaluate the outcome wisely. It is important to objectively assess the progress made without judgment based solely on somebody's preferences, because we are all different. It is better to ask yourself if the result of work fulfills the business requirements: Does it solve the problem that the brief set out?
6 Look at work through the consumer's eyes. Listen very carefully to the input from the account planner, who represents the voice of the consumer in the process. You may not like the color scheme, or the music, but it might be perfect for the target audience.
7 Be honest. Be sure you can clearly communicate the client's priorities and aspirations in order to help creatives understand the context in which they are working. Feedback provided honestly and with the client's point of view in place will be seen as critical but valuable feedback.
8 Don't give or allow inappropriate feedback. By inappropriate feedback, we don't mean critical feedback—that's important. Inappropriate feedback is feedback that is not going to improve the work. Types of inappropriate feedback include:

   - Dictatorial feedback, such as telling the creatives, "You must make the logo bigger," without stating any specific reasons.
   - Feedback from an unexpected source who is not familiar with the brief, such as a client's friend or some other random person.
   - Feedback that changes what was originally asked in the creative brief.
   - Feedback that demotes the creative team to a production role.

## Summary

The account executive's role is to work, and work effectively, with a variety of people in the corporate setting. While agencies are filled with interesting and creative people, the creative team relationship can be one of the most challenging and one of the most rewarding ones in the agency.

## Discussion questions

1 Think about some of the creative people you have encountered during your college career. Do they reflect some of the traits described in this chapter?
2 What are some examples of suggesting versus dictating the creative process?
3 In what ways do you think you are empathetic? Can you think of some examples?
4 What specific strengths relative to what was discussed in this chapter do you currently have? What strengths do you need to work on?

### Case 8.1 JPT Agency

#### *Issue: personnel conflict*

Donna Jackson was excited about her new job at JPT, one of the top creative agencies in Portland, Oregon. She quickly bonded with many of her new colleagues, and started to hear a lot of insider information about the agency. Everyone wanted to talk to her about Andre Williams, the creative director of the office. While he had a reputation of being one of the most creative guys on the planet, he was also one of the most volatile. Donna has known of Andre's reputation before she took the job, and now she had to figure out how to work effectively with him.

For every great idea Andre had, he had many more that ignored the basic marketing strategies established by the client. It seemed that the more off strategy his ideas were, the more protective he became about them. He also found ways not to show the creative to the account team prior to presenting it to clients—he was either working on it up to the last minute or was busy in other meetings so that he couldn't meet with the team members.

In their most recent meeting, Donna and Andre met with top management at one of the agency's most important clients, Zelos, an athletic shoe brand. Unfortunately, Andre clashed directly with the president and marketing director in the meeting, and they had to wrestle control of the meeting back from him in order to appease others in the room.

When they got back to the office, Donna called him into her office to discuss it. She explained to him that she was embarrassed about his performance, particularly in light of the fact that the creative was completely off strategy. She told him she also didn't appreciate his tone.

Andre wasn't happy to be called on the carpet. He started by saying that he didn't appreciate Donna taking the client's side in front of the entire agency account group and creative team. Andre went on to say, "If you're going to undermine me like that, then my value to this account is nonexistent."

But he didn't stop there. Andre went on to say that he thought that the agency and the client had developed the wrong strategy and that his creative would be on strategy if they would listen to his reasoning.

"The next time we present a creative, I don't want anyone else in the room with the client but me," said Andre dramatically.

He stormed out of her office saying, "If you don't let me present the creative that I want, then I'm through here."

Donna took a deep breath. "I need more coffee and then I'm going to figure this out."

### Questions

1 Should Donna have seen the creative prior to having it being shown to the client? What are some ways that Donna can try to make this happen in the future?
2 Should you have Andre resign?
3 Should you discuss Andre's importance to the account with the client before you make a decision?
4 Should you discuss Andre's performance with others in the office?
5 If Andre leaves, how should you handle it with the rest of the staff or the clients?

Chapter 9

# Managing across cultures

## LEARNING OBJECTIVES

This chapter is intended to help you:

- Understand the unique challenges of a multicultural workforce.
- Recognize the importance of cultural intelligence.
- Understand Hofstede's notions of culture.
- Understand the notion of inclusive leadership.

Today's account manager works in a multicultural world. In the United States, for example, the Census reports that more than 13% of the population is Black, about 6% is Asian, and about 1% is Native American. About 60% identify solely as White, with over 18% identifying as Latino, Latina or Latinx. Almost 3% indicate they are two or more races. The Pew Research Institute anticipates that by 2050, Whites will be a minority race in the United States. In addition, the advertising industry today is global, and many agencies have offices and clients around the world. You may someday have the opportunity to work on a global brand, or at an office that is outside of the United States.

In your career, you most certainly will have an opportunity to work with people who come from a culture different from your own, and as a result account managers can face unique challenges. First, studies show that advertising television, print and digital ads rarely show this multicultural mix: the vast majority of people shown in ads are White. This is due, in part, to the racial makeup of many advertising agencies, which tend to be predominantly White. In addition, Americans have a minimal understanding of cultures outside of the United States. Taken together, these two ideas suggest that some agencies and brand people may not recognize the cultural differences that exist in the workplace or understand how these differences can help create strong messages.

Many brand agencies in the 21st century are trying to be more diverse. First, it is likely that diverse workforces will create communications that resonate better with a range of audiences (we'll talk more about this in Chapter 10). There is a strong business case for diversity. A report by the consulting firm McKinsey defined diverse companies as firms with a greater proportion of women and ethnically/culturally diverse individuals and found that there is a direct correlation between diversity among company leaders and two measures of financial performance: profitability and value creation. Companies in the top quartile for cultural diversity on executive teams were 33% more likely to have industry-leading profitability.

Today, there is a strong need for advertising managers who recognize the importance of diversity, and who are comfortable working with and understanding with a large number of cultures and traditions. Those managers who understand other cultures will fare well in the global marketplace. The need to understand Black culture has been heightened by the 2020 Black Lives Matter protests against police brutality. Much of this understanding comes from some of the things we've already talked about: communicating with people effectively and authentically, learning about others by listening, asking the right questions, and having an empathetic mindset. In addition, account managers need to think closely about diversity issues within their own agencies.

## Cultural intelligence

Professor Geert Hofstede, an expert in how different cultures communicate, defines culture as "the collective programming of the mind distinguishing the members of one group or category of people from others." Cultural intelligence (CQ) is the ability to work effectively in different cultural contexts. The construct was developed by researcher P. Christopher Earley in 2002 and was originally defined as a person's capability to adapt as they interact with others from different cultural regions. It is important for agencies and clients alike to have employees with high levels of CQ, as these employees will:

- Bridge divides and knowledge gaps in an organization.
- Educate their peers about different cultures.
- Transfer knowledge among groups to build interpersonal connections.
- Smooth the interpersonal processes in a multicultural workforce.

In the previous chapter, we discussed strategies and best practices for working with and managing coworkers with a creative mindset. Another benefit of having people with high levels of CQ is that they may be able to contribute to increasing innovation and creativity where they work: these people know how to make the best use of the multiple perspectives that a multicultural workforce brings to the workplace.

What exactly is CQ? It's more than being smart, or mature, or having good social skills. CQ has three overlapping components—cultural knowledge, cross-cultural skills and cultural metacognition. These concepts do not operate in isolation, but instead overlap and interact.

- **Cultural knowledge** consists of both the content (what) and the process (how) knowledge of other cultures. For example, different cultures have different ways to express disagreement and different expectations for feedback. Hierarchical structures are also different.

  Cultural knowledge can be developed in many ways. You can choose to expose yourself to media such as newspapers, books, television programs and films from other cultures. You can work closely and get to know people from a culture other than your own. You can travel and experience difference cultures. You should be careful to be mindful during this process, challenging your own cultural biases, analyzing how the culture differs from yours and what this brings to the communication process, and thinking about how this knowledge can be used in the future.

- **Cross-cultural skills** are a range of skills that you can use every day, including the following.
  - Interpersonal skills such as talking and interacting with people from other cultures
  - Tolerance of uncertainty or your ability to recognize that interactions with people from different cultures may be different from interactions that you are used to. Someone with high CQ is ready to accept and celebrate those differences.
  - Adaptability or the ability to change one's own behaviors to be a better fit with a different culture
  - Empathy or the degree to which one can put themselves in a culturally different person's shoes and imagine the situation from their perspective
  - Perceptual acuity or how one understands other people's feelings and subtle meanings during intercultural interactions

  Cross-cultural skills can be developed in different ways, but, in general, come from long-term engagement with different cultures, often in an experiential learning context (studying abroad or working in a culture, whereby you can practice these skills and be OK to fail sometimes). You must be an active participant in this part: sitting back and observing isn't enough.
- **Cultural metacognition (sometimes called cultural mindfulness)** is defined as the knowledge of and control over one's thinking and learning activities when working in a multicultural environment. Specifically, this involves being aware of the cultural context, analyzing the interactions in an empathetic way, and planning courses of actions for different cultural contexts.

  To improve cultural metacognition, it is important to not only observe others and how they communicate but also reflect on your own reactions and subsequent behaviors related to those reactions. Pay attention to how others act and react to you in a number of situations. Reflect on successful as well as unsuccessful intercultural interactions and try to identify what made some work well and others not so well. Did you misinterpret what someone was trying to say? Were there any words and behaviors that were challenging to understand? Are there other tactics you could try?

## Hofstede's cultural dimensions

One of the first places to start in developing CQ is to consider cultural dimensions, which are the different ways that different cultures deal with problem-solving. Many of these dimensions have been identified and closely studied by Geert Hofstede. They include the following.

- Relations between people: Hofstede segments cultures into those that are individualistic and those that are collectivist. Individualistic cultures have a loosely knit social framework in which individuals are expected to take care of only themselves and their immediate families. The majority culture in the United States is highly individualistic. Collectivistic cultures, on the other hand, have a tightly knit framework in society in which individuals can expect their relatives or members of a particular ingroup to look after them in exchange for unquestioning loyalty. Asian culture in the United States tends to be more collectivistic.

People who appreciate individualistic cultures tend to like to work independently, while those who prefer collectivistic cultures prefer working in a team. Most communication firms will require a balance of these preferences; someone who cannot utilize the balance may struggle.

- Power distance: Hofstede describes this dimension as the degree to which the less powerful members of organizations and institutions accept and expect that power is distributed unequally. This dimension reflects how a culture addresses power inequalities. People in societies exhibiting a large degree of power distance accept a hierarchical order in which everybody has a place and which needs no further justification. In societies with low power distance, people strive to equalize the distribution of power and demand justification for inequalities of power.

  Many workplaces have hierarchical structures: staff at the bottom of the ladder, and each ascending rung includes supervisors, managers, directors and executive leadership. When employees embrace or accept this structure within the workplace, they understand that supervisors have a higher level of authority than staff, managers more than supervisors and executive leadership more power than everybody else. Those who prefer a flat structure would like an equal distribution of and may resist the hierarchy and layers of power within that organizational structure.
- Motivational orientation: Hofstede argued that different cultures have different ways to cope with uncertainty. One orientation is masculine versus feminine: masculine cultures are competitive and based on achievement, heroism, assertiveness, and material rewards for success. Society at large is more competitive. Its opposite, feminine cultures, is more consensus oriented and focuses on cooperation and care.

  In the business context, masculinity versus femininity is sometimes also related to as "tough versus tender" cultures. Highly masculine countries include Japan, Germany, and Mexico. The feminine side includes other Latin American countries (Spain, El Salvador, etc.). At the extreme "feminine" side are the Nordic countries including Sweden, Norway, and the Netherlands.
- Uncertainty avoidance: Hofstede saw this as the degree to which the members of a society feel uncomfortable with uncertainty and ambiguity. Cultures with a high level of uncertainty avoidance have rigid codes of belief and behavior, and tend to be intolerant of unorthodox behavior and ideas, while those with less uncertainty avoidance are less rigid and believe that practice counts more than principles. Greek and Portuguese cultures have a high level of uncertainty avoidance, while Jamaica and Denmark have a very low level of uncertainty avoidance.

  In the business context, uncertainty avoidance reflects how comfortable people are with change. Employees with strong uncertainty avoidance tendencies might feel more comfortable in roles where they have a high degree of certainty that the organization and the position will remain steady.
- Attitudes towards time: Hofstede distinguishes between long-term and short-term orientations. Cultures with a short-term or normative orientation maintain time-honored traditions and norms while viewing societal change with suspicion. Cultures with long-term orientations are more pragmatic and encourage efforts in modern education as a way to prepare for the future.

  Managers in long-term oriented cultures are used to working towards building strong positions in their markets, do not expect immediate results, and are allowed time and resources to make their own contributions. In short-term oriented cultures, the "bottom line" is a major concern; control systems are focused on it and managers are constantly judged by it.

- Indulgence and restraint: Some cultures allow relatively free gratification of basic and natural human drives related to enjoying life and having fun, while other cultures are more focused on restraint, where gratifications of needs is suppressed by strict social norms.

  Employees who find it difficult to unplug on family vacations and who stay tethered to the office and their jobs, no matter where they are or what else is going on in their personal lives, may have higher restraint scores on this culture index.

Understanding how different people reflect these different values, based on their cultural backgrounds, can give the account manager some clues on how to best manage people.

## The account manager and the multicultural team

As previously discussed, there is a lack of a diverse workforce in the advertising industry. The advertising industry does not have a good track record of hiring and keeping diverse talent. For example, an article in *Forbes* in 2019 reported that less than 15% of all creative directors are women. According to the Bureau of Labor Statistics, people who identify as African American or Black account for only 8% of those working in advertising, public relations and related sectors, even though more than 12% of the population is Black. About 15% of people in the industry are Hispanic, while about 18% of the population is Hispanic.

At the leadership level, the numbers are even more discouraging. A study of companies belonging to the Association of National Advertisers found that among chief marketing officers of member companies, only 3% were Black, 5% were Asian, and 5% were Hispanic. This lack of diversity affects the internal culture and the work that gets produced.

Without understanding cultural nuances, the account manager may not be able to create an environment where voices—and ideas—are equal. Therefore, an important job of the account manager is to recognize and appreciate the diversity in the account team. If this is done, then the entire account team will share the culture of the company and will also reflect the cultures of the individual members of the team.

This may sound simple, but it isn't. An account manager may not be aware that the non-White members of the team may be hesitant to speak up, and some may not wish to have difficult conversations. As a result, some minority workers report feeling afraid at work. A story in the trade magazine *Ad Age* in June 2020 reported that Black employees experience racism, microaggressions, and unconscious bias at work. Some feel that their work is scrutinized more than that of their White colleagues. Many are afraid to speak out about this in the workplace, as they are afraid of losing their jobs. The account manager needs to proactively engage with all members of the team to be sure they feel heard, respected, and safe.

At the same time, the account manager also needs to recognize that cultural differences among team members may create misunderstanding. This is particularly true in a teamwork-oriented environment, where groups of people work together on a project with a specific goal, since many project management techniques have been developed in individualistic countries. As a result, many project management techniques are based on cultural assumptions that may not resonate with people from more collectivist cultures.

For example, we've stressed the importance of communication throughout this book. One area of communication that account managers will have to deal with is assessing team performance. However, in managing a team with members from collectivist cultures, discussing performance openly may be embarrassing to the team members. As a result, the account manager must understand the values, beliefs and norms of the different cultures represented in the account team. Most importantly, the account manager shouldn't make assumptions about cultural preferences of team members. Making sure the team understands the shared goals, and then talking to individuals on how those goals will be achieved, and how communication will work best, is paramount.

With the 2020 #BlackLivesMatter protests in the United States due to the murders of several Black citizens by police, Black professionals in advertising wrote a statement that demanded action from agency leaders. They indicated several actions that agency leadership could do to address systematic racism and indicated that while the actions applied specifically addressed needs of Black advertising professionals, the same concerns applied to women and members of LGBTQ+, disabled, and other person of color communities. While most of these recommendations addressed senior leadership, several areas apply to account managers specifically, including active participation in company diversity and inclusion initiatives, and establishing a diversity review panel to stem the spread of stereotypes in creative work.

The letter also demanded extending agency outreach in recruiting to more diverse schools. This is an important consideration as the account manager is often the individual sent out to do such recruitment. The Association of Natural Advertisers listed a number of outreach opportunities as well: recruiting at Historically Black Colleges and Universities (HBCU) and Hispanic Servicing Institutions (HSIs), exposing candidates to a diverse interview campaigns, and continuing with diversity-focused internship programs such as the MAIP.

If diversity is getting invited to the dance, inclusion is making sure everyone is dancing. Diversity and inclusion go hand in hand—if you have diverse employees but they do not feel included or valued, you will not retain them. A diverse employee's manager must be willing to advocate on his or her behalf and tell others about the great work the person is doing and assign important projects so that they can raise their profile within the organization. If you notice a diverse employee is quiet during meetings, strategically invite him or her to share their thoughts. Provide feedback and make them aware of the opportunities and tell them they are ready for the next step.

Diverse talent must also be retained. The ANA study showed how the industry is poor at retention of Black talent: while 9% of entry-level professionals are Black, the percentage of Black mid-level professionals decreased to about 5.5 and that of Black senior level professionals decreased to 4%. Among Asians, the percentage of representation increased from 10% at the entry-level professional to 12% at the mid-level before declining to 9% at the senior level. Hispanics represented about 7% of the entry-level and mid-level professionals and 9% of the senior level. The poor retention of Black professionals has been attributed to the predominance of White professionals in management positions who may not create a welcoming environment or may not appreciate or understand the cultural nuances in the work generated by their diverse workforce. In addition, agencies should:

- Have training on inclusive leadership for all managers.
- Promote more Black professionals to management positions to help achieve retention.
- Survey employees to measure their sense of belonging and their perceptions of how agencies value diversity.
- Create a culture of celebration that goes beyond Christmas.

## Inclusive leadership

Writing in the *Harvard Business Review*, Juliet Bourke and Andrea Espedido promoted the value of inclusive leadership, or leadership that develops a workforce that feels included, that they are treated fairly and respectfully, and that they are valued and belong. The authors argued that inclusive leaders share six important traits.

1 A visible commitment to diversity. Inclusive leaders not only talk the talk but walk the talk as they challenge the status quo, hold others accountable for decisions that affect the diversity and inclusion of the company, and make diversity and inclusion a personal priority.
2 A sense of humility. Inclusive leaders can admit what they don't know and when they make mistakes. They also work to create a space for all people to contribute to the goals of an organization, recognizing that their perspectives are limited.
3 Awareness of bias. Inclusive leaders recognize that they have personal blind spots, and that the accumulation of such blind spots can lead to unjust systems. As a result, they work hard to ensure that a meritocracy—rewarding ability—is in place.
4 Curiosity about others. Inclusive leaders have open minds and are curious about others. They know how to listen with judgment and have a highly developed sense of empathy to understand those around them.
5 Cultural intelligence: Inclusive leaders are attentive to others' cultures and adapt their own behaviors as needed.
6 Effective collaboration: Inclusive leaders empower others, pay attention to diversity of thinking, appreciate and foster psychological safety, and focus on team cohesion.

## Summary

The contemporary workforce is a multicultural workforce, and as a result the ways business was done in decades past may not work in the current workplace. Account managers need to develop their own sense of cultural intelligence in order to manage a diverse team well. Hofstede's six dimensions of culture can be a useful tool in identifying why some teams work and some teams do not. Account managers can develop skills in inclusive leadership by building on this knowledge.

## Discussion Questions

1 Consider where you fall in each of Hofstede's six dimensions of culture. Share your results with another student in your class. What similarities do you share, and what differences do you see? Discuss how these results might affect your work.

2 Think about a time that you were on a team that worked well. What values did the team share? How did you work out difficulties? How is that reflected in what you read in this chapter?
3 Think about a time you were on a team that didn't work well. Use Hofstede's six dimensions of culture to understand what might have gone wrong. What might you do in the future to improve that team experience?

## Case 9.1 The Davis Group

### *Issue: hiring*

Jim Davis pondered the three resumes that he had before him. This was a crucial hire for his advertising agency, The Davis Group. Two weeks ago, his top account director had left for another job at a competing advertising agency. As if that weren't enough, the largest account that he was working on, Parsons and Bramble, had said that unless Jim filled the job with a very strong candidate, they would put their account up for review. They also brought to Jim's attention the fact that they had a new diversity program. They were committed to promoting diversity and inclusion by promoting the development and advancement of underrepresented groups through professional development courses and trainings, and to actively create a productive work environment that is free of harassment and bullying.

Due to the nature of the account, Jim also needed someone who had a wide range of experience from packaged goods to retail, and someone with at least ten years of experience. While P&B was a large packaged goods company, they did a lot of retail promotions. The brands that Jim's agency handled also required that the candidate have experience marketing to women as well as to kids.

The Davis Group was also committed to develop a more diverse workforce. At the moment, only two of the 75 people at the agency were people of color—Leslie Markson in the traffic department and Jean Jarrett, a media planner/buyer. Thus, Jim saw this new hire as a great opportunity to make a change that would start to address the lack of ethnic diversity in the agency.

Parsons and Bramble had a very formal culture that required agency personnel to be highly learned as well as very conservative—they wanted the account people to have an MBA, and to dress formally for all meetings. The account people had to recognize that it was a challenge for the creative people to deal with the brand managers of P&B. Jim's creative folks were very liberal and quite artistic, which flew directly in the face of the account's culture. His prior account director was very good at bridging the cultural gap between P&B and the creative group. He needed this candidate to have the same capabilities.

Jim needed to act quickly since P&B would not let much time pass before they made a decision to review their account. Jim couldn't risk that happening. The recruiter that the agency regularly used, Sara O'Connell, came up with a group of possible candidates and sent their resumes over to Jim. After reviewing the resumes, Jim hoped that either Emily Barna or Richard Putnam had what it took to fill the position of the account director. Plus he hoped that either Emily or Richard would not only fit with P&B but would also fit his laid-back culture.

In addition, Jim kept going back to review the resume of a third candidate, Marcus Lattimore. Marcus was the only ethnic minority candidate provided by the recruiter. Marcus didn't have the requisite years of experience, but as the only minority candidate in the pool was of interest to Jim. Marcus seemed very accomplished for a young person who graduated a few years ago from Howard University, an HBCU, and seemed like he had a lot of potential and would fit in with the creative team.

He had interviewed both Emily and Richard over Zoom and Richard was, by far, the best interviewee. He was glib and had a great sense of humor, along with the requisite MBA and experience. Emily seemed very buttoned-up and straitlaced—a good fit for the client, perhaps, but not for the agency.

Jim didn't have a lot of time to make the decision so wondered if the Zoom interviews were enough (Exhibits 9.2 and 9.3).

---

## Exhibit 9.1

Resume: Richard Putnam

### OVERVIEW

Eighteen years of excellent experience as an account executive, account supervisor, and account coordinator with several outstanding advertising agencies. Record of excellence and achievement in advertising, public relations, and general business communication.

### WORK EXPERIENCE

- Platen, Randell, and Plodkin advertising agency, New York, New York
  Supervisor for all aspects of advertising campaigns, with primary responsibility for success of the programs. Responsible for account supervision on numerous accounts in consumer packaged goods and consumer services. Handled plans for several outstanding advertising and promotional campaigns. Produced first annotated campaign planbook for the agency. Received accolades from many clients for superior quality of work.
- Creative Advertising Consultants, Inc., New York, New York
  Directed a staff of more than a dozen people, including copywriters, artists, media planners and merchandisers. Participated in all client meetings and planning sessions. Helped establish experimental marketing effort for new product. Oversaw promotional effort for extraordinary new automotive service firm. Selected personnel incentive programs. Organized original seasonal sales program.
- Rivers, Simon, and Larson advertising, Los Angeles, CA
  Planned and administered entire advertising program for many clients' accounts. Worked with outstanding regional marketers and advertisers.

Created brochures and sales bulletins. Handled all trade show arrangements and business meeting plans. Assisted top management with plans, strategies, and tactics. Credited with "Best of Show" award.

- Hammacher, Herpel, Mangell, Dover Associates, Los Angeles, CA
  Section supervisor and account manager. Responsible for creative and media budget of more than half a million dollars. Managed work for important local manufacturer. Acted as liaison for staff coordination group meetings. In charge of records for plans board.

## EDUCATION

- MBA, University of Wisconsin, Madison
- Bachelor's Degree: Marquette University, $1,500 student scholarship, Dean's List.
- Kappa Mu honorary.

## PROFESSIONAL EDUCATION

- Attended two-week training seminar, Glendale, California. Worked with distributors and wholesalers in research and development program for new and improved products.
- Graphic training course.
- Management planning seminar, New York City.
- Dale Carnegie Institute.

## Exhibit 9.2

Resume: Marcus Lattimore

Experience

- Marketing consultant with Gothan, Rainer Marketing Consultants, New York City (two years)
  Involved in the planning and execution of advertising and marketing programs for Ideal Toy Company, Burlington Industries, and SCM Corporation.
- Advertising manager, Butler Brothers discount store chain, Trenton, New Jersey (two years)
  Responsible for budgeting, media selection, special promotion planning, and marketing coordination for 17 large discount stores in Pennsylvania, New York, Maryland, Delaware, and New Jersey.
- Account coordinator, Blandell & Rupee advertising agency, Pittsburgh, Pennsylvania (two years) Supervised accounts for small local retail store, for regional dog food manufacturer, for fast-food chain operation and for agricultural custom fertilizing service.
- Account trainee and copywriter, Blandell & Rupee advertising agency, Pittsburgh, Pennsylvania, (one year)
  Wrote copy and created promotional campaigns and advertisements for various accounts, including a ski shop, a small automotive parts supplier, and an industrial packaging distributor.

Education: BS degree in business, Howard University

## Exhibit 9.3

Emily Barna
Account Director

### EDUCATION

- MBA, UCLA
- Bachelor's Degree: UC San Diego. $1,500 California student scholarship, Dean's List, Kappa Mu honorary.

### EXPERIENCE

- GlobalSodas, Inc.: Senior Brand Manager (four years)
  - Directed all brand activities for a portfolio of beverage products representing over $25 billion in annual sales
  - Managed a staff of 15
  - Liaised with advertising and PR agencies
- Tobias and Christopher Advertising (six years)
  - Account Director on GlobalSodas account
  - Responsible for all advertising activity on the Loco Cola, Sipsy Lemon-Lime and Rockin' Root Beer brands.
  - Managed a staff of 12
  - Promoted from Account Director
- Big Bang Advertising (six months)
  - Associate Account Director
  - Worked on Blue Bear cookies

### *Questions*

1. Do you think that Jim Davis has enough information to make a decision?
2. What are the pros and cons of Richard and Emily as candidates?
3. If you had to select one of the two, whom would you select? Why?
4. Do you think he should hire one of the two, or should he keep the search open?
5. Should Marcus be considered for the position?

Chapter 10

# Handling tricky situations

## LEARNING OBJECTIVES

This chapter is intended to help you:

- Learn how to work with multiple clients effectively.
- Understand how to run a meeting.
- Understand the challenges of managing remote workers.
- Be empathetic when dealing with ethical challenges.

There is no typical day in the life of an account manager. This chapter will provide an overview of a variety of different situations you might encounter in an average day and will provide you with tools to help you do your job effectively.

## Day-to-day management

Every workday is likely to have multiple meetings with different clients and agency personnel. Here are some situations you are likely to encounter in the daily work of account management.

### *Juggling multiple clients*

In your career, there may be a time where you will be working on several different clients at the same time. This could be due to the size of their business (which does not allow a dedicated account team), or you may be helping out on a new business pitch. With multiple clients, you will have to deal with multiple deadlines, often at the same time, multiple projects and account teams, and multiple client expectations. At the same time, while many clients understand you will work on business other than their business, they want to know that you are always on top of their account. What do you do?

This is where your outstanding organizational, time management, and follow-through skills will come into play. You will have to have a way to make sure that you are on top of each client's work every moment of the workday. This may be via a to-do list organized by deadline, client, and time needed for the tasks. You should encourage your team members to do this as well and share these lists so that you know where everyone is at any phase of the process.

Here are a few tips.

- **Be extra organized**. Set up your schedule at the start of each week so that you know which clients you're working with and how much time you'll need on each. Plan to put a certain number of hours in for each client during the week.
- **Keep track of hours closely**. Make sure your billing is accurate and can be supported by your work output.
- **Keep an eye on deadlines**. Keep deadlines in mind and come up with a schedule that works best for you and allows you enough time to perform well for each client.
- **Communicate!** Having regular update meetings with your clients each week could help them understand that their business is being well cared for.
- **Use a digital tool**. See if your agency has a digital project management system—many agencies and clients use digital project management systems like Asana or Basecamp. These systems allow you to organize tasks by project and will also provide deadlines. Some of these systems will also notify you when deadlines are coming up. Such systems will also allow collaboration with your team.
- **Be focused**. Try to focus on one task at a time. If you're constantly shifting between a couple of different client projects, you will lack the focus to do an excellent job on one.
- **Put out fires, judiciously**. Sometimes, of course, you'll be interrupted in your daily tasks to deal with a "fire" that needs to be doused immediately, but oftentimes a request from a colleague can be put off for an hour for you to finish up an important task for a client.
- **Take care of yourself**. Recognize when your client load gets too large and talk to your supervisor about getting some additional help. Don't compromise your quality account service or attention to detail by overloading your schedule.

### *Managing remote workers*

The 2020 COVID-19 pandemic resulted in most agencies mandating that employees work from home. Even as the pandemic eased, many agencies continued to allow remote work. As a result, you may find that some of your team may be working remotely in the same city as you, while others may be working in other offices. There are ways to make the remote-work experience productive and engaging—for employees and the organization

- **Start from a place of trust**. It is natural to think that someone working from home may be goofing off. However, you should put utmost trust and confidence in your employees that they will do the right thing—which they will if employers provide a supportive structure. Don't micromanage, as this will only disengage and fatigue already stressed employees.
- **Recognize that remote can be challenging**. Acknowledge that virtual communications are different—and won't be perfect—but should still be professional and respectful of others. Understand that for some employees, virtual communications are less comfortable and effective.

- **Model good work**. Help employees understand how to work well remotely and how to have effective interactions by modeling them in meetings and through exchanges with them.
- **Help people be successful**. Make sure employees have the technology they need to be successful, which may be more than just a mobile phone and laptop. For example, if you expect employees to attend virtual meetings, do they have adequate cameras? Make sure that everyone has access to the tools they need to do their job.
- **Promote organizational values**. Always keep in mind that your team members are key stakeholders and keep communicating to them how important they are to the team and to your clients.
- **Be clear about your objectives**. One of the challenges of remote work is that role definitions get blurry, leaving employees unsure of where to focus. Be sure to reinforce what each member of your team should be accomplishing. Think about emphasizing objectives over processes to create greater clarity for employees—and drive greater engagement levels as employees see how their work contributes to the company's goals.
- **Celebrate successes**. Effective recognition of the work that people are doing motivates team members and models good practices for other employees. Publicly acknowledge great performances regularly—perhaps more than you would in an in-person situation where a simple "thank you for this" would be enough.
- **Communicate—and communicate some more**. Two-way communication will provide the team with the information and perspectives they need. It will also help you to understand how employees are handling remote work. When you meet with employees, ask them what barriers they have overcome or how some of their colleagues have helped them. This will help you be an empathetic leader, and also you will find things to celebrate with the team.
- **Be attuned to employee challenges**. Use both direct conversations and indirect observations to get visibility into employees' challenges and concerns. Use every opportunity to make clear to employees that you support and care for them.

### *Running a good meeting*

Many account people think their lives are spent in meetings. Meetings are an important part of agency life, and there are ways to make these meetings efficient. Here are some things you can do to make meetings work well.

- **Have an agenda**. Know the clear sense of purpose for bringing people together. You can send out the agenda in an email before the meeting starts, or you can write it on a whiteboard in the meeting room, or you can simply state it at the start. Everyone should know why they are gathered and what they are supposed to accomplish.
- **Stick to the agenda**. Think of the agenda as the compass for the conversation. Often, meetings get off track—that can serve a purpose too by bringing people together and letting them build relationships. You will need to get the meeting back on track, so use the agenda to pull everyone back to the topic at hand.
- **Start on time, end on time**. Be the first person in the room—this shows that you respect everyone's time and effort to be at the meeting. Showing up late is going to be seen as an obnoxious power play and waiting for the meeting leaders is a waste of

agency resources. A definitive end time will help ensure that you accomplish what's on your agenda and get people back to their work promptly.

- **End with an action plan**. The last few minutes of every meeting should be used to discuss next steps. This discussion should include deciding who is responsible for what, and what the deadlines are.

### *Managing remote meetings*

Even before the COVID-19 pandemic, many agency and brand people participated in a variety of meetings held via a platform like Zoom or Skype. Meeting remotely saves time and money in travel costs. However, these meetings require a few specific changes from in-person meetings.

- **Invite the right people**. While 12 or 15 people in an agency conference room may be fun and energetic, when moving to a remote platform smaller meetings are better. It's difficult to hold a remote meeting with lots of people, as technological options make it difficult to "see" everyone in the meeting with larger numbers, and people may choose to not speak up.
- **Have a more specific agenda and share it in advance**. Have a plan with specific items to cover and stick to that plan. It is better to share the agenda ahead of time to those who will participate so that everyone can prepare. It may be harder for some people to speak up and engage in meetings, so being able to prepare a response may encourage fuller participation by everyone on the meeting.
- **Develop protocols for meetings**. Whether it is a brainstorm session or a presentation of a media plan, set up the rules and circulate it to participants before the meeting. Do people need to mute themselves, or will you mute them and control their microphone? If people want to contribute, do they just start talking, use a feature (like a "hand raise" feature) available through the platform, send a message in the "chat" section that they want to talk, or send you a text? Any one of these will work, but using just one will make it much easier for you to chair the meeting.

  You may want to remind people to avoid side conversations and background distractions. Just like in high school when you didn't like someone whispering behind your back, side conversations can be confusing and leave people out. Clarify that participation is expected and call on people who you haven't heard from. Mention them by name and repeat the questions—you don't want to "catch" them, you want to engage them.
- **Acknowledge each participant**. At the start of the meeting, make sure that you introduce the participants, that you have each participant introduce themselves, or that you mention each individual by name. Which one to go for depends on whether the people know one another or not—in an agency meeting you can probably just acknowledge, but in a client meeting you may wish to introduce everyone. People are more willing to participate and are more open when they know who's on the call. If someone feels like their role in the meeting is important, they are more likely to engage with the group.
- **Chat for a bit**. Start with a few minutes of small talk to help people make their presence felt on the remote meeting and to get people feeling connected.

- **Clarify the goal at the start**. Since you've sent the agenda out in advance, it's always good to have a quick reminder why you are all there and what you want to accomplish.
- **Give people things to do**. You may consider asking people in the meeting to take on different roles. The facilitator runs the meeting and probes for conversations, the timekeeper keeps track of the time and reminds the group how much time is left, and the scribe can keep track of action points and decisions made; the scribe can then send their information to you so that you can send out a summary of the meeting. This helps involve participants in the meeting. For a recurring meeting, change the roles between participants from meeting to meeting.
- **Call on non-participants**. Asking directly for input really helps team members feel engaged. And remember, listeners can only hear one person at a time clearly, so take turns sharing with each other.

## Managing interpersonal difficulties

Working with people is often energizing, but it is also unpredictable. Dealing with different personalities and interpersonal difficulties isn't necessarily a fun part of the job, but it is a necessary one.

### *Managing difficult coworkers*

No matter where you work, there always seems to be at least one coworker who is difficult to deal with. Some people are bullies. Sometimes, personalities clash. Sometimes, you simply have nothing in common with another person. Sometimes, they just have characteristics that, in your view, hurt the workplace situation: they may tend to gossip, they are always late with work, they never take responsibility for errors. Here are some techniques to deal with difficult coworkers.

- **Step back**. Your first step is to figure out specifically what the issues are that you perceive, and what might be able to be addressed. Check your own attitudes to see if there is something that you are doing that is causing the relationship to be antagonistic. If someone has come to you with a problem concerning a coworker and asks for your help, step back to determine if both people are somehow contributing to a problematic situation.
- **Talk to a friend**. Talking over your coworker situation with a friend can be helpful, not only because you can vent your own frustrations but because your friend can give you an objective opinion on what is going on and how to handle it. Be careful about talking with other coworkers about problematic people. Complaining to others in the office might get you branded as a problem yourself, so keep any complaining down to those in your family or a close friend outside the office. Going public with grievances is always a bad idea.
- **Talk to the difficult person**. Think about having a calm discussion, outside of the office, to get to know the person a bit more and discuss some of the concerns with the working relationship. Some people do not realize the adverse impact their statements and actions have on others. Sometimes, this is enough to get them to change their behavior, but at other times this is not.

- **Plan your daily interactions**. If difficulties continue, try to be pleasant, smiling and polite every time you talk with the difficult person; this can improve another person's attitude towards you. At the same time, try to limit the amount of time you have to spend with the coworker—set time limits for the meetings where you interact with them.
- **Document issues**. Make notes to keep track of the issues that you have with the person in case the situation escalates. Take notes on how this person's actions are affecting your work and productivity on projects and write down exactly what that person is doing to adversely affect your work.
- **Go to your boss**. This is the path of last resort, as in most cases your supervisor will want you to fix things yourself. If you do decide to take the matter up with your supervisor, make sure to go armed with the information you need to make your case. Also, bring in some options for how the situation can be resolved.

### *Managing internal conflicts*

A fact of agency life is that people disagree. The creatives may want to produce something that the media people would say is too expensive. The creative director wants one model and the account team wants another. While many of these issues get "talked out" and a decision can be made, other conflicts can lead to people taking things personally and this can escalate quickly and disrupt the work process. Here is what to do when you hear someone say, "I can't work with that person" or "I will never be in a meeting with that person again."

- **Listen carefully**. Find out what happened and avoid interrupting. Try not to react. After the person finishes speaking, rephrase what they said to make sure you understand it, and ask questions to fill in any gaps. If the reason is something that goes against agency policy (like one person is harassing another), then bring HR in immediately.
- **Summarize the areas of agreement and disagreement**. See if you can point out places where there isn't conflict ("You and Pat worked together well in the past.") and where there is conflict ("But when Pat made a flippant remark you felt that your work was insulted."). Ask if the person agrees with your summarization, and if they don't, keep discussing until they do. Then, identify which areas of conflict are most important to each of you to resolve.
- **Focus on the future**. Prioritize the areas that can be worked on. Ask yourself: *What needs to be done so that the people can work together well again?* One of your key jobs is to maintain a collaborative, "let's-work-out-a-solution" attitude.
- **Develop a plan**. Should you talk to the other person, or do you schedule a time when all three can meet? Help the employee know what to say.
- **Have a supportive discussion**. Discuss the situation with the other party in a supportive and collaborative way. Don't accuse the other employee, try to focus on empathy for both individuals.

### *Managing difficult clients*

Everyone will run into a difficult client at some point. They may be mean, they may be not good at their job, they may try to blame the agency for their problems or they may be asserting their "power" over the agency. As the person tasked with servicing clients, you will be in the center of any client issues. Here are some tips.

- **Stay calm**. Clients might yell at you because you did something wrong, because they're having a bad day, or for any other of a dozen reasons. Do your best to stay calm and not stoop to their level of hostility. Try to have a calm voice and demeanor. Many people will mirror the emotional signals you send out, and so if you're calm, you'll encourage others to be calm as well.
- **Listen**. Sometimes, a client feels that they've lost control of a process and just want to be heard. Listening without getting defensive could de-escalate the conflict quite easily. Be sure your client understands that you're focused on their problem. Like with an internal conflict, ask follow-up questions, repeat their statements back to them, and acknowledge that you've heard and understood.
- **Respond promptly**. As soon as a client raises an issue, make it a priority to get it sorted out. You don't have to accept blame, but you're establishing good communication while validating the client's point of view. Promise you will look into the problem and get back to them quickly.
- **Figure out what happened**. Client problems can arise when they have expectations that are out of alignment with what you've been contracted to do or when a miscommunication has occurred. Talk to the relevant parties at the agency and check your emails and status reports. Find out where things went wrong (if they did, in fact, go wrong), and how you might be able to improve processes or communication in the future.
- **Offer a solution**. Find a way to solve the problem. If you made a mistake, admit it up front, and show the client how you'll make amends and get their project back on track. If the client is in the wrong, it gets trickier. Point out the information you found—did the client expect something that wasn't agreed to at the last status meeting? Do you have an email that said you were to do the opposite of what the angry client is saying? If miscommunication is the problem, offer alternative ways to communicate so that the client feels included. Give them options—a daily phone call, email update, face-to-face meeting, or regular check-ins via your client management dashboard—so that they can choose what works best for them.
- **Deal with any financial fallout**. Your reputation and integrity are more important than the agency's bottom line. Fixing the problem—even if that solution comes at a price—will have benefits for you and the agency in the future. Your previously difficult client may turn into a dream client, fiercely loyal and excited to tell all their associates how you went the extra mile to resolve the issue.
- **Review and learn**. After the problem is solved, take a step back and evaluate what happened. Ask yourself:

    - *Why did this problem arise in the first place?*
    - *What could I have done to prevent it?*
    - *What lessons have I learnt that I can apply in the future?*

    Figure out if there are changes to your processes that can avoid such a situation in the future.

### *Managing expectations about clients*

What happens when someone at the agency has a problem with the client's business? Many people may not want to work on tobacco, alcohol, or pharmaceutical accounts. Others may be concerned about working for gas and oil companies, or companies that contribute money to a political party whose ideologies they don't agree with. The distinctions between what someone considers a "good" and "bad" company are highly nuanced and personal. If we look closely, we can find challenges with every client: a packaged good company producing breakfast cereals with high-sugar content that can lead to obesity, or a clothing company or retailer that sells products made with child labor, and an electronics company producing weapons for modern warfare. The list goes on and on.

Most of us want to work for organizations that we feel good about, and to work on business that we can be proud of. Once we consider that companies, like people, are fallible and always have the ability to do better, we can start to think differently about our own engagement with the brand. At the same time, companies bring lots of benefits to society: they provide employment, they make products that make people's lives easier, and they pay taxes that support infrastructure. Each individual needs to make a personal determination about what a particular company means to them, and whether their engagement with the company can make a positive difference.

### *If a client asks for something unethical*

Most clients are ethical and will never ask you to do something that is immoral or illegal. There are some clients who will try to skirt the bounds of ethicality, for example by asking you to highlight a benefit in a way that is not authentic or is untrue, or asking you to show a response to a societal crisis that is inappropriate for the mission or the vision of the brand. In these cases, remember the following.

- You are bound by any ethical standards that your agency has agreed to, such as those outlined by the American Association of Advertising Agencies (4A's).
- You are bound by various truth-in-advertising laws regulated by the Federal Trade Commission.
- You are not in this alone. Anything that a client asks you to do that seems uncomfortable should be taken immediately to your supervisor, with whom a frank discussion of the situation must ensue immediately. Additional agency management must be brought in to make sure the situation is dealt with appropriately and expediently.

## Summary

Dealing with challenging people and situations is part of life—and a part of the workplace. One of the first steps in dealing with a difficult situation is to listen empathetically: identify the different sides of the story or conflict, fill in the gaps with necessary additional information and commit to take action to improve the situation.

## Discussion questions

1 Think of a few times when you had a conflict with another person. What are the different tactics you used to address the conflict? What worked, and what didn't? How can these tactics work in the workplace?
2 Have you ever been asked to do a task that you felt was legally or ethically wrong? How did you handle that? How did you feel after? Would you do anything different in the future?
3 Have you taken classes online? How was it different from in-person classes? What did you learn that can be translated to working in a remote meeting?
4 Visit the website of the 4A's and the code of conduct: https://www.aaaa.org/4as-member-code-conduct/. What aspects do you think might be most challenging to uphold?

## Case 10.1 The Leaky Oil Company

### *Issue: new business trade-off*

Last Friday, Nate Clark, president of Nate Clark and Associates, was invited to meet with the top marketing executives of a major oil company. They stressed to Nate the need for secrecy, and then told him that his agency was just one of three agencies that had been prescreened for this account review. The oil company was to embark on a public policy campaign as well as a branding campaign for their 3,000-store retail brand.

This was a very heady opportunity for Nate's agency, which had suffered a loss of a major oil company account through consolidation just two years ago. The marketing director of this prospective oil company went on to discuss the retail branding effort, which would be twice the level of spending of any other brand in the category. This was more than $40 million in advertising. That alone would be twice the size of any existing account in Nate's agency.

Then the marketing director went on to discuss the need for a public policy campaign. He said that the company, which had been a joint venture between a U.S. company and the Venezuelan government, was now going to be majority owned by a private company based in Venezuela.

The marketing director said that he and his U.S. counterparts would run the marketing but the board of directors of the company would all be from Venezuela. While he assured Nate that there was a need for marketing, he indicated that he did not know how the tensions between the United States and Venezuela would ultimately play out. He also said that this information was strictly confidential. He had made a point of having all the three agencies sign an NDA (non-disclosure agreement) so that if something was leaked to the press, his company would sue them. "My client has very deep pockets," said the marketing director. That was a warning to not say a word on this sensitive topic.

Back at the office, Nate convened a meeting of the agency's top executives representing each discipline. He described the situation to them and told them that it is highly confidential. If word leaked out, there would be significant penalties. He acknowledged that while this is an unusual situation, the size and magnitude of the account would greatly enhance the agency's profitability.

"We have always talked about landing the big one," Nate told the team. "While there is some risk in this, it is unlikely that there will be another account of this size coming down the pike anytime soon."

Not everyone shared Nate's views on the account. A couple of the top executives were very put off that Nate would even consider this account given the political implications. The South American country has been spiraling downward for years with growing political discontent further fueled by skyrocketing hyperinflation, power cuts and shortages of food and medicine. The United Nations has accused the government of using a strategy of instilling fear in its population to retain power. And while the marketing executives said the oil company was now in private hands, the lack of confidence in whether this was true or not caused many to be worried about the relationship.

Judy Chen, the head of the public relations division, said, "Can you imagine the fallout from our other clients if we take this on? Why, we will be called the anti-American agency."

Nate thought about this over the weekend. On Monday morning, he prepared to call the marketing director of the prospective oil company. As he picked up the phone, Nate's administrative assistant told him that three of his top executives want to see him now.

The spokesperson for the group, an old-line account manager, told Nate that if the agency decides to pitch this account, they would leak the news of this to the press and would try to persuade the rest of the staff to quit. They also threatened to tell their other clients about the company that the agency might do business with.

### *Questions*

1. Do you decide to pitch the account or do you withdraw from the review?
2. If you decide to pitch the account, how do you deal with the disgruntled faction that doesn't want to pitch it?
3. Should you discuss this potential client with any other clients to gauge their reaction?
4. Should you seek legal counsel regarding the faction that is threatening to leak the news to the press?
5. If you decide not to pitch the account, do you retain the faction that is threatening you?

# Chapter 11

# Management and creative strategy

## LEARNING OBJECTIVES

This chapter is intended to help you:

- Understand what strategy is.
- Understand the different strategic choices a brand has.
- Learn about the concept of a creative brief and the account manager's role in developing one.
- Identify what a good creative brief is.

Strategy is a key component to every advertising campaign, and to every brand. When talking about brands, there are many different strategies at play. The first is the long-term strategy of where a brand fits into a company's (and an agency's) business. There's a medium-term strategy of what the brand wants to achieve in the next year. And, finally, there's the short-term strategy of what the brand wants to achieve with the upcoming campaign.

The advertising strategy is the plan to reach and persuade a customer to buy a product or a service. In order to develop a strategy, the following elements have to be considered.

- The product itself and its advantages
- The customer and his or her characteristics (demographic, psychographic)
- The relative advantages of alternative routes whereby the customer can be informed of the product
- The optimization of resulting choices given budgetary constraints

To begin developing a strategy, the business goals must be clear, the environment where the brand is competing must be understood, and the available resources to support the brand (such as the budget) have to be clearly identified.

Regardless of the type of strategy (short term, medium term and long term) that is being discussed, the role of strategy does not change: it provides a brand with focus. At many levels, strategy is about the choices that brands and their agents make: for everything a brand decides to do, it is also deciding what not to do. Decisions about demographic and psychographic target audiences, about which attributes to highlight and which to avoid talking about, about whether the packaging will be updated next year or in five years—all these are choices that emphasize one aspect and deemphasizes another. These trade-offs are some of the major decisions that a brand or account manager will make.

The most successful organizations tend to have a strategic focus. A strategic focus exists when a company or a brand is clear about its mission and vision, and has a clear direction on how the mission and vision are manifested. Coke's mission, for example, is to inspire moments of happiness and optimism. Given that mission, the strategy of Coke is based around the idea of a simple strategy of pleasure. Having a Coke is a pleasurable part of your day, one that you can enjoy alone or share with others.

Selecting this strategy involves a deep understanding of the brand and of consumers' relationship with the brand. Beyond that, it involves a series of decisions by the brand management team.

## Strategy as trade-offs

Michael Porter is a business scholar who focuses on competitive advantage, or that which puts a company in a favorable or superior business position. Porter argues that there are two basic strategies that any brand can use.

1 Overall cost leadership: a brand produced and sold with greater cost efficiencies than other brands.
2 Differentiation: superior products or services, not related to cost.

Brands that are successful at the first strategy, overall cost leadership, are generally focused on large markets (like the full United States) and must have efficient processes in place (particularly in terms of manufacturing, distribution, and marketing). Walmart, for example, has cost leadership because of the volume of products it sells, and this allows the brand to have a powerful position relative to both vendors and its competition. This strategy is particularly effective for market sectors where buyers are price sensitive and there is minimal opportunity for differentiation.

One of the drawbacks of pursuing a cost leadership strategy is that if a brand gets in competition with other brands, prices and profits can be driven to very low levels. Think about the dollar menus offered by most fast food brands. Dollar menus are a way to get people into a restaurant with plans to "upsell" more expensive options to them. However, reliance on dollar menus can cause is profits to decrease, and as a result the brand may have less money to spend on research and development or marketing.

In contrast, many of the brands you are familiar with use a differentiation strategy, which consists of finding something unique about the product to promote in messaging. This uniqueness means that price is less of an important factor in the consumer's mind, and some consumers may pay more for the special product. The uniqueness of the brand may be based on numerous qualities: the design of the product (such as the iPhone or the MacBook from Apple), the distribution (Ikea products are only available at Ikea stories), the way the product makes one feel (the way one feels like an athlete when one wears Nikes), the actual benefit of the product (Simply Orange Juice provides more calcium than other brands).

When using a differentiation strategy, brands must be sure that consumers see the unique aspect as truly unique from the brand's competitors. In addition, the uniqueness must be something that is important to the consumer, especially if the brand is asking a higher price than competitors.

Differentiation can be risky. First, competitors can copy the differentiation, making it less unique in the market. Competitors can also come up with a differentiation that is even more appealing to consumers. Consumers are fickle, and their tastes may change, and once that happens, the brand's uniqueness may be less compelling.

Occasionally, low cost and differentiation strategies can be combined: for example, Southwest Airlines has combined low-cost fares with differentiation. The company has done this with a mix of fun advertising and cost-cutting measures (no assigned seats, no meals). At the same time, it offers its consumers benefits in terms of free checked bags. A brand of sunscreen called Equate offers an SPF sunscreen for a very low cost, yet it protects better than all other sunscreens (according to Consumer Reports). However, these products tend to be few and far between.

## Strategy as discipline

Michael Treacy and Fred Wiersema, two other business experts, created the value disciplines model. They argue that a brand has to consider cost leadership *and* differentiation as well as focus. In fact, in their book *The Discipline of Market Leaders*, they offered four rules that competing companies must obey with regard to strategy.

1 **Provide the best offer in the marketplace, by excelling in one specific dimension of value**. Strategy must begin with a value proposition: an innovation, service, or feature intended to make a company or product attractive to customers. The value proposition must be both compelling to consumers and different from competition.
2 **Maintain strong standards on other dimensions of value**. Even though the brand will focus on a unique value, the brand's performance in other dimensions can't be neglected. A luxury car that is fun to drive can't break down on a regular basis. A hoodie can't fade after three washes.
3 **Improve on value every year**. The focus on a single value will allow energies to be pushed to making that value better every day through finding cost efficiencies, new packaging opportunities, or new brand offering.
4 **Deliver unmatched value to consumers**. In a competitive marketplace, the customer value must be improved. This is the imperative of the market leader. The operating model is the key to raising and resetting customer expectation.

## Three value disciplines

Brands have three different value disciplines in which they can choose to focus: operational excellence, product leadership, and customer intimacy. Similar to Porter's idea of trade-offs, brands must select one of these values to focus on.

- **Operational excellence** is characterized by excellent operations and executions. This can often lead to a good-quality product at a low price. Many fast-moving consumer goods brands focus on this value.

- **Product leadership** is characterized by innovative development and design, and a fast time to market, and high margins in a short time frame. Company cultures are flexible to encourage innovation. Companies like Google and Apple represent this value.
- **Customer intimacy** is a value where companies excel in customer attention and customer service. They tailor their products and services to individual or almost individual customers. There is large variation in product assortment. Starbucks is an example of this type of company, providing ever-changing options of food and drink to their customers.

## Developing a strategy

A brand strategy is not developed in a vacuum. It is the result of significant consumer and competitive research, an understanding of positioning (see next chapter) and hard discussions on the current and future status of the brand. Some key aspects of strategy development are as follows.

- **Inspire collaborative development**. Developing strategy is a collaborative exchange. It's meant to encourage dialogue from the outset. Be open to working together on a strategic direction of trust and mutual respect. Talk about your strategies with your agency, exchange ideas and develop a strong strategy together.
- **State a challenge, not a solution**. The strategy must attempt to solve the stated program or business challenge through the campaign. All stated objectives should be SMART—specific, measurable, achievable, relevant and time-bound. As a result, the strategy will inspire the agency to build on ideas, challenge perceptions of the audience or media and think creatively about the course of action for sharing a message.
- **Invest time for feedback**. Always seek input from a variety of stakeholders on the strategy including brand marketing, product, sales teams and other decision-makers or stakeholders.
- **Standardize and streamline the approval process**. Establish clear ownership of the approval process.

## Creative briefs

Once the overall strategy is developed, specific campaigns can start to be created. Often, these campaigns begin with a creative brief, which sets the goals and guidelines for the specific executions. These briefs are guided by overall business goals and by the brand strategy, and also by the specific brand positioning (see next chapter on a discussion of positioning).

Briefs are collaborative documents developed by brand and agency teams. A good brief is a living document that is inspirational to the account team. The creative brief is the foundation on which the work of any creative project will be done. Good briefs can lead to exceptional work, but all too often projects fall short because of poorly written, bloated, non-actionable, ambiguous creative briefs.

Briefs provide numerous benefits to both the client and the agency. Some of the benefits to the client are as follows.

- The brief clarifies all of the project objectives and goals.
- The brief ensures that all the facts and assumptions are communicated clearly.
- The brief enables all the stakeholders to provide input on the project.
- The brief provides clear assessment criteria and holds your creative and media team accountable for the results.

Some of the benefits of briefs to the agency are as follows.

- The brief introduces the agency to the brand.
- The brief provides all the necessary background details for both creative and media teams.
- The brief illustrates customers' personalities and preferences.
- The brief keeps everyone focused and on the same page.
- The brief provides assessment criteria.

### *Goal and components of a creative brief*

Creative briefs serve very specific goals. A good creative brief:

- Outlines clear objectives that the campaign is supposed to achieve.
- Provides all relevant information about the project.
- Gives a reference point for the entire team, and all personnel involved in the project.

A well-written creative brief should include a wealth of relevant information and should be clearly organized. At the same time, it should be *brief*—about a page. Many agencies have a standard template for creative briefs that contain a fairly consistent range of information such as:

- An overview of the scope of the project, along with the problem that brand is facing.
- Concrete business and communication goals.
- Target audience: Who the audience is, not only from a demographic perspective (age and gender) but also their mindset?
- Current perceptions: What do consumers currently think and feel about the product?
- Value proposition or positioning: What differentiates you from the competition? The next chapter reviews elements of positioning.
- Core message: single most important message that consumers will take away.
- Timeline (start and end dates).

Some briefs may also include:

- Key performance indicators (KPIs): exactly how success of the project will be assessed.
- Competitors: What do you know about them?
- Past insights: what worked and what didn't.

### *Writing the brief*

One person at the agency may be responsible for drafting the brief, generally either the account manager or the account planner. In many cases, the account manager and the account planner work together on the brief. Some guidelines to drafting the brief are given below.

- Don't make assumptions: Assume that people who read the brief are coming to the brief with no preexisting notions of the brand or the product. This will help you lay out the situation and explain the project as fully as possible. Focus on both big and small issues and synthesize your knowledge into the key information that the team needs to know.
- Focus on the problem and how you're solving it: The problem isn't "how do we make an ad?" but rather "how do we make an ad that meets the needs and solves a problem." The brief provides the starting point for creative and media teams to solve the problem. All decisions should be informed by the established primary goals and objectives, so it's crucial that everyone is crystal clear on exactly what they are.
- Keep it brief. We've said this before; a brief is called a brief because it needs to be brief. It is often easier to provide lots of information; narrowing all the information to what is relevant for solving a problem is more challenging but more valuable to solving the problem.
- Use clear, unambiguous writing: Use as little jargon as possible. Plain language will help insure that everyone will get the most important concepts.
- The brief is a living document: As people read and comment on the brief, their thoughts can be integrated into the document. You will gain insights that you wouldn't have thought of otherwise (Exhibit 11.1).

---

## Exhibit 11.1

Creative brief example:

- An overview of the scope of the project, along with the problem that brand is facing: BeeEnergy is a new energy drink that uses the power of honey to deliver a punch of energy. It is the only honey-based energy on the market. The challenge the brand faces is that most energy drinks are consumed by young men, who have no interest in a honey-based drink.
- Concrete business and communication goals: increase awareness of BeeEnergy to 25% of women aged 35+ in the first six months.
- Target audience: who the audience is, not only from a demographic perspective (age and gender) but also their mindset: The Queen Bee: Women aged 35+ who value natural ingredients and enjoy a sweet treat in their busy workday.
- Current perceptions: What do consumers currently think and feel about the product? The Queen Bee lives a busy lifestyle and avoids traditional energy drinks even when she's exhausted because of the chemicals and because the brands don't fit who she is. There is no drink especially for her.

- Value proposition or positioning: What differentiates you from the competition? Honey-based energy drink that is as opposite from the other energy drinks as it can be.

Core message: the single most important message that consumers will take away: Honey is nature's energy drink, and so it is a good fit for me.

## Assessing creative briefs

The role of the account manager may be writing the brief, collaborating with the account planner on the brief, and/or assessing the brief. For great work to happen, good feedback on the brief is needed. Ask yourself:

- *Is the brief single minded and focused?*
- *Is it logical? Is it easy to be the story that begins with the brief?*
- *Is there a compelling insight or brand truth?*
- *Does the brief work specifically for our brand?*
- *Does the brief commit to a point of view?*

## Summary

A single brand can have a variety of strategies that all serve to build brand value in the minds of consumers and positively affect sales. Brands often choose either a low price or differentiation strategy. Three key values, namely, operational excellence, product leadership and customer intimacy, can also influence brand strategy. Strategy is communicated through creative briefs that keep both the client and the agency on the same page.

## Discussion questions

1 Think about what short-term, medium-term and long-term strategies might work for iPhone and McDonald's.
2 Think about brands you buy regularly and whether you purchase them because of low price or differentiation. If it is because of differentiation, what aspects of differentiation make the products appealing?
3 What is an example of customer intimacy that you've experienced?
4 Google "creative briefs" and find examples from a few different agencies. How do they express ideas similarly, and in what ways are they different?

## Case 11.1 Go Organic Company

### *Issue: market segmentation*

Go Organic Foods, based in Omaha, Nebraska, was one of the newest packaged foods companies to jump on the organic bandwagon. Go Organic offered a variety of products that could be found in grocery stores, specialty health food stores, and even some restaurants and other food-service establishments.

One of the best-selling brands in their product line was Go Organic frozen food. This was the brainchild of founder Robert Sierra, who had learnt of a method called "flash freezing," where you could retain all the nutrients in the food even though it was frozen. Mr. Sierra was tremendously excited about this process since he believed that it would solve a large public health problem in America, that of obesity. Mr. Sierra had studied America's eating habits for years and realized that much of the country's diet consisted of high-fat and high-sodium frozen-food meals. In fact, Mr. Sierra had seen his own mother and father gain considerable weight and later develop heart disease as a result of their poor dietary habits. All Mr. Sierra could remember was that their diet was driven by frozen food.

Mr. Sierra used this new technology to develop a line of frozen dinners that were low in fat, sodium, and cholesterol, and high in nutrients. Even with this seemingly large breakthrough, grocers were reluctant to carry his products. They didn't believe that there was a large consumer demand for natural or organic foods. They told Mr. Sierra that it was a niche item.

Undaunted, Mr. Sierra finally convinced the president of a small independent chain of high-quality stores to carry the products. Sales of the Go Organic dinners began to take hold. The flavor of Go Organic products exceeded expectation, and soon those who wished to eat a low-fat, nutritious meal without sacrificing flavor were flocking to the brand. Retailers who had previously been reluctant to carry the brand began to call Go Organic.

Although men tend to eat frozen dinners more often than women, the Go Organic line of frozen dinners was aimed primarily at women over the age of 40. However, the company soon learned that men also liked the Go Organic dinners as well. This popularity spurred Go Organic to expand their product line to include more frozen dinners, some breakfast items, and even desserts. The strategy focused on the idea that working couples over 40 could make a delicious and nutritious meal—and have more time for one another. The "dinner date" campaign was very successful among members of the target audience.

Naturally, the competition in the frozen food category did not stand still while Go Organic captured its market share. They also focused on health in their advertising, and soon introduced their own organic or part organic frozen food products. The frozen food marketplace was becoming an organic and natural foods battleground.

Carol Hart, the vice president of marketing for Go Organic, looked at the trends of the business with some trepidation. The competition had significant capital compared to the small, privately held, Go Organic. Carol was concerned about the growth of the brand and if they could keep up with the constant battle for their market share.

While she was mulling things over, Mr. Sierra entered her office and tossed an article on her desk. He said that this article summed up the market segment that he felt was still untapped by his brand. He asked Carol to read the article and to provide him with a point of view on the best way to develop consumer segmentation for the brand (Exhibit 11.2).

## Exhibit 11.2 Information according to a recent government report

| *Demographics* | *Frozen dinner consumption* | *Organic food consumption* | *Obesity likelihood* |
|---|---|---|---|
| Average index | 100 | 100 | 100 |
| Gender | | | |
| Men | 110 | 50 | 80 |
| Women | 90 | 150 | 120 |
| Age | | | |
| Teens 13–17 | 65 | 20 | 120 |
| Adults 18–24 | 120 | 30 | 110 |
| 25–34 | 110 | 100 | 70 |
| 35–54 | 80 | 110 | 70 |
| 55–64 | 70 | 140 | 90 |
| 65+ | 130 | 60 | 120 |
| Ethnicity | | | |
| Caucasian | 100 | 130 | 70 |
| African American | 100 | 50 | 140 |
| Hispanic | 70 | 40 | 150 |
| Asian | 110 | 150 | 60 |
| Native American | 20 | 30 | 180 |
| Education | | | |
| High school or less | 115 | 30 | 150 |
| High school grad | 105 | 70 | 120 |
| Some college | 100 | 100 | 100 |
| College grad | 95 | 130 | 75 |
| Grad school | 60 | 180 | 50 |
| Income | | | |
| $50k or less | 100 | 40 | 150 |
| $50k to $100k | 120 | 80 | 110 |
| $100k or more | 90 | 170 | 60 |

*Note*: Index to average is 100. Above 100 is m.

Two facts leaped out:

- According to a recent government report, obesity among adults had doubled since 1980, while being overweight had tripled among adolescents. One study cited rates as high as 15% of teenage boys and girls being overweight.
- Hispanics and African Americans had a much higher prevalence for being overweight than the Caucasian population. Women were more likely to be obese compared to men.

Mr. Sierra turned to Carol and said, "Look at these statistics. We need to rethink our advertising and marketing. Why, homes that have teens and ethnic audiences are totally untapped markets for us! I'm pretty sure the 'Dinner Date' campaign isn't working for them. I would like a report on how we rethink the strategy within the next week."

As Mr. Sierra left, Carol felt very conflicted. She knew that he was passionate about wanting to help people who had a high proclivity for being obese, yet she was looking at other demographic information on frozen food purchasers and organic food buyers that was very different from this information.

Given the recent amount of competition in the marketplace, she knew that they had to be right in the strategy they would develop. She began to quickly review the data and assemble a presentation. She hoped that she was right.

## Questions

1. Do you think that the information gleaned about segmentation is enough to develop a segmentation scheme for the brand?
2. Which information do you consider more valuable, the trends Carol was looking at or the facts in the article? Why?
3. What trends would you consider if you were to develop a segmentation strategy?
4. Do you feel that the segmentation strategy should be based on adding new purchasers to the brand or adding frequency to current buyers?
5. What would be the ideal information to have to make this decision?
6. Would you go with the information you have, or recommend that you take more time and do primary research on the market before making a decision?

Chapter 12

# Making strategic decisions in advertising management within a brand perspective

## LEARNING OBJECTIVES

This chapter is intended to help you:

- Learn about the concept of positioning.
- Understand the relationship between positioning and the 4Ps.
- Understand the relationship between segmenting, targeting and positioning.
- Understand the value of perceptual mapping.

In the previous chapter, we discussed different strategic options for the brand and reviewed the elements of the creative brief. One of the key elements of the brief is brand positioning. This chapter will focus specifically on making your brand distinctive, using the concept of positioning. The most important takeaway from this chapter is this: positioning is not something that anyone does to a brand, but rather a thing that occurs in the mind of the consumer.

The concept of positioning was developed by Al Ries and Jack Trout in their book *Positioning: The Battle for Your Mind*. The authors argued that a brand must identify and attempt to "own" a marketing niche for itself. They suggested that there are numerous ways to own the niche, and many of these relate to the concepts discussed in the previous chapters.

## Positioning and the 4Ps

The traditional marketing "4Ps" can be used as a jumping-off place for looking at alternatives for positioning. Thus, a brand would evaluate whether their unique niche involves the 4Ps.

- Product: the attributes of the brand. For positioning, a unique attribute or benefit of the product is selected to be highlighted. For example, Apple's products are technically advanced, but most people see them as beautifully designed products.
- Pricing: how much the brand costs, for example, being either the lowest cost or the highest cost. For example, Dollar Shave Club positions itself as a low-cost brand, L'Oréal hair products position themselves as more expensive ("Because I'm worth it").

- Distribution (also known as "place"): where the brand is available. Whole Foods Market stores position themselves as a higher-end choice by building stores in upscale neighborhoods; Trader Joe's selects less upscale neighborhoods to position themselves as a local grocery.
- Packaging: how the brand is physically packaged. Crown Royal whiskey comes in a purple velvet bag to reinforce the "royal" aspect of its name, as it was first blended for King George VI's royal visit to Canada.

Brand positioning is an important part of the marketing process, as a strong brand position can communicate brand uniqueness relative to different brands, as well as reasons for purchasing and using the specific brand. Brand positioning also pushes the account people to make sure that everyone on the team possesses a deep understanding of consumers. It is one thing that sets your brand apart from others.

It is important to note that brand positioning occurs regardless of whether or not a company is proactive in developing a position. Consumers will make their own assumptions about the brand based on where they see it in the store, who else is buying it, and whatever information they hear from other users. Therefore, it is important to be proactive to make sure that consumers are seeing the brand in the best light.

## Segmentation, targeting and positioning

To build a brand, three crucial decisions must be made: segmentation, targeting and positioning. The first two, segmentation and targeting, are fairly straightforward. Segmenting is dividing the market into relevant groups. A brand like Nike has product segments such as running, basketball, tennis and golf. There are also segments that are people-based, such as professional athletes, people who watch sports, people who play sports, and people who talk about sports.

Targeting is selecting the group that makes the most sense for the brand in terms of what the product offers and what the business goals are. Nike believes that anyone can be an athlete; thus, someone who is engaged in a sport would be the target.

Next comes the hard part: positioning. This focuses on the message that will be delivered. Advertising and other type of brand communication can serve to suggest the type of positioning that a consumer will take up; indeed, many marketers see positioning as the process by which an image or identity is created in the minds of the target audience.

### *The process of positioning*

Jack Trout provides four steps to implement positioning.

1 Study your competitors and identify the attributes they own in the mind of the consumer. This is important since your brand should not select a positioning that is already in use by other brands.
2 Assess your brand's strengths and weaknesses, and look for that differentiating idea. What things have the competitors not chosen to highlight? What are the strengths and weaknesses of those options?

3 Think long term: can you support your differentiating idea with facts attributed to the brand? Are these facts likely to remain consistent over time?
4 Promote the positioning: develop a campaign to communicate the differentiating idea to your target audience.

One method to identify possible brands is through a perceptual map. Perceptual brand mapping is the visual plotting of specific brands against two axes, where each axis represents an attribute that is known to drive brand selection. For example, one axis may be cost (low cost on one end, high cost on the other) and the other may be quality (low quality on one end, high quality on the other). Different competitors can be assessed and placed at various places on the map.

Because brand mapping creates such a concise summary of significant amounts of information, it has three key benefits for marketers.

- First, it can unlock insights about your competitors and the industry overall. It shows the relative position of competing brands based on how those brands are perceived by consumers.
- Second, it can communicate where the brand should be headed.
- Third, it can gain alignment with business strategy. Does the perceptual map reflect the various strategic decisions that the brand has chosen?

Let's say you had a client who had a regional chain of coffee shops. The vast majority of the coffee shops are located in downtown urban areas. However, the client wants to have more presence in college and university areas, given that students drink coffee all day long (and sometimes all night) and like to have places they can gather. Your client asks you for thoughts on positioning.

You visit a college campus near your office and identify five different coffee places that currently exist. After having a latte at each location, you put together a chart that describes each coffee place on three aspects: cost (high, medium or low), quality (high, medium or low) and nearness to campus (see Exhibit 12.1).

**Exhibit 12.1 Coffee places near campus**

| *Name* | *Quality* | *Price* | *Location* |
|---|---|---|---|
| Starbucks | High | High | Near |
| Campus Coffee | Low | Medium | Far |
| Java Shack | Medium | Medium | Less far |
| Le Café | Medium | High | Near |
| Coffee Love | Low | Low | Less far |

The next step is to map each of three pairs of aspects: cost and quality, cost and nearness to campus, quality and nearness to campus. Exhibit 12.2 displays these maps.

## Exhibit 12.2 Perceptual maps for coffee places near campus

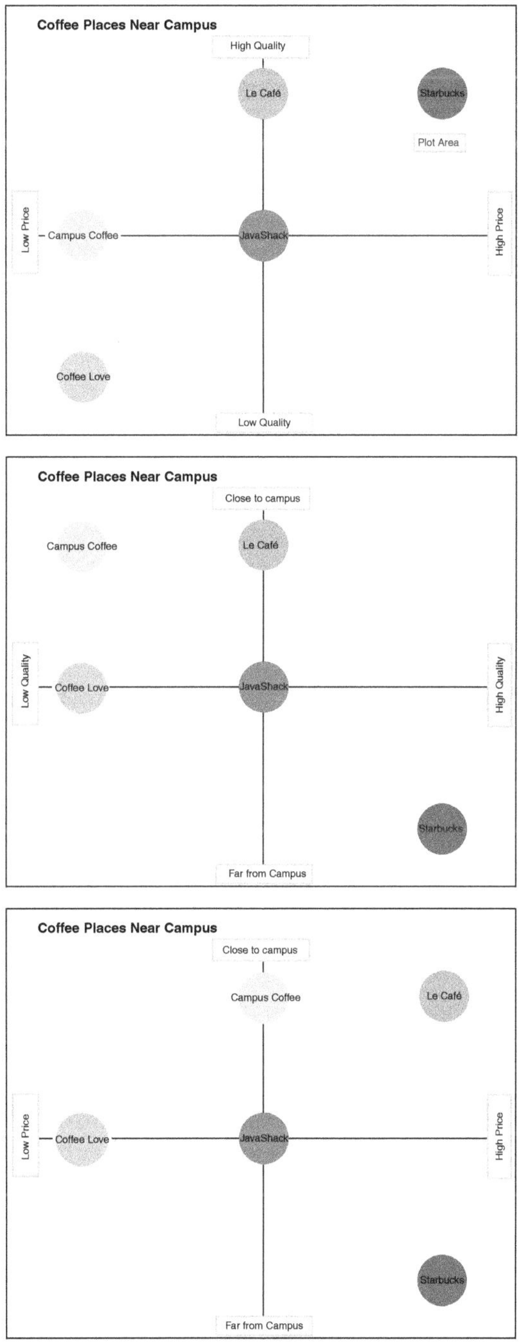

The first map compares cost and quality. By reading this map, you can see a strong correlation between cost and quality—the more expensive the coffee, the higher the quality. The map doesn't show a lot of reasonable options for unique positioning except for high quality and low price (which may or may not be economically feasible), and low quality and high price (which does not seem like a strong option).

The second map shows quality and location relative to campus. Here, we see an opportunity for high-quality coffee close to campus. The third map shows cost and location relative to campus. This shows two opportunities: one for low price and close to campus, and the other for low price and farther from campus.

In this case, a good recommendation would be a café that offered high-quality coffee close to campus. It could be that since other high-priced offerings close to campus aren't seen as high quality, the positioning would be unique.

## A consideration set

In most cases, the positioning of a brand is all relative to other products in the consumers' choice set. Our coffee example includes a variety of places near to campus that a consumer might consider. Therefore, the location/convenience creates the choice set. If the consumer is looking for mustard for a Fourth of July picnic, for example, the choice set might include French's, Grey Poupon, and Heinz. If the customer is looking for desserts for that same picnic, the choice set might include Popsicle, Betty Crocker, TOLL HOUSE, or Klondike. Notice in this second group, there are several different categories included in the choice set: frozen ice cream, frozen fruit treats, baking products (TOLL HOUSE chips) and box brownie mix.

Thinking about a larger "choice set" is important because it will help you identify the target consumer's reason to buy your brand instead of others. Brand positioning must make sure that:

- The brand is seen as unique and different from the competition.
- The brand is seen as important and valuable to consumers.
- The brand promise can be promoted in a variety of channels.
- The brand positioning will allow the company to achieve its goals.
- The brand positioning promotes the mission and values of the organization.

The temptation is to always communicate everything your brand has to offer. There is only one problem: people have selective memory and tend to attach only one "label" to a brand. For example, Google is "search," FedEx is "overnight delivery" and Volvo is "safety." The more the number of elements you are trying to communicate, the less the people remember your brand.

Nike, for example, wants consumers to have a distinct "feeling" that transcends the product: that the individual who wears the product is an athlete. When someone wears the brand, they feel that they are wearing the same product that all great athletes wear. Nike's tagline, Just Do It, became a rallying cry that got people off their sofas and onto streets and basketball courts.

Going back to our coffee example, the perceptual maps can be used for a new brand to think about what is lacking in the market or for an existing brand to think about changing some of the things it does to be more appealing to consumers. In our coffee example, there seems to be a lack of very high-end coffee. There's also an opportunity for a high-quality, low-cost option. A high-end coffee place might work well in a university town, even without a high-end retail establishment from which to see the coffee—a brightly painted truck might work.

## What is a brand positioning statement?

A positioning statement is a framework that communicates your brand's unique value to your customers in relation to your main competitors. It is very similar to a creative brief—however, a creative brief is the direction for a campaign, while a positioning statement is used in the brief for advertising work as well as for other decisions made about the brand. It is likely that the brand positioning statement will be true for the brand for several years (if not longer), while a creative strategy is focused primarily on an upcoming ad campaign.

Most brand positioning statements contain four aspects.

1 **Target customer**: What is the demographic and attitudinal description of the group your brand wants to appeal to and attract?
2 **Market definition**: What category is your brand competing in, and how is your brand relevant in this category?
3 **Brand promise**: What is the most compelling (emotional/rational) benefit to your target customers that your brand can own relative to your competition?
4 **Reason to believe**: What is the most compelling evidence that your brand delivers on its brand promise?

After thoughtfully answering these four questions, you can craft your positioning statement. A template is found in Exhibit 12.3.

### Exhibit 12.3 Brand positioning template

| *BRAND NAME* | |
|---|---|
| To | *THE CONSUMER* |
| *BRAND NAME* is | *CURRENT DESCRIPTION* |
| That | *VALUE PROMISE* |
| That's because | *REASON TO BELIEVE* |

The brand positioning statements for Target (Exhibit 12.4), Tesla (Exhibit 12.5), Disney (Exhibit 12.6) and Jet Blue (Exhibit 12.7) show the connections between consumers, products, and messages.

### Exhibit 12.4 Brand positioning statement for Target

| *Brand position: Target* | |
|---|---|
| To | Value-oriented shoppers |
| Target is | The cheap and chic retailer |
| That | Offers high-end style at low-end cost |
| That's because | Of our partnerships with famous designers |

### Exhibit 12.5 Brand positioning statement for Tesla

*Brand positioning: Tesla*

| | |
|---|---|
| To | Luxury car buyers |
| Tesla is | The only long-range, eco-friendly and electric vehicle |
| That | Is difficult to get |
| That's because | It is the only luxury car that helps the planet |

### Exhibit 12.6 Brand positioning statement for Disney

*Brand positioning: Disney*

| | |
|---|---|
| To | Anyone who is young or young at heart |
| Disney is | The only destination |
| That | Will make your magical dreams come true |
| That's because | It is the happiest place on earth |

### Exhibit 12.7 Brand positioning statement for Jet Blue

*Brand positioning: Jet Blue*

| | |
|---|---|
| To | "Underserved customers"—those looking for better features and benefits that aren't provided by low-cost carriers and at a reasonable price that aren't provided by larger carriers |
| Jet Blue is | The only airline |
| That | Provides the range of amenities that travelers are looking for at a low cost |
| That's because | The flight experience is the most important thing |

## Evaluating your brand positioning strategy

Your brand positioning statement can be a powerful tool to bring focus and clarity to your marketing strategies, advertising campaigns, and other branded communications such as public relations efforts and social media. Here are some questions to ask to make sure your statement is as strong as it can be.

1 Does it differentiate your brand in the mind of the consumer? The brand positioning has to be unique from that of your competition.
2 Does it match customer perceptions of your brand? The positioning has to connect to an existing consumer truth, or else it won't seem valid to consumers.
3 Does it identify your brand's unique value to your customers? Will your core customers find it easy to understand? The positioning should be simple and clear.

4 Will core customers find it memorable? The brand positioning should be not only different from competitors but interesting to consumers, and connect to a consumer truth.
5 Can it be used consistently throughout brand activities? The positioning should work not only for advertising campaigns but for public relations activities, point-of-purchase displays, packaging, sales promotions, and other activities.
6 Is your brand promise believable and credible? The positioning should be able to reflect real truths of the brand that anyone could research and prove.
7 Can your brand own it? In a perfect world, no other brand would be able to have your positioning.

## Problematic positioning

Not all positioning choices work well. Some poor choices include:

1 **Under positioning**. In this case, the positioning is not strong, so customers will have a blurred and unclear idea of the brand.
2 **Over positioning**. In this case, customers awareness has not been established to the degree that a positioning will resonate with them. Customers have too limited an awareness of the brand or a category for a unique positioning to be meaningful.
3 **Confused positioning**. In this case, consumers do not see competition as distinctive. As a result, customers have a confused opinion of the brand.
4 **Double positioning**. The positioning seems too similar to a competitor's, and as a result customers do not accept the claims of the brand.

## Brand repositioning

When a brand is positioned incorrectly, or just to make an old brand feel new, brands reposition themselves. Repositioning can occur for different reasons. Research may show that consumers have no defined perceptions about the brand. A competitor may have a value proposition that consumers see as more valuable than your brand's. Other reasons include that the core market is becoming smaller, or that aspects of the brand are no longer appealing.

Brands often need to evolve, adapt and sometimes radically change depending on what is going on in society. For example, Quaker Oats owns a pancake mix and syrup brand, which for over 130 years was known as "Aunt Jemima." According to a story in the New York Times, the brand was named after a 19th-century minstrel song called "Old Aunt Jemima." The imagery associated with this brand was one of a Black woman in a servant position; when introducing the brand in 1893, Quaker hired a former slave to represent the brand. As a result, the positioning of the product was Southern-based comfort food, like a household servant could prepare.

Over the years, Quaker replaced the character's headscarf (which connected her to slavery) with a headband and added jewelry to her image in the 1980s. After the Black Lives Matter protests of 2020, Quaker retired the character and changed the name to Pearl Milling Company. Other brands with problematic imagery, such as Mrs. Butterworth's syrup, also were planning to reposition their brands.

Repositioning is a very tricky and sensitive exercise. Even when the positioning is problematic, people have internalized the positioning and it is very familiar to them. When a brand is rebranded and its positioning changes, significant resources must be committed to the repositioning.

## Summary

Brand positioning is the place that the brand exists in the mind of the consumer. Perceptual mapping is a tool that can help account managers understand how consumers see brands, and how this perception aligns with current brand strategy. A brand strategy statement helps to bring all parties aligned with the specific strategy to be undertaken. Repositioning can be done if brand strategy is somehow failing the brand in a contemporary market.

## Discussion questions

1 What are some examples for brands that you think have strong positioning? Also, give some examples for brands that you think have weak positioning.
2 See if you can determine the positioning for the following brands: Southwest Airlines, Ritz Carlton hotels, Mercedes Benz, Kia.
3 Select a brand category and draw three or four perceptual maps, using at leave five brands in the category. Possible categories include athletic shoes, trucks, shampoo, candy and vacation destinations.
4 What is an example of a brand that has repositioned itself?

## Case 12.1 Boston Life Insurance Company

### *Issue: advertising strategy*

Boston Life Insurance was founded in 1890 as one of the first life insurance companies in the United States. As with most insurance companies, Boston Life had diversified into a financial services company through a variety of acquisitions. Boston Life had an extensive marketing sales force throughout the United States.

Boston Life was the third largest life insurance company, offering traditional life insurance policies as well as annuity products and other financial instruments. The top insurance company was Peoples Insurance, followed closely by Mutual Insurance. Metro Insurance was the fourth largest insurance company in the category, but they were far down the line from the top three in terms of market share.

### *Boston Life strategy*

Boston Life management believed that the company had evolved over the years from one that provided only life insurance to one that provided for the entire family's financial foundation. According to a recent study, Boston Life customers found the company to be:

- Responsive to their needs.
- Good to do business with.
- A moral and ethical company.
- Solid and stable.

However, even though Boston Life had some positive attributes, Sho Ito, the advertising director of Boston Life, wanted to take it up a notch. His goals for the company as well as for the agency handling their account were to ensure the positioning of Boston Life as the leader in the category and to increase its awareness among a younger population of potential families. Sho was concerned that Boston Life was missing out on the younger end of the market by not marketing to them effectively and by not aggressively using the sales force to call on this audience.

Sho was also not convinced that the current advertising campaign, "Special Moments for Special Families," was hitting the mark. He felt that it was nice but it wasn't truly a breakthrough campaign or that it really differentiated Boston Life from its competitors.

### *Advertising tracking research*

Liam Kelly, the account director of Peabody Agency, began to survey the recent results of the advertising research for Boston Life. He had taken many calls from Sho Ito regarding the Boston Life campaign. Liam knew that Sho wanted more from the campaign.

**Exhibit 12.8 Top-of-mind awareness (in %)**

| *Company* | *Wave 1* | *Wave 2* | *Wave 3* | *Wave 4* |
|---|---|---|---|---|
| Boston Life | 17 | 21 | 18 | 17 |
| Mutual | 8 | 11 | 13 | 15 |
| Metro | 13 | 12 | 11 | 11 |
| Peoples | 25 | 24 | 25 | 24 |

*Sample*: 1,000 respondents per wave.
*Source*: Boston Life Insurance.

### Exhibit 12.9 Top-of-mind awareness by key demographics

| | *Demographics* | *Boston Wave 4 (%)* |
|---|---|---|
| Gender | Men | 24 |
| | Women | 15 |
| Age | 18–34 | 9 |
| | 35–54 | 19 |
| | 55+ | 26 |
| Education | Less than college | 17 |
| | College+ | 19 |
| HH income | Less than $50K | 15 |
| | $50K to $100K | 18 |
| | $100K+ | 20 |
| | Overall | 17 |

*Sample*: 1,000.
*Source*: Boston Life Insurance.

However, Liam also knew that every time that Peabody Agency had suggested a change in strategy, the CEO of Boston Life had turned it down. He was very conservative and wanted to stay the course with the advertising.

As Liam looked over the advertising research, he saw things that did not make him happy. The first thing that he reviewed was the top-of-mind awareness numbers from a national survey that Boston Life did with over 1,000 consumers. The study had surveyed both customers and noncustomers to understand where they stood in the market in terms of overall awareness and advertising awareness compared to the key competitors.

The top-of-mind awareness numbers for Boston Life continued to go down (see Exhibit 12.8). They had peaked in Wave 2 of the study, but now they were actually back to where they had started in Wave 1. What was even more disturbing was that Mutual Insurance was beginning to gain momentum. They were closing in on Boston Life. The top brand, Peoples, continued to retain its number one position (Exhibits 12.9 and 12.10).

### Exhibit 12.10 Boston Life creative testing

| *Diagnostics* | *Boston Life score* | *Financial services norms* |
|---|---|---|
| Recall of ad | 20 | 21 |
| Playback of key message | 10 | 15 |
| Likability of ad | 35 | 22 |
| Positive image | 31 | 28 |
| Unique to advertiser | 15 | 18 |

When Liam turned the page of the study to the demographic breakdown of the awareness numbers, his heart dropped further. He started to see where the Boston Life advertising campaign was having an impact and where the impact was sorely lacking.

It was obvious from this chart that Boston Life was being effective with older, more upscale men. However, they were woefully underdeveloped with the younger end of the family set and with women.

*No wonder Sho Ito is concerned with our advertising campaign,* thought Liam.

### *Creative testing research*

Liam Kelly wasted no time in calling his team together after the tracking study research was in. He said, "We must determine if our media plan or our message or both are on track." Liam felt that this was a critical time for the agency to do something on the account. So he commissioned creative testing research that the agency paid for at its own expense.

The creative testing research was done with Boston Life ads put into the advertising medium with other ads. This was done for Boston Life with both television and print advertising. For the television ads, they were placed within the context of a 30-minute television program and in commercial pods with other ads. Consumers were then asked to recall ads in the program and then replayed the Boston Life ad for specific feedback. A similar test was done with newspapers where a consumer was asked to read the newspaper and then asked about the ads within it.

The scores of the consumer responses were then compared against other financial services companies that had also done this type of creative testing. These were called normative values. Liam Kelly was anxious to understand if the Boston Life ads were better than the normative values (Exhibits 12.11 and 12.12).

**Exhibit 12.11 Competitive media spending (millions of dollars)**

| *Company* | *Year 1* | *Year 2* | *Year 3* |
|---|---|---|---|
| Boston Life | 15.0 | 18.0 | 21.0 |
| Mutual | 6.0 | 8.0 | 9.0 |
| Metro | 8.0 | 8.0 | 8.0 |
| Peoples | 20.0 | 22.0 | 24.0 |

What Liam found was a mixed bag. The overall recall of the Boston Life ad was right on norm, but consumers didn't play back the key message of the commercial. Consumers really liked the ads, yet they didn't feel that they were unique to Boston Life.

Liam wasn't sure what to do with the results. The campaign was a series of warm family moments, so he wasn't surprised if consumers liked them. "Who doesn't like cuddly kids and their pets," he thought. What bothered Liam was the diagnostics on uniqueness. That was what Sho Ito of Boston Life had been harping on about. Yet the CEO of Boston Life loved the ads. "I feel so good when I see them," said the CEO.

### *Media analysis*

The bigger news in analyzing the advertising strategy for Boston Life was in the competitive media analysis. Boston Life had steadily been increasing its advertising expenditures for the past three years. It was closing in on the category leader, Peoples Insurance.

**Exhibit 12.12 Media mix analysis (in %)**

| *Medium* | *Boston Life* | *Mutual* | *Metro* | *Peoples* |
|---|---|---|---|---|
| Network TV/cable | 30 | | 10 | 70 |
| National/spot radio | | 60 | | |
| Magazine | 30 | | 40 | |
| Newspaper | 30 | | | |
| Out-of-home | | 30 | | |
| Sponsorships | 10 | | 40 | 20 |
| Online | | 10 | 10 | 10 |
| Total | 100 | 100 | 100 | 100 |

As Liam reviewed the media expenditure information, he also saw that Mutual Insurance had increased their spending, yet they were still spending less than half of Boston Life's total.

We have been spending more, yet we seem to be getting nowhere in terms of top-of-mind awareness, thought Liam. Liam knew that this chart alone was a condemnation of an ineffective advertising program. He mused, I don't think too many clients are willing to spend more and get the same thing.

As Liam dove deeper into the information, he began to see where differences emerged in the way the media dollars were allocated by each of the brands. His media group had provided a breakdown of the four insurance companies and the major media in which they invested their advertising dollars.

Boston Life had had the same media mix for years. They had been very print-focused. This was due to the Boston Life's CEO, who felt that a product like life insurance should have a medium that is tangible. "Print conveys that we are a real company. Plus it is great to send those ads to our sales force," commented the Boston Life CEO.

The past few years, Boston Life had developed a series of television ads that were placed in golf and tennis programming. Boston Life also sponsored a series of yacht races that began in Boston Harbor. The Boston Life CEO was an avid sportsman and he enjoyed being associated with yachting, golf, and tennis.

Liam found it interesting that Peoples Insurance spent the majority of their dollars on network television and cable television. One expected that type of media plan from the category leader. Mutual Insurance took a different tack. They have developed a funny character that had a recognizable voice. As a result, they put their money into radio and also used outdoor advertising in selective markets.

### *Advertising decisions*

Liam felt that he had all the information he needed to help craft a point of view on Boston Life. He wondered how he should put it together and what he should actually reveal to the client. This was going to be a difficult meeting, since much of the advertising strategy had been directed by the Boston Life CEO. Yet Liam knew that the agency was ultimately responsible for the advertising program.

Liam also knew that Sho Ito wanted results and would not be satisfied unless something was changed to make the program more effective. Liam saw issues with both the creative and the media—but which one was really driving the lower awareness numbers? Liam wondered if wholesale changes were needed or if he should just redirect some dollars into different media. He was particularly troubled by the program in light of the lack of response of younger families.

Liam had a week to prepare for a meeting where he would address both Sho Ito and the Boston Life CEO with some answers. He started to work that afternoon on the agency point of view.

### *Questions*

1 What do you think the agency point of view should be regarding the Boston Life advertising?
2 What changes would you recommend to reach younger families?
3 Do you think that the media plan should be significantly changed? If so, what changes would you make?
4 Do you think that the creative should be changed?
5 How do you think Liam Kelly should handle the issue of creative testing with the client? What should he tell the client, if anything?
6 What should Sho Ito, as a client, demand from the agency?
7 Knowing the Boston Life CEO's involvement, how much should Sho Ito hold the agency responsible for the advertising results?

Chapter 13

# Aligning strategy to cultural differences in advertising management

## LEARNING OBJECTIVES

This chapter is intended to help you:

- Understand the cultural aspects of today's society.
- Understand the similarities between multiculturalism, polyculturalism and "whole market" approaches in advertising.
- Understand the nature of process and perspective in adopting a multicultural approach.
- Discover the importance of specific tactics for building a multicultural workforce, which can then lead to better multicultural messages.

Working in the advertising industry—or most industries today—you will be working with people from a variety of culture. In Chapter 6, we talked about strategies for managing people in a multicultural workplace, and the value this brings to an agency. In this chapter, we'll talk about being an account manager on campaigns that exist in a multicultural world, and the role the account manager plays in making sure that culturally appropriate messages are created and that best hiring practices are adhered to by the agency to create a diverse workforce.

Most people understand that this country is on a straight line path towards becoming a minority-majority nation. This new demographic reality means that brands may have to rethink their current marketing strategies to remain profitable. Research findings from the Association of National Advertisers (ANA) indicate that consumers are generally more responsive to ads featuring people they can relate to. This may be, for example, people of their age, their race, their gender, or their involvement with social causes.

If people don't see themselves in ads, they won't relate to brand messages. However, the vast majority of people who appear in advertisements tend to be White. The demographics of the U.S. market is changing, and ads that don't show an accurate picture of this market are missing out on important consumers.

In addition, the ANA study showed that people are much more likely to want to learn more about a brand, as well as much more likely to buy from a brand for the first time, if the messages they receive are culturally relevant. The ANA defines culturally relevant as accurately reflecting the culture, not showing, for example, only one ethic group. The ANA study also showed that consumers are 50% more likely to repurchase from a brand and three times more likely to recommend a brand that uses culturally relevant ads.

## Beyond the majority

There are several different terms that are used to describe the current marketing environment. They all recognize that many messages have traditionally been crafted for the "majority" market in the United States—majority from a racial perspective, meaning White consumers. Today, race is one of the many ways advertisers and marketers segment individuals. At the same time, most advertisers understand that a campaign targeted to the "majority" market is going to miss the mark with other segments (such as consumers who identify as Black, Hispanic/Latino, Pacific Islander or First Nation).

Some key issues that account managers need to recognize that influence marketing decisions are as follows.

- Brand messages often don't reflect society. A study by Adobe found that nearly three in four Whites believed their race/ethnicity is represented in the ads they see, but only 26% of Black and 10% of Hispanics/Latinos believe their race/ethnicity is represented.
- Ethnic groups are not homogeneous. For example, in the United States, an individual's Hispanic identity is strongly tied to an individual's culture of origin. This means there isn't one typical type of Hispanic consumer, but rather dozens, depending on their cultural roots: someone from Mexico has a different cultural lens than someone from Puerto Rico or someone from Brazil. Also in our society today, an increasing number of Hispanics are becoming more interested in the Spanish language, and many Hispanics believe the Spanish language is more important today than it was five years ago.
- Millennials, in particular, tend to reject the traditional society and demographic labels that most advertisers use on a regular basis, and instead embrace what has been termed a polycultural identity: the mix and match cultural rituals, values, and belief systems to create their own versions of self. How to address what Facebook called "Omni-cultural Identities"—the idea that people will embrace more personalized, complex and fluid means of self-identifying—is a huge challenge. Agencies are often challenged to understand how to include polyculture in their marketing.
- Messages are just the beginning. Advertising and brand managers need to understand different cultural audiences, how they use media, what their interests are and how they communicate among one another and with the brands they like. Do they engage directly via Twitter, or do they share content on Facebook?

## Different perspectives on marketing

### *Multicultural marketing*

One term you may have heard is multicultural marketing. The term multicultural marketing assumes that any target audience—such as women aged 25–54 years—contain several cultural or ethnic groups. In a multicultural society, people from these different cultural or ethnic groups live and work alongside one another, and each individual experiences the interaction of different cultural influences on themselves and their community. The goal of multicultural marketing is for brands to look deeper into their target consumer demographics and identify specific motivations, aspirations, and purchase drivers for each segment.

Multicultural markets generally have different campaigns/efforts for different segments. Multicultural marketing provides opportunities for brands to engage with their consumers outside of the "majority audience," looking at specific consumer segments based on ethnic and sociocultural patterns in order to build a deeper emotional connection that increases the chance of a conversion.

Consumers outside of the majority audience make up nearly 40% of the U.S. population. Yet only 5.2% of the total advertising and marketing spends is directed towards them. A multicultural approach starts with ethnic segments to develop marketing programs that cross over into the general market. Multicultural ads can run on mainstream and ethnic media, and may include languages other than English.

### *Polycultural marketing*

Polycultural marketing is different from multicultural marketing in that it assumes the world is somewhat segment-free. Instead, each individual creates their own identity by borrowing from a variety of cultures, creating their own unique polycultural reality. The majority of babies born during the early part of this century—meaning the 18-to-24-year-olds of 2020—are not White. Because of this fact, advertising and marketing are changing. Americans, particularly younger ones, see themselves as inclusive and have blended their views of culture, self-identification, and ethnicity. Advertising can no longer rely on using what used to be the dominant culture—White culture—as the primary message in advertising.

Polycultural marketing, then, puts demographics (particularly ethnicity) aside, and looks at the values and motivations that match well with the values and benefits of the brand. For example, the Converse campaign "Day-jobbers" focused on the fact that many people who are artistically inclined need to have a mundane "day job" to support their passion. In one ad, shots of a young Latino man wearing a bee costume to pass out fliers on a busy street are interspersed with the same young man performing with his band. The words "this is my job" appear on an image of the man in his costume, while the words "not what I do" appear on an image of the man playing drums. The spots end with the hashtag #whoIam. This campaign speaks to key motivations of younger people in society.

Advertisers who focus on polycultural marketing view advertisers who use the multicultural method of creating messages to be at risk of producing tone-deaf messages. Having a "mainstream" campaign (e.g., one directed at White Americans) accompanied by a "Black" and a "Hispanic" campaign may not resonate well, particularly with younger consumers.

In reality, many brands and advertisers use a combination of approaches to marketing that consider an entire market with an appreciation of how cultural forces can shape trends and consumer behavior. Large brands across the country consider both multicultural and polycultural strategies in order to make sure ads are seen as culturally relevant.

### *The whole market/total market approach*

A blend of the abovesaid two approaches is known as the whole market or total market approach. A total market approach does not consider ethnic differences in the marketing message but seeks to reach as many people as possible with the same message. A total market approach often uses diverse talent in messages but goes beyond that.

A whole market/total market campaign delivers relevance that cuts across the broadest possible audience, that are otherwise disparate consumer segments. This is based on a universally shared insight—one that captures their realities, values and needs. With an insight that underpins a strategy, the whole market idea can be expressed in different ways and implemented differently depending on the segment. In marketing communications, this could lead to either one fully integrated approach, individual segment approaches, or both in many cases, but always aligned under one overarching strategy.

Whole market campaigns can create marketing efficiencies of a total market strategy. The efficiencies often rely on the media reach of their campaigns, but they also include internal team collaboration and support. It can also increase brand equity through integration, coherence and message repetition; this builds the brand across all consumer segments, regardless of race or ethnicity. Brand equity is built on the number of consumer touch points as well as the quality of the message.

Two concepts are important to understand the whole market approach: process and perspective.

- **Process** is about starting with ethnic segments versus "general market." This sounds simple and almost trivial, but it's neither. The vast majority of advertising developed in this country is done from a general market-*first* perspective. This is a result of who drives these decisions at the highest levels at large brands and advertising agencies.
- **Perspective** is about deeply understanding and leveraging ethnic consumers. This is more difficult. Perspective comes from working in the trenches, from deeply understanding Hispanic, African American, Asian and other ethnic consumers. Many times, it comes from being an ethnic consumer yourself. As with the point about process, this lack of perspective is a structural issue in Madison Avenue. This is where multicultural marketers shine.

One example of the total market approach is the fast-food chain Denny's. The brand is looking to target young, multicultural diners with their campaign "See You at Denny's." The advertising in this campaign focuses on illustrating a diverse, relaxed, and comfortable brand. The campaign shows Denny's as a place where people of all backgrounds, races and religions can come together, be themselves and make connections. John Dillon, the chief brand officer at Denny's, explained that Denny's is a family brand that recognizes that the American family has evolved. The company has hired three agencies with expertise in diversity—fluent360, Conill and EP+Co—to bring its message to life, targeted at different audiences. One ad features a young girl saying, "If you look around, we're not all so different. We all want a friend we can talk to. We all want somewhere where we can be ourselves, a place where it's OK to be different. And, sure there's tension out there. But here, you leave that all at the door."

## It all starts with a universal insight

New approaches to marketing begin with what is a referred to as a cultural orientation mindset. The cultural orientation mindset includes two unique values: cultural attachment and cultural openness.

- Cultural attachment addresses the idea of how individuals experience and find security and comfort in different cultures, be it their own native culture and/or other cultures they have extensive exposure to.
- Cultural openness is the degree to which people to navigate within and across different cultural groups, absorbing the elements that work within their preferred lifestyle, but not necessarily at the cost of pride and participation in their native culture.

Finding these touchpoints can allow for the development of more nuanced campaigns.

Earlier, we discussed the importance of cultural intelligence in the workplace, and it is also important to deal with developing a campaign that targets a wide variety of customers. You will recall that cultural intelligence is the ability to read the world without feeling threatened in the presence of someone who is different, either because of race, socioeconomic status, appearance, personal abilities or sexual orientation. Superior cultural intelligence takes it up a notch with the ability to relate to those who are different, engage in dialogue, work together or develop personal relationships.

This can be enhanced by a concept called color bravery, that was introduced in a TED Talk by Mellody Hobson. Color bravery means being realistic about race issues and addressing them directly. This is important since many U.S. Consumers, including ethnic minority consumers, believe businesses are too concerned about offending the general population and hence fail to take a stand on issues that matter to minorities.

A universal insight recognizes that cultural attachment and cultural openness are important ways to find commonalities between different people. This recognizes that each individual has a unique set of "tribes" that they feel they belong to, as well as a range of "tribes" that they feel like they understand and would like to be part of. There are universal values that people hold, such as security, tradition, freedom, and benevolence. These values might get manifested in different ways but finding those values in different cultural contexts is a good first step to developing a universal insight. Denny's, for example, used the universal value of benevolence and friendship to position itself as a place where all kinds of people can come together. The campaign was produced in both English and Spanish.

## Campaign development

As an account manager, there are several things you can do to shepherd the campaign process that addresses the new reality.

- Recognize that brands need to do more, not less, and a multicultural approach is not a method to save money. Many brands might think that with a whole market campaign, in particular, they can reduce resources allocated to ethnic marketing. However, the whole market philosophy means that ethnic marketing requires a bigger investment, from media spending to strategic planning.
- Language is perhaps one of the most sensitive aspects to be considered when considering messages. If not addressed correctly, language can be a huge source of misunderstanding: a word which is completely neutral in a certain language can be offensive or even obscene in another. Also, within the same language, there may be different dialects with different nuances that have to be taken into account.

- The development of niche ads that are highly segmented and delivered in a language other than English can suffer from a generic treatment that doesn't resonate with the target audience because the creative process gets interrupted once the words have been translated from English. Furthermore, the language needs to be addressed in developing advertising for a multicultural world.
- Marketers need to avoid using stereotypes all the time, but especially when developing a multicultural campaign. Stereotyping is defined as the oversimplification of something that is more complex than it's portrayed. In reality, people are complex and cannot be defined by single role. In advertising, labels are commonly used to portray an individual or group of people in a very specific light. The dad who can't take care of the kids, the really smart Asian student, the silly blonde woman—all of these stereotypes can be seen in advertising today, and none of these reflect the complex nature of human beings.
- Build empathy. Your strategy should display a genuine understanding of consumer needs and their roots in their cultural/socioeconomic background. In fact, the best multicultural marketing campaigns aim to build empathy by showing how well the brand understands the consumer.
- Recognize and respect multicultural social norms. Some advertising may try to take a short cut and utilize social norms from a culture in an ad, but these can be problematic because people would get offended if they see that their own social norms are not being respected. In order to avoid this, it is, first of all, important to understand the cultural values that people hold dear. People from certain religions, for instance, don't accept jokes related to their belief. References to politics and other social aspects in advertisements may be appreciated by some groups, but others may not appreciate them at all.
- Understand the importance of visuals. Any type of image or scenario can be interpreted in different ways by different people—this is all due to their cultural perception of life. Something as simple as a color choice can be imbued with implied meaning: black symbolizes death in some cultures, while in some cultures white symbolizes death, and in other cultures red does.
- Media choices are important considerations as well. It is imperative that the communicator understand that different cultures have different ways of attending to and interpreting advertising messages, and vary in terms of the media channels they engage with. For instance, print media might be better for a campaign directed towards consumers in the 60–75 years age bracket, while interactive platforms like Snapchat or TikTok are better suited to Gen Z.

Media selection should be guided by research, and your media department colleagues should be clear about the data they use to make decisions. For example, if you are planning a mobile campaign, you should learn that research by Nielsen uncovered that Black consumers aged 35 and over are much more active mobile phone users than Whites and Hispanics. Different cultures use different types of digital platforms. Hispanic adults are highly involved in digital activities—much more than non-Hispanic Whites, non-Hispanic Black, or Asians. For example, over 85% of Hispanic adults do as many as 14 different digital activities (such as watching YouTube videos or listening to Spotify) every month, compared to the seven digital activities of non-Hispanic whites and the six digital activities that non-Hispanic African-Americans do each month.

- Become familiar with culture clubs: One interesting way to consider multicultural audience is to think about the notion of "cultural clubs." Culture clubs are digital platforms with in-culture content. Respondents would be more likely to pay more attention, trust the brand more and buy from a brand if their ads were placed in culture club communities.

  According to Digital Lives 2018, ads promoted in "culture club" places have more power across ages and languages.
- Focus on the three R's—real, relevant, and respectful. These three elements should be present in every marketing campaign, but even more so in those that are targeted at diverse audience. The brand message should be real and authentic, and communicated in a culturally relevant way that respects your audience. If the message misses one of these aspects, it should be reconsidered.
- Have a multifaceted strategy, as the "one size fits all" approach isn't going to work well. Work with your account planners to identify the key types of research that will inform insights to guide your strategy and creative. Be sure diverse voices are reflected in the research—make sure you know who the audience is and, most importantly, what motivates different individuals in the target audience. Remember, these individuals may be first-generation Americans or from a family that has been here for decades. They may be straight or LGBTQ. They may speak English, they may speak Spanish, they may speak Urdu—and they may be bilingual or trilingual. They may be entrepreneurs, teachers, construction workers, doctors, athletes, artists and engineers—multicultural means multidimensional. This is a great opportunity for brands as they have multiple points to connect with consumers.
- Be the wave. Many brands use multicultural marketing to make a splash—to have a quick hit to show as many people as possible that the brand is engaged and involved with diverse consumers. What's more impactful and lasting than a splash is a wave.

  Picture a wave in your mind. Waves create ripples. Brands create ripples when they seek out diverse talent in tune with culture and emerging trends. These people know how to create waves—unlike brands that are opportunistic and tend to ride the waves, they create their own waves. These newly created waves will better reflect culture.
- Expand the table. Have seats at the table for more people to be sure that the best people are informing these decisions from start to finish. Brands and agencies need multicultural minds and diverse voices to effectively shape strategies.

## Expanding the table: the importance of a diverse workforce

Concerning this late point, the bottom line is that marketers, advertisers and messages should focus on the ability to unite rather than divide people. Marketers can't be afraid to have real, and sometimes uncomfortable, conversations with brands to develop messaging and programming that resonates with diverse consumers and respects their cultures.

In Chapter 6, we discussed about the importance of a diverse workforce, and this is a critical best practice to remember when launching a multicultural or whole market campaign. A message directed at one consumer group shouldn't be perceived as offensive to another. The decision-making team requires contributions from multiple voices across gender, age, economic, cultural, and locational divides. As explained in Robin D'Angelo's book "White Fragility"—the question asked shouldn't be whether a claim is true or false: or to say another way, the question isn't whether an ad is racist, or sexist, or ageist. Instead, we should investigate the ways that a message might perceived as racist (or sexist or ageist). Bringing diverse viewpoints to the table is one way to make sure that happens.

If existing decision-makers are not adequately diverse, agencies should consider following the practice that Denny's used in developing their new campaign—they hired several different agencies to work together to make sure that diversity was represented at the table.

The lack of a diverse workforce might be seen in what happened with a Dove ad that showed a Black woman removing her top to reveal a White woman underneath supposedly after using Dove body lotion. Dove spokespeople insisted that the ad was not meant to be a "before and after" ad and said that they "... do not condone any activity or imagery that intentionally insults any audience." However, the damage to Dove had been done, with thousands of people indicating their displeasure on social media.

Some key considerations to building a diverse workforce are as follows.

- Start by asking the people in the agency: "Do we want to be diverse or look diverse?" Just because a diverse employee has a seat at the table, it does not mean they have influence at the table. Employers need to commit to listen to the people they invite to the table.
- Ensure that the job description is written in an inclusive manner. Job descriptions should include language that not only appeals to a broad range of applicants but also highlights institutional goals of creating an innovative and vibrant community where diversity of thought and experience is welcomed and encouraged.
- Widely disseminate the opportunity. To find diverse candidates, employers need to get out of their community—and their comfort zone. Employers must put in the work to actively research and tap into diverse community groups and encourage their leadership and hiring managers to get affiliated with diverse nonprofits, boards, local and national industry groups, schools and vendors.
- Utilize their internal recruiting resources: their employees. Many internal employees are well-respected in their communities, especially in communities of color. The most important thing is, by utilizing this source, it endears the employees' loyalty to the firm to a much greater extent. This loyalty is paid off by a referral of a case that has made worldwide headlines.
- Actively reach out to diverse candidate pools. The best talent needs to be headhunted and made aware of the opportunity. Many high-performing candidates are currently happy in their jobs and aren't regularly reading job postings and ads. Recruiters are specially trained to reach out to a range of candidates, particularly those who aren't actively interested in a new job.
- Consider asking for blind resumes. Blind resumes help avoid unconscious bias against non-White names or certain schools or backgrounds. Employers should not be hiring from only certain schools, their alma maters and so on. Try to focus less on whether you "like" the person. The emphasis should be on the skills and experience they bring to the table: "What would this person add to the team that we're missing?" as opposed to "This person is just like us. They'll fit right in!"
- Establish a consistent interview panel trained to check bias, A bias is just part of a larger story played in your mind. We must control our own stories in our heads. Don't fight it. Instead, acknowledge it, put it out there and talk through it.

- Interviews should pose the same set of questions in the same order to all candidates, allowing clearer comparisons between them. This may seem like an obvious approach, but, incredibly, it remains underused. Some people find that if interviewers score each answer immediately after it is provided, it can neutralize a variety of biases: Evaluators who wait until the end of the interview to rate answers risk forgetting an early or less-vivid but high-quality answer.
- Consider comparing candidate responses horizontally—that is, comparing the answers on question one across all candidates. This reduces the chance that one answer will influence the scores on subsequent questions. Comparative evaluations, arguably, can decrease the reflex to rely on stereotypes to guide our impressions.
- Be transparent about the culture of the organization. Candidates want to see diversity at the senior levels. No diverse candidate wants to feel like they are the "token" hire. Tokenizing the diverse staff members instead of elevating them and including them in the same way as all other staff should be avoided.
- Think about identifying and introducing possible mentors during the interview. A mentor will serve to check in with the person regularly and make sure things are going well. A new environment can sometimes lead to loneliness, isolation and a sense of not belonging. A mentor would ask them what they want or need, listen to their response, then give them the tools they need to succeed while giving them challenging work and valuing their contributions.

## Summary

Today's society is a multicultural society, and successful advertising often shows a recognition for the importance of diversity and inclusion in order to appeal to the range of people who live in the United States. A consistent strategy is essential to the brand; once the strategy is established, brands can consider whether executions can appeal to a whole market or if separate campaigns to reach specific groups are warranted.

## Discussion questions

1 Do you see yourself represented in media today? If yes, in what ways?
2 What are the different ways the media (and advertising) present college students? Does this reflect your reality?
3 What types of images of college students would you like to see portrayed?
4 What brands do you think are doing a good job of showing people from different cultures in messages? Which ones are doing a bad job of the same?

## Case 13.1 Barrands Agency

### *Issue: advertising spokespeople*

Lisa Blunt, account director of the Barrands Agency, couldn't believe her eyes when she surfed the Internet for the news headlines that morning. She quickly turned on the television to see if she could confirm it. Yes, it was true.

Taylor Lively had been stopped for erratic driving at 3 o'clock that morning in Los Angeles. Her blood alcohol level was at 0.10%—much higher than the 0.08% limit in California—and the arresting officer found cocaine in the glove box. This wasn't the first time that Taylor had been in trouble with the law. She was a known kleptomaniac and had taken a wig and four coats last month from a dress shop in Beverly Hills. She even was caught shoplifting a cigarette lighter from a convenience store just two weeks ago. But, until now, she had never been caught with drugs. Various outlets reported that Taylor was heading to rehab immediately.

Taylor was the spokesperson for one of the Barrands Agency clients, Glam Girl, a new beauty product line-up, that was taking the teenage market by storm. The Glam Girl line included skin care products such as cleanser and moisturizer, as well as make-up products including tinted moisturizer, lip gloss, and mascara. Taylor was the perfect spokesperson since she had a No. 1 hit single record and was in a variety of television sitcoms watched by teenage girls. Taylor had cultivated that "clean-cut teen idol" image that fit with what Glam Girl was all about.

Tim Barrands, founder and president of the Barrands Agency, came into Lisa's office with Bobbi Hazeltine, the creative director. Tim said, "Lisa, we need to call our lawyers and begin to cancel Taylor's contract with Glam Girl and alert the media team to immediately cancel our ads. We need to be proactive on this issue before the client calls." Bobbi Hazeltine said, "Thank goodness that girl got caught. I hated working with her and her agent. Frankly, I was thinking about quitting because of her. Now we can move ahead and make Jamila the primary spokesperson."

Jamila was an up-and-coming singer and model. Born in Chicago, she had a musical style that was a mix of soulful vocals with retro-funk influences. She wrote many of her own songs and worked with some of the top hip-hop producers. She had a dancer's body, and very long dreadlocks that were part of her signature style. She had been a secondary spokesperson for Glam Girl, and was featured in their make-up ads for Black and Hispanic girls. She was easy to work with, and both Bobbi and Lisa agreed she could easily replace Taylor.

The phone rang, and Judi Mitchell, the head of marketing for Glam Girl, was on the line. Instead of being upset with the situation, she was upbeat:

> Lisa, this is the break we were looking for. Glam Girl needs to have a bit more 'bad girl' image and this is our break. And if we stay with Taylor while she is down, we can be there as she rises out of rehab. You know, they say that any publicity is good publicity. Well, we can get millions of dollars of publicity for Glam Girl out of this.

Lisa took a deep breath: "Well, Judi, that's an option, but another option is Jamila. She's very popular with the minority markets and her last single really pulled her into the mainstream. She is already on contract, and she's so easy to work with. What do you think about Jamila?"

After a long pause, Judi said,

> I don't know, Lisa. Jamila is fine for the minority make-up campaigns but we need a star for the mainstream campaign. I'm not sure suburban cheerleaders can relate to Jamila. And our current skin care line hasn't been formulated to work on a variety of skin types—do we know it would work well on Black skin? Think about Taylor and call me back.

### Questions

1 What should Lisa counsel her client to do?
2 What is the most ethical course of action?
3 Is the ethical course of action the best business strategy?
4 Is this an advertising issue or a legal issue or both?
5 How would you change a spokesperson without damaging the brand?

Chapter 14

# Managing the brand's digital assets

## LEARNING OBJECTIVES

This chapter is intended to help you:

- Understand what a digital asset is.
- Understand what digital asset management entails.
- Understand why it is important to manage assets.
- Learn how to manage assets.

Most brands are collections of stories. For these brands, digital media and content play important roles in telling that story. The longer a brand has been around, the more digital assets would be in existence.

Everyone tends to have their own individual way to organize the information that is important to them, but this method may not be the best way for agencies. While advertising, branding, creative and marketing agencies may have different offerings, there's one thing they share in common: they all create a ton of assets. They create files for design concepts, pitch decks and marketing campaigns, and must distribute them to their clients efficiently. With hundreds of assets and multiple clients, this can be a real challenge.

## What are digital assets?

Agencies and clients create many different types of content during the course of a campaign, and if these digital files contain the rights to use them, they are considered an asset. The idea of rights means that the digital asset cannot be shared without consent of the entity that owns the asset—usually the client.

Agencies may also buy assets, such as stock photos, for use in campaigns.

Basic asset types include the following.

- Emails
- Photos
- Slide decks
- Excel spreadsheets
- Word documents
- Brochures
- Sales letters
- Blog posts
- Articles

- Logos
- Videos: these can include product demos, product review, video ads, interviews, video testimonials and live streaming
- Images: photographs and drawings
- Audio recordings (such as podcasts)
- PDFs
- White papers

There are several key elements that make any single file a digital asset. A digital asset must:

- be a digital file.
- provide value to the company.
- be unique. It should be automatically associated with your brand (not your competitor's brand) in the minds of consumers.
- be directly connected and recognizable for your brand.

Here are some examples of digital assets.

- The Nike Swoosh
- Images of the Aflac Duck
- The designs for the Coca-Cola bottle
- Drawings of "Tony the Tiger"
- Images of the McDonald's golden arches
- Kit Kat's "Give me a break" jingle
- Sephora's podcast #liplines

## What is digital asset management?

When a communications effort is being developed, new digital assets may be created and existing digital assets may be incorporated into a new piece of communication. As iterations are discussed and reviewed internally at the agency and externally with the client, agencies may need access to stock photos (i.e., photos purchased for use from an external source), stock video, and specific images, as well as to copy, brand imagery, and logos. The development of a single campaign may require the use of several dozen assets—some created by the agency, some purchased from external sources and some provided by the client.

Keeping all these organized is the goal of digital asset management (DAM). A DAM system keeps branding materials relevant by centrally storing large amounts of contents. The files will be stored on the cloud and backed up. In addition, the files are tagged with information that allow for quick and easy search and retrieval.

A DAM system is valuable at four different points of the advertising and marketing process.

1 Design and creation: copywriters, art directors, and others involved in content creation can review how the brand's style has evolved in regard to copy, layout and graphic design. Editing of content can also occur in a DAM system.

2 Approvals: creative directions, account people, legal representatives, and clients can access work to approve copy and design.
3 Storage and maintenance: management and legal representatives can understand the scope of assets available to the brand, and can also track usage of different assets.
4 Customization and distribution: management, franchisees, and clients outside of brand management can utilize assets to maintain a consistent brand look while localizing and personalizing content.

## Benefits of DAM

There are many benefits to having a DAM program at both the agency and the client.

- Everyone involved with a brand knows what you have and where they can find the assets. Without a management strategy, your digital assets will be spread across many computers and file systems. With a DAM program in place, content access is democratized as everyone can have access to the content that they use on a regular basis.
- Anything associated with your brand will have a level of consistency. DAM helps your organization ensure brand consistency. In turn, it encourages brand loyalty. User adoption can be a challenge within agencies, which is why leadership endorsement is essential for a successful implementation. Art directors and writers inherently dislike process and often may prefer email, social communities or Basecamp-like applications for sharing and reviewing files. If your company is going to invest in digital asset management, you need to communicate how important it is to own and use, and that there is value in collaborating on it.
- DAM improves client relationships as client requests can be answered quickly and efficiently. Clients require a lot of individual attention and effort. As content is being developed, sharing of the content with clients can turn from a simple process (e.g., sending an email with a logo) to a complex situation fairly quickly. Clients can lose or misplace emails, and you'll get messages to resend the content. But if the designers have done additional work, it may be unclear what should be sent out. A DAM system allows for a more controlled process where you can control what clients are looking at.
- Tagging assets with keywords allow for an easy-to-understand system. A DAM system allows people to find and share images more easily. The system includes a way to tag and organize assets by keywords to improve searchability. Agencies have to deal with a lot of files and a lot of clients. Clients, meanwhile, often have multiple people on staff, and sometimes other contractors and parties, who all have to access different digital assets. Far too often, the marketing agencies themselves get stuck with the hassle of having to try to manage files, and distribution and access to these files.
- It becomes possible to track usage of different assets over time, providing information on asset popularity. DAM systems also support extensive logs of all activities so that you can track changes to individual files, and also be informed when files are uploaded to the system. If something is moved, sent to the trash, uploaded or whatever, as an administrator you'll be able to find out who did what and when. This can come in very handy when a situation arises.

- DAM eliminates redundancy. Instead of creating new photographs of a 30-year-old woman using fabric softener, a quick check of a DAM system can indicate that there are currently a dozen such photos in existence, eliminating the need for an additional photo shoot. The DAM allows agencies and clients to more efficiently repurpose assets for other markets outside the one where the asset was created; the cost of campaigns can be reduced if existing assets can be reused.
- A DAM system helps to ensure the outdated assets aren't used. Using an outdated asset is not only embarrassing, but it can derail a client's brand consistency and appear unprofessional. Helping a client maintain a consistent brand image is crucial for agencies and using a DAM software ensures brand consistency across both in-house content as well as creatives developed by agency partners. The platform serves as a central source of truth: No matter what a user needs, they will get an asset that is current, and can convert it to whatever format they need to complete the project.
- A DAM system can improve collaboration between the ad agency and the client, and among a client's agencies. DAM allows you to collaborate on project workflow from creation to approval and execution. Let's say your creative team has developed a 32-page brochure for your client, and you've sent them the first draft for review. Now, multiple parties start reviewing and commenting on each page. It is very easy to lose control of the overview when emails with comments start flowing back and forth between multiple parties. Some digital asset management solutions have built-in commenting and online proofing features that makes it easy to track changes on a wide variety of documents. These features enable you to add comments and markers on each page, pointing out exactly where changes are needed. And everybody invited to the process can see exactly who has asked for which changes. Finally, when the changes have been implemented and a new version is uploaded, you can approve each page. And again, it is clear to everybody who has approved or rejected each specific page.
- A DAM program improves privacy and security. DAM enables secure file transfer and file backup. With an online digital asset management system, you can organize all of your clients' files easily and securely. This reduces the risk of files ever being lost, deleted, or destroyed. For example, most DAM systems operate with a trash feature, where selected users are allowed to delete files, but only administrators can actually empty the trash. This makes it much less likely for a file to be accidentally deleted by a client who is not so tech-savvy. Additionally, a DAM system ensures that anyone who leaves a company will not take the assets with them.

## Managing digital assets

Often, agencies manage their digital assets (i.e., images, design files, videos, and other rich media) using systems and protocols they have developed themselves. These methods cost valuable time to maintain, and also come with very few—if any—safeguards against redundancy, version control, or the loss of digital files due to storage malfunction, physical damage or accidental deletion.

### *Identify who has assets*

Many people on both the agency and the client side are likely to have assets stored in laptops and desktop computers. Reach out to everyone in the agency who has ever worked on the business to find out what assets they have. Arrange a simple way for them to send the assets to you—either through some type of file transfer protocol or through email. Ask a client contact to do the same thing with their assets. As people move on to work on different brands, be sure you request them to include their assets in the DAM system.

### *Centralize your media library*

Collect all of your assets so that you can know what you have and how each asset has been used. It usually makes sense to put all your assets in a type of cloud storage location, such as a formal digital asset management software program or some consumer option like Google Drive or Dropbox. This ensures that the assets aren't spread out over the agency and client offices.

### *Name and tag your assets*

This part of the process is likely to take a long amount of time. It will also require a level of agreement among different stakeholders in the DAM system. This process allows each asset to be properly identified so that it can be found quickly.

The information used to describe a digital asset is known as metadata, which technically means "data about data." The idea is to describe a digital asset by using terms that are associated with it, which could include:

- The year the asset was created
- The name of the asset (such as Coke bottle label)
- A description of asset (such as packaging label)
- The color of the item
- The author/creator's name
- Keywords

As you're deciding on your tagging scheme, think of the following.

- Consider your users: think about the information that users (such as agency and brand personnel) are likely to associate with assets. This is what they are likely to search for when using the digital asset database.
- Be consistent when you decide on your names: if you use data created for a few assets, use it on all your assets.
- Think about keywords and provide some guidance on how keywords can be connected. Keywords can be very subjective, so for a large group of assets, it might be helpful to create a robust list of possible keywords that could possibly be used to tag assets.

This can be a somewhat tedious activity but very important for the strength of the system. Be sure the naming process is clearly documented.

### *Track your assets*

Once your database of assets is developed, be sure to track what assets are accessed and used most often. If you know how frequently a product image is downloaded by users or staff, for instance, you might be able to decide to produce more or fewer images in the future.

### *Promote the system to potential users*

You will need everyone to get excited about the software, systems and protocols. An introductory email with some type of training program might work well. Think about identifying "experts" in various departments who can serve as point people for the system.

### *Consider a software program*

DAM software programs aren't inexpensive, but they can provide value to an organization. DAM programs include offerings from Adobe, Brandfolder and Cloudinary.

These software programs can:

- Organize digital assets in a central location.
- Automate workflows to promote creativity.
- Quickly find digital assets using sophisticated search capabilities.
- Manage press kits and picture collections.
- Automate watermarking for images.
- Tag images automatically, even using facial recognition for headshots.

## Summary

Brands have many, many digital assets, and finding a way to organize them is important for brand success. Digital asset management allows people to quickly and efficiently find and use assets they need, and also keep assets from "leaving the office" when people move on to different jobs.

## Discussion questions

1 Digital asset management is often an overlooked function. What is the value of DAM?
2 Why should DAM be part of an account manager's responsibilities?
3 Do an online image search for a brand you like (e.g., Coca-Cola, Heineken, or Forever 21). Take five images that come up on the search and identify the types of tags that you might give to these images in order to organize them. Think of three or four broad categories (such as the type of product, or the location of the ad) and then assign hashtags to each image to show how that image might be categorized.

## Case 14.1 AdLeaders

### *Issue: digital asset management*

Joonghwa Lee is an account executive at AdLeaders, a large global agency based in Los Angeles. He works on several medium-size clients, and oversees the creation and implementation of both the traditional and digital content that his agency develops. He has a dedicated assistant account executive working under him on each of the following accounts.

- Kookaburra Coffee: a chain of 50 coffee shops located in California, Nevada, Arizona and New Mexico. About a fourth are franchise stores, where franchisees pay in about 3% of their sales to participate in advertising campaigns. Marketing messages include seasonal (holiday) television ads, radio ads, in-store signage, and a variety of digital content.
- First Health Credit Union: a national credit union for people who work in the health care industries. Credit Unions differ from traditional banks as all members are stakeholders. Members select the board of directors, and the board sets the vision and direction of the brand. As a nonprofit, any profits are used to support members and the locations of the Credit Unions by fewer and reduced fees, increased saving rates, and lower loan rates. Marketing messages include television, radio and newspaper ads, digital content, out-of-home including billboards and taxi tops, brochures talking about various types of accounts offered by the Credit Union.
- Baker's Best: a line of high-end kitchen products that are sold in specialized kitchen and gourmet stores. Their products include stand mixers, cold-rolled steel baking pans with nonstick surfaces, and silicone baking mats. They run print ads in high-end cooking magazines and digital ads on a variety of online baking sites. They also provide in-store signage to the retailers who sell their products.

Joonghwa has been overseeing the development of digital asset management systems for all three brands for the past two years. AdLeaders has a DAM policy that states that only people who are currently working on the account from the agency and client side have access to the assets stored in the DAM. Every asset that is created by the agency—whether produced and presented to the public or not—is entered into the DAM system.

A typical day for Joonghwa includes the following types of interactions.

- Colleen Case, the brand manager at Baker's Best, is putting together a presentation for the 50th anniversary of the brand and asks for Joonghwa's help. Joonghwa knows that the DAM has more than 65 years of assets that have been digitized.

What keywords might Joonghwa use in order to come up with assets to highlight in Colleen's presentation?

- Joonghwa creates a new file in the DAM system where he copies some of the assets that might be useful for Colleen's presentation and Colleen is very appreciative. She does note that she has an asset that is not in the system that she wants to include. On receiving the asset from Colleen, Joonghwa checks the DAM system and identifies that the asset was not created by the agency—it was one that was created by one of the retailers that sells Baker's Best products. As he looked at the asset, Joonghwa felt that the brand and product information is not getting communicated in the way desired by the agency and agreed to by the client.

What should he do?

- Kookaburra Coffee's newest big idea is to have a personalized campaign—they want the agency to create coffee sleeves that read "John bought me a coffee" or "Lauren bought me this coffee" in order to encourage people to buy coffee for friends. Using data collected by Kookaburra Coffee, the agency has come up with 200 most-used names that people give when ordering their coffee. These 200 different coffee sleeves are scheduled to be produced soon. Mark Marshall, the traffic manager, doesn't think each individual coffee sleeve needs to be entered into the DAM system.

Should Joonghwa agree with him, or not? What reasons should Joonghwa give for his opinion?

- Joonghwa's boss, Alice Martinez, saw an ad for a competitor of Kookaburra Coffee that looks like an execution proposed by a former copywriter, Len Black. Len left AdLeaders for another agency six months ago. Alice questioned whether the competitor's ad was developed while Len was at AdLeaders.

Is this something that the DAM system could help answer?

- One of the Kookaburra Coffee's franchisees calls Joonghwa to report of a great opportunity—she can purchase a mobile ad on the app of a local county fair that she's willing to pay for out of pocket. She has some old mobile ads that she used a few years back that she really likes and wants to be sure it is OK to use them.

What should Joonghwa do, and how can the DAM system help him with it?

- A new campaign for First Health Credit Union features a car loan rate that changes every week—one week the APR might be 3.09, while the next week it might be 3.16. The agency sends print ads directly from the DAM system to the local newspaper, *The Pacific Times*, every Thursday to run in the Friday issue of the paper. The print ads contain the most recent rate. If the rate is incorrect, First Health Credit Union must honor the rate until a new rate appears in the newspaper.

One Friday, the assistant AE on First Health Credit Union brings in a copy of the day's issue to Joonghwa—*The Pacific Times* has run the wrong ad.

How can the DAM help Joonghwa determine what happened?

- A copywriter on the First Health Credit Union account has emailed Joonghwa asking for access to the First Health DAM system in order to get some inspiration for a new campaign.

What are the pros and cons of Joonghwa granting the copywriter's request? What would you do if you were Joonghwa?

Chapter 15

# Advertising management when things go wrong

## LEARNING OBJECTIVES

This chapter is intended to help you:

- Understand the notion of brand reputation and reputation management.
- Identify the skills necessary to manage reputation.
- Understand the role of social media in reputation management.
- Understand how to plan for crises.

As careful as one can be with their planning, there will always be a time when something goes wrong. A number of situations can have a negative effect on a brand, and the account manager must be ready at a moment's notice to deal with any and all unexpected problems.

Most—virtually all—problems can and will be solved. The challenge to a brand is that in today's world, consumers have immediate access to all kinds of information about brands, and most of this information contributes to a brand's reputation. The idea of reputation management suggests that a brand's reputation can contribute huge value, and our reputations can be key differentiators. Every day, our reputations are bringing opportunities to create a competitive advantage.

## Elements of brand reputation

The account manager should have a firm grasp on the status of the brand's reputation, particularly online. The key elements to understanding (and, if needed, improving) brand reputation include the following.

- Advertising: understanding the key takeaways that your campaign messages provide to consumers
- Public relations: Strong mentions in the press and in the public eye, such as through thought-leadership articles in online and traditional content, as well as through public speaking opportunities, can improve brand perceptions. A strong PR program positions brands and their representatives as thought leaders and experts in their field.
- Search engine optimization (SEO): When customers search for resources and solutions to timely problems, brands should be ready to offer help. SEO uses strategic keywords and content to drive traffic to a brand website.

- Content marketing: Producing lead-generating content such as white papers, blogs, and industry report across an array of channels raises awareness about your brand and benefits of your products.
- Website development: An easy-to-navigate website that provides an enjoyable user experience will improve brand loyalty.
- Social media: Social media is a great way to make your business accessible, personable and focused on the customer.

Some clients may hire specialized agencies for these projects, while other agencies will offer full service and clients may see them as a one-stop shop. The account manager's role will be to ensure that the strategic message is consistent across all efforts, and that the brand image is not diluted as it moves from platform to platform. The brand positioning statement can provide the touchstone for a variety of efforts to be sure that the brand image is consistent: This is the fastest way to a strong brand reputation.

## When things go wrong

Everyone makes mistakes. Things that are out of our control may happen. Unexpected happenings can either help or hurt a brand but being poised to deal with an unexpected event can help make sure that brand reputations stay intact.

In general, a brand manager has to deal with three broad categories of unexpected events.

- Issues about the work
- Issues about the client
- Societal issues

### *Issues about the work*

What types of things can happen that can affect the work? Here are a few: a great creative can move to a competitor's agency, a media planner can mess up the placement of a print ad or television spot, or a digital designer can put the wrong price on the product featured in a digital ad.

The most important thing an account manager can do is to understand what went wrong, figure out how to fix it, and then get in touch with the client to let them know what is happening. No one at the agency feels good when a mistake is made, and the account manager has to make sure that everyone knows that mistakes are part of life, and quickly mobilize the people involved to fix the problem.

For example, if a deadline is missed and a television ad won't run, the agency needs to quickly figure out how to make up the impression that the television ad would deliver. If the wrong price is published in digital content, the agency must quickly correct the price.

Both of these situations may cause a financial loss to the client. If the television ad was promoting a short-term event, and the lack of the ad limited the number of people who might attend, then the client would lose money. Similarly, the client has to honor the price in the digital ad until it is corrected. They may lose money from this as well. The account manager and the client might have to negotiate some type of cost renumeration for the agency's mistake.

The account manager's efforts in the immediate aftermath of discovering a mistake will show their interest and engagement in the business. Afterwards, the account manager should investigate the root causes of the mistake in order to make sure they won't happen again. Fixing the root causes of the mistakes takes determination and a willingness to see things in a new light.

Clients and agencies share the responsibility when consumers don't like ad messages; at the end of the day, the client should take the ultimate responsibility for the work it airs. For example, the beer brand Heineken started using the tagline "sometimes, lighter is better," featuring it in a television spot showing a bartender sliding a beer past three black people to a lighter-skinned woman. Chance the Rapper was one of several celebrities who spoke out against the ad. Having a prominent voice amplify criticism of your marketing campaign in this way is one of the quickest ways for your brand to come under pressure. In the same vein, Dolce & Gabbana's advertising campaign showed a Chinese model trying—and failing—to eat different Italian dishes with chopsticks. Consumers were angry that the ad portrayed Chinese people as lacking in refinement and an understanding of other cultures.

In these cases, the agency and brand teams should come together quickly to see what went wrong. The two cases described above may be due to the fact that the ads were developed and approved by people who were not in the audiences that were portrayed in the messages, and the agency and client did not attempt to get feedback on the portrayals. If the agency and client agree a mistake has been made, they should quickly apologize. Then the agency and client should ask what will make sure the situation will not happen in the future.

However, many agencies choose to stand side by side when advertising become problematic. Agencies and clients don't always have to apologize for their choices even if they are controversial.

Nike came under fire when it hired NFL player Colin Kaepernick for a campaign. Nike selected him because the brand found him to be inspirational in his actions protesting racial injustice and police brutality. Kaepernick knelt during the national anthem, a choice which angered many people while inspiring others.

When Kaepernick's Nike ads first aired, there were calls to burn Nike products and boycott the brand. Nike supported their decision to hire Kaepernick and ended up with a sales increase despite the protests. The strong association between the athlete and the brand came off as very authentic for many consumers.

### *Issues about the client*

Beyond advertising, brand reputations can be hurt by actions of the brands and of their leaders. For example, in 2019, Facebook came under fire and had to answer to legislators around the world about how it shares users' data with third parties, the role it plays in spreading disinformation, and the vulnerabilities it has to hacks. Elon Musk, the CEO of Tesla, derided the SEC, missed a Wall Street delivery goal, tweeted unexpectedly that he would take the company private, and smoked marijuana on live TV. Often, such missteps are addressed as part of a crisis communication plan, which will be detailed in upcoming pages.

### *Societal issues*

In addition to problems with the brand messages and problems with the company, there are always events that are out of everyone's control. Weather events such as hurricanes and wildfires, a pandemic, and worldwide protests over racism and social injustice happened in just the first six months of 2020. These types of crises may have a direct impact on brands in terms of shutting down production, or an indirect impact due to larger societal impacts such as consumers losing income or becoming seriously ill.

Account managers have important roles in addressing all these issues. In general, there are a few guidelines that crises call for.

1 Have a crisis communication team. The account management team is probably an optimal group to have at an agency, and a representative from the account team is probably an ideal person to have at the client's office as well.
2 Anticipate ahead of time. Bad things happen and knowing that at some point a bad thing will happen can allow for the account manager to proactively prepare for a crisis. Having occasional brainstorming sessions among a select group of people on a crisis management team can make the agency nimble in responding to crises, allowing for a variety of responses to be developed and discussed before a crisis happens. In addition, having such brainstorming sessions can help identify what types of situations are preventable by changing existing processes.
3 Identify and train spokespeople. During a crisis, only authorized people should speak on behalf of the organization and the brand. These individuals should be well-spoken and confident, and familiar with the organization. This does not have to be the CEO, except in cases where a loss of life has occurred. Spokesperson training teaches you to be prepared, to be ready to respond in a way that optimizes the response of all stakeholders.
4 Establish ways to notify key stakeholders quickly when decisions are being made. The Virginia Tech campus shooting catastrophe, where email was the sole means of alerting students initially, proves that using any single modality can make a crisis worse. Some of us may be on email constantly, and others not so much. Some of us receive our cell phone calls or messages quickly, and some do not. If you use more than one modality to reach your stakeholders, the chances are much greater that the message will go through.
5 Identify and know your stakeholders: Who are the internal and external stakeholders that matter to your organization? I consider employees to be your most important audience, because every employee is a PR representative and crisis manager for your organization whether you want them to be or not! But, ultimately, all stakeholders will be talking about you to others not on your contact list, so it's up to you to ensure that they receive the messages you would like them to repeat elsewhere.
6 Develop holding statements: While full message development must await the outbreak of an actual crisis, "holding statements," messages designed for use immediately after a crisis breaks, can be developed in advance to be used for a wide variety of scenarios to which the organization is perceived to be vulnerable. Examples of holding statements by a hotel chain with properties hit by a natural disaster, before the organization's headquarters has any hard factual information, might be:

- "We have implemented our crisis response plan, which places the highest priority on the health and safety of our guests and staff."
- "Our thoughts are with those who were in harm's way, and we hope that they are well."
- "We will be supplying additional information when it is available and posting it on our website."

  The organization's crisis communications team should regularly review holding statements to determine if they require revision and/or whether statements for other scenarios should be developed.

The key thing to remember though is that the holding statement is merely a place holder—it signals to stakeholders that more information is coming. You must then provide more information in order to keep your stakeholders informed and up-to-date on how you're handling the issue. The holding statement buys you time to take a deep breath, review the situation, review your options, and pick the best direction for your brand.

## Assessing social media reputation

Many clients love social media—it enables them to get messages out to targeted consumers quickly, and it is fairly simple to assess how consumers are responding to messages. Social media can also get quickly out of control, especially when consumers start talking about brands in negative ways; these conversations can often spiral out of control.

Social media reputation management is the process of posting strategic social media content, monitoring social media channels (Facebook, Twitter, Instagram, etc.), and engaging with customers who talk about the brand. It can also include assessment of digital spaces where customers have a say about their experience with a business, such as online review sites like Yelp. Brands should have a continual plan to assess their reputation on social media, and it is important to track this closely during and after a crisis.

Not every piece of feedback is positive. If customer issues come up on social media and online review sites, make sure you address the situation and get back to them. When responding to negative reviews and social media comments, be as specific as you can about the customer's experience and communicate any changes or improvements you have made as a result of their feedback. The sooner you can get back to your customer, the greater your chances of improving the situation.

### *The role of social listening*

Brands should be willing to engage with your community of fans and followers by liking, commenting on, and responding to their activity on the brand's social media. Marketers have always paid attention to social media to listen and respond to what customers are saying about the brand in the social media space. They also use social media posts to gauge sentiment about the brand.

Among the most used sites where customers post online reviews are Google and Facebook. Google is the online review site where consumers are reading the most reviews: 63.6% of consumers read reviews on Google before visiting a business. This means that a priority should be to understand consumers' perceptions on these two platforms.

However, given the scope of the Internet, it can be challenging to track every single conversation about your business happening on every social media channel. Investing in a social listening tool allows you to track conversations and mentions, and monitor online reviews. During and after the pandemic, when society was disrupted by business closures, stay-at-home orders, social distancing, and job losses, consumers demanded that companies pay more attention to key social issues of the day. Consumers desire businesses to do more, and consumers can provide insights into what types of activities will be most appreciated by marketers.

According to research conducted by Gartner during a March 2020 webinar, 51% of marketing leaders worldwide turned to social listening platforms to keep up with consumers' changing desires during the pandemic. This is likely to rise, as more consumers spend more time online, and brands put more effort into their social media platforms.

Most companies use a social media listening tool, which is a software program that monitors and analyzes online conversations about brands, specific topics and competitors—really, anything that is relevant to the brand. By providing keywords to the tool, the software identifies mentions of the specified keywords and provides some analysis of the mentions. While every brand will have a different list that will evolve over time, a list of important keywords and topics to monitor right from the start is provided below.

- Your brand name and any "handles" (#brandname) that you use
- Your product name(s), including any misspellings that are regularly used
- Your competitors' brand names, product names, and handles
- Industry buzzwords
- Your slogan/taglines and also those of your competitors
- Names of key people in your company and your competitors' companies (your CEO, spokesperson, etc.)
- Campaign names or keywords
- Your branded hashtags and those of your competitors
- Unbranded hashtags related to your industry

  The keywords and topics you monitor will likely evolve over time. Using social listening tools, you will learn what kinds of words people tend to use when they talk about your business and your industry. You'll also start to get a sense of what kinds of insights are most useful for you.

Depending on the tool, not only can social media listening occur on the key social media sites like twitter and Facebook, but it includes posts and comments on blogs, forums and many websites. A big part of the value of the social media listening tool is the volume of data that the tool can generate. Given the large amount of information, social listening allows you continually track how well your company is doing and what your consumers think of your brand and its messages. This insight will allow you to amplify or change social media messages on the fly, respond to concerns, and inform the strategy for future brand communications.

Social listening is different from social media monitoring. **Social media monitoring** looks at some specific metrics like engagement rate (such as likes and follows) and how often people share or repost social media posts. **Social listening**, in contrast, looks beyond the numbers to consider the mood behind the data. This mood is called social media sentiment.

Understanding this social media sentiment allows you to understand how people feel about your brand and allows you to respond right away to positive or negative posts. As you track the sentiment in real time, you can make subtle adjustments to posts and respond to negative feedback—either by responding directly to people who post something negative about the blog or by making a more general post addressing the negative topic. This will also prepare you well to quickly address any negative events or crises that the brand encounters.

Some options for social media tools include the following.

- Hootsuite: a dashboard that allows you to social listen and respond directly to consumers and influencers
- AdView: a tool that focuses on social listening on Facebook and Instagram ads
- ReviewTrackers: a tool that quickly monitors reviews from more than 50 review sites like Tripadvisor and Google Maps within 15 minutes of being posted
- Talkwalker: a tool that draws on more than 150,000 sources for data
- Synthesio: a tool that provides a social media reputation score based on its social listening data collection
- Reddit Keyword Monitor: Reddit garners more than 120 million unique views a month. It's filled with web forums (subreddits) allowing for in-depth discussions and reviews. You'll also be able to monitor unlimited keywords across reddit and respond to and engage with different posts that discuss your brand and keywords.

## Developing resilience

As we write this book, the world is still immersed in the COVID-19 pandemic, and no one knows the ultimate impact the pandemic will have on society, or on business, or on us as individuals. In times of societal disruption, people's priorities shift drastically and rapidly. The previous section showed how the pandemic affected consumer social media engagement. Some brands reacted well, and some brands faltered. In times of crisis, many brands may wonder what their role is in helping to solve the crisis.

Resilience is the ability to adapt, problem-solve, and respond to unexpected challenges. Resilience is a central part of the survival of us as individuals and our societies.

We have found that in a time of disruption, people are fine with hearing from brands—it gives them a sense of normalcy in their lives. At the same time, brands often can't continue communication as normal—it has to recognize that society is striving for authenticity, support, and assurance.

To build resilience, brands can undertake a variety of tactics.

- Brands should build memory salience, which means creating and/or reinforcing positive memories and association in the mind of consumers. This means messages need to stay true to a brand's unique values and positioning. People will quickly identify those brands that are being opportunistic and taking advantage of a situation rather than actively engaging.
- Brands should focus on strong emotional engagement with their messages rather than product attributes. During a crisis, people aren't worried about which paper towel is more absorbent—they're worried about how the world will continue. That doesn't mean a paper towel can't have a role in the conversation—a paper towel

could remind consumers that the brand will be consistent in an upside-down world. People want to know what the brand will do to help—or what the brand will do to help them.

- In times of crisis, people may be more attuned to what is happening in their local community versus what is happening on a national or global level. If possible, introduce some local aspects to your messaging.
- Continually think about ways by which the brand can be a source of inspiration and optimism.
- While it is often the quickest to put out messages on social media sites and through the brand's own web page, social media, often, isn't enough. Use trusted traditional channels in addition to the social media presence.

## Summary

It probably isn't a matter of if something bad will happen to a brand; it is really a matter of when. Brands can easily have their value diminished, but planning in advance for a range of scenarios can help brands be more prepared for a crisis. Account managers should ensure they keep connected to how people are talking about their brands, and as brands recover from crises, this information can be used as a benchmark to help brands get back to a position of value to consumers.

## Review questions

1 What are some issues that account managers encounter that are within their control, and those that are beyond their control?
2 What is reputation management and why is it important?
3 What are the different ways that a brand's reputation can be hurt?
4 Pick a brand and identify seven to ten keywords that you might use for social media listening.
5 What is the role of social media in hurting reputations and in restoring reputations?
6 What is a resilient brand, and how can advertising make brands more resilient?

## Case 15.1 Phoenix Power Company

### *Issue: advertising message strategy*

Phoenix Power's electricity rates were among the highest in the country, a fact that was resented by many of the company's customer base. However, as the company had a monopoly on providing electricity to the area, there wasn't much customers could do about it.

However, in an attempt to overcome this negative public opinion, Phoenix Power had borrowed a technique that has proven to be effective for other energy marketers. This involved developing an advertising campaign that demonstrated how customers could save energy costs by using better insulation in their homes or by purchasing more energy efficient appliances, including air conditioners.

By using all of these conservation methods, homeowners could save up to 20% on their cooling bill. In Phoenix, where the summer temperatures are continually above 100 degrees, that could be a substantial amount of money.

While the campaign was seen positively by some, others were concerned that Phoenix Power was putting all the onus on customers to save money. Many customers said that Phoenix Power was making so much in profits that they could afford to lower energy costs to consumers.

More recently, though, Phoenix Power made plans to invest in a new nuclear power plant. The company applied for a rate increase to help offset the increasing cost of doing business due to the costs of building the nuclear reactor. The same customers who complained in the past now had a new cause to complain about: Most people in the state were concerned about having a nuclear plant close to them.

Regardless of the consumer sentiment, the legislature approved Phoenix Power's plans to build the nuclear reactor and appeared likely give the company permission for at least part, if not all, of the requested rate increase. Managers at Phoenix Power believed that once the nuclear power plant is built, energy prices might be reduced, since the company will no longer have to import energy from power plants in California. "Once the nuclear plant is built, Arizona will have a total in-state energy solution," said a Phoenix Power spokesperson.

Now, Phoenix Power wanted to develop a short-term advertising campaign to explain to customers why rates will be rising and to prepare customers for the anticipated rate increase. They were looking for a creative strategy that could be used to help communicate this unpopular message to a very skeptical and unreceptive audience.

### Questions

1 Should Phoenix Power advertise at all, or should it put its efforts into public relations to help tell its story?
2 If Phoenix Power does advertise, what medium do you believe would serve best to tell the story?
3 What type of creative execution do you believe would be the best approach?
4 What type of research might you consider before coming out with a campaign?

# Index

AAU study 72
accounting 48, 55, 60, 91; working with 52
account manager 107, 108; assessing creative work 111–112; brand reputation 179–180; campaign development 164–166; challenges 115; issues about client 181; issues about work 180–181; managing responsibility 109; and multicultural team 119–121; societal issues 182–183; supporting creative colleagues 109–111; writing briefs 141
action plan 7
adaptability 117
adhocracy model 26
AdLeaders 177–178
administration 35; and management 28–29
Adobe Experience Cloud 75
Adverting Review Council 45
advertiser 12, 15, 51, 162, 166
advertising 53, 179; DAM system 172–173; social impact of 43–44
advertising agency 12–15, 97; ethical standard of 42; position their culture 26; profit and loss statement 53–54
advertising budget: allocation 50–51; developing media plan 51–52; methods 49–50
advertising campaign 10, 11, 34, 43, 50, 53; common digital measures 76; key performance indicators for 68; message strategy for 69–70; personnel issue 91; strategy in 136; value of 78
advertising industry, diverse workforce in 119
advertising management 1, 9–10; action plan/next step 7; contingency plan 7–8; external factors for problems 4; foundation principles 10; impact of digital advertising 15–16; impact of globalization 16–18; internal factors and personnel problems 4–5; people, the product 10–11; planning 11; process 11; process of generating alternatives 5–6; profit 12; recommendation/rationale 6–7; roles and organization structure 12–13; titles and structures 13–15
advertising manager 1, 18, 27, 96–97; advertising process and campaign measurement 68, 72; becoming 97–99; being player/coach 100–101; budgeting 48; cash flow statement 55; challenge for 17; challenges and opportunities for 88; conflict 91; dealing with ambiguity and stress 99–100; finance 56; global currency 59; integrate ethics 38; job of 10; in leadership communication 30–31; to manage people 93; media planning 51–52; need for 116; role in social media 42; roles and titles 13; SG&A 58; trick for 75; where to go from here 101–102; working with accounting 52
advertising measurement 68–69; copy testing 71–72; media measurement 75–77; message and creative execution measurement 69–71; perception and reputation tracking 72–74; return on investment 74–75
advertising messages 37, 41, 44
advertising organization 97, 101
advertising personnel management: conflict in workplace 90–92; diversity in workplace 88–90; employee/management job perceptions 85–86; evaluation of employee 87–88; in organization 92–93; personnel evaluations 86–87
advertising program 12, 51, 52, 68
advertising strategy 111, 136; *see also* strategy
AdView 185
Allstate Insurance 41–42
ambiguity 99–100
American Association of Advertising Agencies (4A's) 133
amortization 57
annual performance reviews 87–88
assets 54, 55
Association of National Advertisers (ANA) 119, 160
Association of Natural Advertisers 120
Aunt Jemima 153

background/situation analysis 3; advertising problems 4
balance sheet 54–55
Barrands Agency 168–170
Better Business Bureau 45
*Beyond Disruption* (Dru) 26
bias, awareness of 121
big idea 70
Black culture 116
Black professionals 119–121
blind resumes 167
Boston Life Insurance Company 154; advertising decisions 159; advertising tracking research 155–157; creative testing research 157; media analysis 158; strategy 155
Boswell Agency: Dallas Office's agency structure (conventional) 21–24; Dallas Office's client roster 20–21; structuring of advertising agency 19
bounce rate 76
Bourke, Juliet 121
brand 4, 74, 137; briefs 139; campaign development 164; cost leadership and differentiation strategy 138; 4Ps 146–147; repositioning 153–154; resilience 185–186; social listening tool 183–185
brand communication 147
brand health studies 72
brand management approach 15
brand manager 15
brand mapping 148–150
brand message 161, 166, 182
brand positioning 147, 150, 154
brand positioning statement 151–152, 180; strategy evaluation 152–153
brand purchase funnel 72, 73
brand reputation 181; elements of 179–180
brand reputation studies 72
brand strategy 154
briefs: assessing of 142; benefits to agency 140; benefits to client 139–140; goal and components of 140; writing of 141
broadcast companies 13
budgeting 48, 60; *see also* advertising budget
budget management 12
Bureau of Labor Statistics 119
business: advertising manager role in 75; fundamental objective 111–112; impact of advertising 69; masculinity *vs.* femininity cultures 118

Cameron, Kim S. 25
campaign, development of 164–166; *see also* advertising campaign
capital 56
case analysis: procedure 2; purpose of 2–3
cash flow statement 55
Cheerios 43
chief executive officer (CEO) 13–14, 92
chief financial officer (CFO) 14
chief information officer (CIO) 14
chief marketing officer (CMO) 14
chief operating officer (COO) 14, 92
clan model 26–27
C-level 13–14
click through rate (CTR) 76
client: DAM system 173; day-to-day management, multiple 126–127; expectations about 133; interpersonal difficulties management 131–132; issues about 181; unethical question 133
client-driven solutions 110
Coca-Cola 70
cognitive empathy 98–99
collectivistic cultures 117, 118
color bravery 164
communication 4, 68, 70, 74, 89–90, 93, 101; assessing team performance 120; effective written 33–34; formal 33; intercultural 32; internal 30–31, 33; issues in 32; leadership 30–31; marketing 41; persuasive 43; two-way 128; unofficial 92
communication technology firms 16
company *see* brand
company-wide communication 34
comparative advertising 44
comparative evaluations 168
compassionate empathy 99
compelling communication 11
competition 4, 108, 137
competitive advertising spending situation 7
conflict 93; internal 131; in workplace 90–92
conflict of interest 37
confused positioning 153
consumer 4, 15; confidence of 37; multicultural marketing 162; responsive to ads 160
contemporary workforce 121
content marketing 180
context 32
contingency budget 51
contingency plan 7–8
convention 33
Converse campaign "Day-jobbers" 162
copy testing 71–72
copywriter 96–97, 110
core values 27–28
cost efficiency 76
cost per click/cost per action (CPC/CPA) 76, 77
cost per thousand (CPM) analysis 76
COVID-19 pandemic (2020) 18, 127, 185
CQ *see* cultural intelligence (CQ)

creative brief 110–112; assessing of 142; benefits to agency 140; benefits to client 139–140; goal and components of 140; writing of 141
creative execution measurement 69–71
creative mindset 107–109
creative people 108, 110, 112
creative space 109
creative strategy 151; *see also* strategy
creative team 108–112
crisis 93, 182, 183, 185, 186; health 18; societal 133
crisis communication plan 181
crisis communication team 182
cross-cultural skills 117
CTR *see* click through rate (CTR)
cultural attachment 163, 164
cultural dimensions 117–119
cultural intelligence (CQ) 116–117, 121, 164
cultural knowledge 116
cultural metacognition 117
cultural nuances 32–33, 119
cultural openness 163, 164
cultural orientation mindset 163
culture: advertising agency, position their 26; Black culture 116; collectivistic 117, 118; and core values 28; high-context 32; individualistic 117, 118; long-term oriented 118–119; low-context 32; masculinity *vs.* femininity 118; short-term oriented 118–119; in United States 117
culture clubs 166
curiosity 121
customer intimacy 139

daily balancing act 17
DAM *see* digital assets management (DAM)
D'Angelo, Robin: "White Fragility" 166–167
The Davis Group 122–125
day-to-day management: juggling multiple clients 126–127; managing remote meetings 129–130; managing remote workers 127–128; meeting 128–129
deferred tax liability 54
Denny's 163, 167
depreciation 57
dictatorial feedback 112
differentiation strategy 137–138
digital advertising 76; impact of 15–16
digital assets 171–172, 174
digital assets management (DAM) 172–173; benefits of 173–174; centralize your media library 175; identification of 175; name and tag 175; promotion to potential users 176; software program 176; track 176
digital campaigns 77; *see also* advertising campaign
Digital Lives 2018 166
digital media 15, 75, 76
digital media company 13
digital platforms 165
digital project management system 127
Dillon, John 163
*The Discipline of Market Leaders* (Treacy and Wiersema) 138
disruption 33
*Disruption* (Dru) 26
"disruptive ideas" 27
diverse workforce 166–168
diversity 43, 93; direct correlation between 115; and inclusion 120; visible commitment to 121; in workplace 88–90
diversity-focused internship programs 120
double positioning 153
Dove 44, 167; Campaign for Real Beauty 43, 70
Drucker, Peter 68
Dru, Jean-Marie: *Beyond Disruption* 26; *Disruption* 26

Earley, P. Christopher 116
earned media 75, 77
EBITDA 57, 58
econometric modeling 75
effective collaboration 121
effective written communication 33–34
emotional empathy 99
empathy 98–99, 117, 165; leadership communication 30–31
employee: evaluation of 87–88; indulgence and restraint 119; interpersonal difficulties management 130–131; job perceptions 85–86; remote-work experience 127–128; unofficial communication between 92
endorsers 45
engagement 77
English language 89–90, 164–165
enthusiasm 111
equity 56
Espedido, Andrea 121
ethical advertising 44–45
ethical practices 38
ethical problems 37; in advertising, personal and organizational 38–39
ethics 37; global differences 42–43; social media 41–42
ethics programs 37–38
ethnic groups 161
ethnicity 88–89
ethnic segments *vs.* general market 163
external communication 34

Facebook 161, 181, 183
Facebook engagement 77
facilitate work, leadership communication 31
false advertising 44
Federal Trade Commission (FTC) 44, 133
feedback: dictatorial 112; inappropriate 112; time for 139
feeling based conflict 91
finance 56, 60; growth of 56–57
financial management 12
financial performance 115; manager 5
fiscal year 52–53
flash freezing 143
formal communication 33
4Ps: of advertising management 10–12; positioning and 146–147
freelance work 101
FTC *see* Federal Trade Commission (FTC)
functional/department management 13
fundamental advertising management 1

Gartner 184
gender 88–89
General Motors 12
global advertising campaign 59; measurement plan 73
global currency 59–60
globalization, impact of 16–18
global measures 78
goals: advertising manager 30; business 136, 139, 147; of campaign 109, 110; communication 50; of creative brief 140; of digital asset management 172; of diversity 89; of multicultural marketing 161–162
goodwill 58
Google 27–28, 183
Go Organic Company 142–145
gossip 92
Gotham Media 104–106
GSD&M 26–27

*Harvard Business Review* 121
hierarchy model 26, 27
high-context culture 32
high effort categories 77
hiring 85; copywriter 96; diverse talent 119; for entry-level positions 86; practices 42
Hispanics 119, 120, 161, 165; campaign 162
Hispanic Servicing Institutions (HSIs) 120
Historically Black Colleges and Universities (HBCU) 120
Hobson, Mellody 164
Hofstede, Geert 116; cultural dimensions 117–119
holding statements 182–183
Hootsuite 185
humility 121

inappropriate feedback 112
inclusion 120, 121, 168
inclusive leadership 121
individualistic cultures 117, 118
indulgence 119
industry groups 45
in-house operation 15
inspirational account manager 111
inspiration, leadership communication 31
intercultural communication 32
interest 57
internal communication 30–31, 33
internal conflicts 131
internal recruiting resources 167
interpersonal difficulties management: client unethical question 133; difficult clients 131–132; difficult coworkers 130–131; expectations about clients 133; internal conflicts 131
interpersonal skills 117
inventories 54
IPortal Media Company 94–95
issues: about client 181; about work 180–181; in communication 32; longer-term 90; personnel 91; short-term 90; societal 182–183

Japanese advertising agencies 42
job descriptions 167
JPT agency 113–114

Kaepernick, Colin 181
key performance indicators (KPIs) 75–76, 140; for advertising campaign 68
KMF agency 46–47

language 89–90, 164
leaders: interpersonal communication 35; *vs.* managers 29; traits 121
leadership: inclusive 121; management and 29–30
leadership communication 30–31
The Leaky Oil Company 134–135
learning orientation environment 109
LGBT 89
liabilities 54, 55
limited liability company (LLC) 13
liquidity 55
listening skill 98, 132
Loduha, Michael A. 28
longer-term issues 90
long-term oriented cultures 118–119
long-term strategy 136

low-context culture 32
low effort categories 77

"majority" market 161
management: administration and 28–29; and leadership 29–30; *see also* advertising management
management job perceptions 85–86
manager: activity for 28; financial performance 5; leaders *vs.* 29; operations 5; personnel 5; *see also* account manager; advertising manager
margin 58–59
market capitalization 57
marketers 165, 166, 183
marketing: DAM system 172–173; multicultural marketing 161–162; polycultural marketing 162; whole market/total market approach 162–163
marketing communication 41
market measures 78
market model 26
McDonalds 9
media 13, 15, 69; conflict in workplace 90; measurement of 75–77
media company 15, 25
media metrics 78
media selection 165
medium-term strategy 136
meeting 128–129; remote 129–130
message 68, 78, 161, 166; and creative execution measurement 69–71; execution of 71–72
message platform strategy 34
metadata 175
Metropolitan Media Company 103–104
millennials 161
misleading claims 44
motivational orientation 118
multicultural marketing 161–162
multicultural social norms 165
multicultural team 119–121
multifaceted strategy 166
multiple clients 126–127
Musk, Elon 181

need based conflict 91
Nike 29, 39, 147, 150, 181

objective-and-task method 50
objective, fundamental 111–112
Ogilvy, David 85
Ogilvy & Mather 85
Omnicom 26
"Omni-cultural Identities" 161
"one size fits all" approach 166
operational excellence 138
operations, manager 5
organization: advertising personnel management in 92–93; categories of 12–13; core values and personal values 27–28; ethics program 37–38; personal growth in 93
organizational culture 25; fundamental types of 25–26
organizational ethics 38–39
organizational structure 14, 15, 92
out-of-home companies 13
overall cost leadership strategy 137
over positioning 153
owned media 75, 76
ownership, structure 13

packaging 147
page views 76
paid advertising 41
paid media, fundamental measures for 75–76
pay 85–86
pay-per-click specialist 16
people, the product 10–11
perception based conflict 91
perception, tracking of 72–74
perceptual acuity 117
perceptual brand mapping 148, 150
performance review 87–88
personal ethics 38–39
personal values 27–28
personnel: evaluations 86–87; issue 37, 91; manager 5
perspective 163
persuasive communication 11, 43
Phoenix Power Company 186–187
place (distribution) 147
planning 11
player/coach model 100–101
polycultural marketing 162
Porter, Michael 137
positioning: consideration set 150–151; process of implementation 147–150; and 4Ps 146–147; segmentation, targeting and 147–150
*Positioning: The Battle for Your Mind* (Ries and Trout) 146
power based conflict 91
power distance 118
pricing 146
Prime Media Corporation 35–36
privately owned company 13
private managers 13
problematic positioning 153
process 11, 163
product 146
product leadership 139
profit 12
profit and loss statement 53–54

profit margin 58–59, 75
profit margin ratio 58
project manager 28
publicly traded company 13, 57–58
public managers 13
public relations (PR) 179
puffery 44–45

Quaker 153
Quinn, Robert E. 25

Randall White Dog Food 78–83
recommendation/rationale 6–7
Reddit Keyword Monitor 185
relationship dilemmas 39–41
remote meetings, management of 129–130
remote workers, management of 127–128
repositioning 153–154
reputation, tracking of 72–74
resilience 185–186
responsibility 109
restraint 119
retail 26
retail campaign 74
retailer 52, 71
return on investment (ROI) 74–75
revenue 56
ReviewTrackers 185
Ries, Al: *Positioning: The Battle for Your Mind* 146
"run of the mill" conflicts 91

search engine optimization (SEO) 179
security 85–86
segmentation 147–150
senior leadership 97
senior management 6, 13, 14, 92
SG&A 58
short-term issue 90
short-term oriented cultures 118–119
short-term strategy 136
Sierra, Robert 143–145
social advertising 44–45
social listening tool 183–185
social media 180, 183; digital campaigns, use of 77; options for tools 185
social media ethics 41–42
social media monitoring 184
social media reputation management 183; role of social listening 183–185
social media sentiment 184–185
social media specialist 16
societal issues 182–183
The Southern Rice Company 60–63
speaking skill 98
specialty vendor 13
stereotyping 43–44, 165
stock price 57
strategy 136–137; creative briefs 139–142; development of 139; as discipline 138; three value disciplines 138–139; as trade-offs 137–138; *see also* advertising strategy
stress 99–100
Synthesio 185

Talkwalker 185
targeting 147–150
TBWA 26, 27, 33
teamwork-oriented environment 119–120
television ad 180–181
three R's 166
Tide 70, 71
time 32; attitudes towards 118–119; for feedback 139
time spent 76
Tinsdale Agency and Design 83–84
tolerance of uncertainty 117
total market approach 162–163
traditional advertising 16
Treacy, Michael: *The Discipline of Market Leaders* 138
trial 74
"tribes" 164
Trout, Jack 147; *Positioning: The Battle for Your Mind* 146
2020 #BlackLivesMatter protests 116, 120, 153
Twitter engagement 77
two-way communication 128

uncertainty avoidance 118
under positioning 153
unexpected events: issues about client 181; issues about work 180–181; societal issues 182–183
unique visitors 76
United Kingdom's Advertising Standards Authority (ASA) 43
United States: advertising campaigns 43; culture in 117; ethical standard of advertising agency 42; ethnic groups 161; global currency 59; globalization impact 17; "majority" market in 161; minority race in 115; 2020 #BlackLivesMatter protests 116, 120
universal ethics 42–43
universal insight 163–164

values based conflict 91
vendors, confidence of 37
Vineyard Agency 64–67
vision 33

Walmart 70
weather events 182

website development 180
website page views 76
Wells Fargo 39
"White Fragility" (D'Angelo) 166–167
white paper 2
White professionals 120
whole market approach 162–163
Wiersema, Fred: *The Discipline of Market Leaders* 138
work: issues about 180–181; valuing 109
workforce, contemporary 121
workplace: conflict in 90–92; diversity in 88–90
World Advertising Research Council (WARC) advertising award 75
writing skill 98; creative briefs 141
written communication 33–34

Zimmerman 26, 27

For Product Safety Concerns and Information please contact our EU representative GPSR@taylorandfrancis.com
Taylor & Francis Verlag GmbH, Kaufingerstraße 24, 80331 München, Germany

www.ingramcontent.com/pod-product-compliance
Lightning Source LLC
LaVergne TN
LVHW080809011026
849160LV00015B/1582
* 9 7 8 0 3 6 7 6 2 0 7 4 5 *